Abigail Pope

Jonathan Rosen is the author of *The Talmud and the Internet* and the novels *Eve's Apple* and *Joy Comes in the Morning*. His essays have appeared in *The New York Times* and *The New Yorker*. He is the editorial director of *Nextbook* and lives in New York City.

THE
LIFE
OF THE
SKIES

JONATHAN ROSEN

PICADOR

FARRAR, STRAUS AND GIROUX

NEW YORK

www.picadorusa.com

Picador® is a U.S. registered trademark and is used by Farrar, Straus and Giroux under license from Pan Books Limited.

For information on Picador Reading Group Guides, please contact Picador. E-mail: readinggroupguides@picadorusa.com

Designed by Gretchen Achilles

Portions of this book appeared, in different form, in *The New York Times, The New Yorker,* and *The American Scholar.*

Grateful acknowledgment is made for permission to reprint the following material:

"Mother," from *Burnt Pearls: Ghetto Poems of Abraham Sutzkever,* translated by Seymour Mayne, copyright © 1981 by Seymour Mayne. Reprinted with permission of Mosaic Press, www.mosaic-press.com.

"The Oven Bird," from *The Poetry of Robert Frost,* edited by Edward Connery Lathem. Copyright © 1916, 1969 by Henry Holt and Company. Copyright © 1944 by Robert Frost. Reprinted by permission of Henry Holt and Company, LLC.

"Who will remain, what will remain?" from *A. Sutzkever: Selected Poetry and Prose,* translated by Barbara and Benjamin Harshav, copyright © 1991 by Barbara and Benjamin Harshav. Reprinted with permission of The University of California Press.

Owing to limitations of space, illustration credits appear on pages 325–326.

ISBN-13: 978-0-312-42819-8
ISBN-10: 0-312-42819-7

First published in the United States by Farrar, Straus and Giroux

First Picador Edition: January 2009

10   9   8   7   6   5   4   3   2   1

FOR THE ALBANY FLOCK—
ANNA, JON, ISAAC, CELIA, AND ELLA—
WITH LOVE

Birds are the life of the skies, and when they fly,
they reveal the thoughts of the skies.

—D. H. LAWRENCE

CONTENTS

THE LIFE OF THE SKIES

PROLOGUE (BIOPHILIA)

"Do you know what the name of that green bird up above us is?" she asked, putting her shoulder rather nearer to his.

"Bee-eater."

"Oh no, Ronny, it has red bars on its wings."

"Parrot," he hazarded.

"Good gracious no."

The bird in question dived into the dome of the tree. It was of no importance, yet they would have liked to identify it, it would somehow have solaced their hearts.

—E. M. FORSTER,
A Passage to India

Everyone is a birdwatcher, but there are two kinds of birdwatchers: those who know what they are and those who haven't yet realized it. In the United States, a lot of people have realized it—47.8 million Americans, according to the Fish and Wildlife Service—and yet my passion is constantly greeted with surprise. *You?* Perhaps it is because I live in a city and lead an urban life. But why should people wonder that I watch birds? It's like being surprised that someone has sex or goes to the bathroom. The surprise reveals ignorance not so much about birds—their beauty, their abundance, their wild allure—as about human nature. We need, as the great biologist Edward O. Wilson has argued, to affiliate with nature in order to be happy. He calls this phenomenon "biophilia."

The urge to watch birds is all but instinctive, dating, no doubt, from a time when knowing the natural world—what could be eaten and what could eat us, what would heal us and what would bring death—was essential. It is fed by our urge to know, as strong as our urge to eat. Could you imagine a lion stalking prey not out of hunger but out of curiosity? We name things, we classify them. In the Bible Adam gives names to the natural world, imposing a human order on a chaos of life, a kind of second creation.

Birdwatching is as human an activity as there can be. We have one foot in the animal kingdom—where, biologically, we belong—but one foot in a kingdom of our own devising. As Walt Whitman said of himself, we are "both in and out of the game / and watching and wondering at it."

As it turns out, living in a city and watching birds is hardly a contradiction. Modern birdwatching is virtually an urban invention. Institutions of higher learning where bird skins were available, not to mention collection curators who brought their indoor learning outdoors, were virtual prerequisites as birdwatching came of age.

To be bored with London is to be bored with life, said Dr. Johnson. I live in New York City, a metropolis greater than Johnson's London, and I feel the same way about my city—but I feel this way partly because it was in New York City that I discovered birds. More and more I realize that to be bored with birds is to be bored with life. I say birds rather than some generic "nature," because birds are what remain to us. Yes, deer and coyotes show up in the suburbs, you can see grizzlies in Yellowstone Park, and certainly there are bugs galore. But in Central Park, two blocks from my apartment, hundreds of species of birds pass through by the thousands every spring and fall, following ancient migratory routes as old as the Ice Age.

If herds of buffalo or caribou moved seasonally through the

park, I'd no doubt go out to see them. But the only remaining wild animals in abundance that carry on in spite of human development are birds. The rain forest is far away, but these birds, who often winter there, bring it with them. Here is the nature my biophiliac soul needs to affiliate with. In our mother's womb we float in water, a remnant of our aquatic origins that we somehow took with us when we left the oceans that spawned us eons ago. But where are the woods, the fertile forests that also constituted the womb of our species? Birds bring us fragments, not in their beaks, but on their backs. Tiny fragments, to be sure, and not enough to reconstitute a world—but something.

Emerson said that if the stars appeared in the night sky only once every thousand years, we would "preserve for many generations the remembrance of the city of God." But the stars come out every night, and as it is, many of us scarcely look up; if we do, we find a sky so crowded with artificial light that we hardly notice what else is up there.

The stars suddenly came out for me twelve years ago. I was at lunch in Manhattan in late March when I overheard a man say, with great excitement, "The warblers will be coming through Central Park soon." Somehow, for reasons I still can't explain, I knew right then and there that even though I wasn't sure what warblers were, I was going to go and find them.

With uncharacteristic follow-through I signed up for an introduction to birdwatching at the local branch of the Audubon Society in the West Twenties in Manhattan (who even knew such a place existed in New York City?). There were two classes and two field trips. In the classes we were shown slides of birds and then asked, after the image vanished, to draw what we had been shown. I was appalled to discover how bad I was at remembering—that a wood duck has a helmet of feathers almost like a Greek warrior; that a cedar waxwing has a band of yellow at the base of its tail, and a tiny splotch of red on its wing, like sealing wax, from which it gets its name. Even the obvious cardinal—a bird I'd seen my whole life—surprised me; I had never noticed it has not merely a red body but a red bill, and that its face is masked in black.

"Try to be one of the people," said Henry James, "on whom nothing is lost." As a writer I considered myself observant, but how much was lost on me! Birds may be everywhere, but they also—lucky for them—inhabit an alternate universe, invisible to most of us until we learn to look in a new way. And even after I had been shown them, aspects kept eluding me.

It wasn't my eyes, of course, but some larger quality of vision, a capacity for noticing that was like an unused muscle. As a boy I'd loved Sherlock Holmes stories, and my favorite moment was always when Holmes dazzles Watson by telling him that the murderer must have been a tall man with a limp and unclipped fingernails who smoked a cigar (brand always specified). Of course, Sherlock Holmes also explains to his disbelieving friend that he makes a point of not knowing many things—for example, that the earth revolves around the sun. According to Holmes, the attic of the mind can't be too cluttered with extraneous information and ideas if you are going to fill it with important things like details.

Sitting in the classroom I already felt the furniture in my head getting rearranged, a great emptying out and a great filling up—of names and pictures. Is there anything more pleasant than looking? Birdwatching is sanctioned voyeurism. Heading for the subway afterward, I wasn't entirely surprised to see one of the men in the class dart into a topless bar across the street.

Knowledge itself, like looking, has an erotic component. Freud claimed that all curiosity is at root sexual, since the ultimate answer to the ultimate question—where do we come from?—leads us back to our mother's genitals, the sex act that produced us and the womb that harbored us before birth. Birding *is* bound up with the question of origins, leading us back not between our mother's legs but to equally awkward places of beginning, bound up as they are with primordial anxieties about creation and evolution, divinity and mere materialist accident.

Birds are the closest living relatives of the dinosaurs—a shocking fact. Who would have believed that those little feathered beauties have so much in common with the hulking skeletons in the American Museum of Natural History that so enthralled me when I was a child? Perhaps birding is the adult fulfillment of a childhood fascination. Except that birds aren't extinct (though many species teeter on the brink). They're as close to a velociraptor as I'll come. The more you look at birds, the more you feel remnants of their cold-blooded reptile past; the pitiless round eye and mechanical beak somehow tell you that if you were the size of an ant they'd peck you up in a second. And who are *our* nearest relatives? Chimpanzees, with whom we share more than 95 percent of our genetic material. Why else do we feel so drawn to the woods?

None of these thoughts was in my head as I began birding. On the two birding field trips that came with my introduction to birding class—one to Central Park, the other to Jamaica Bay Wildlife Refuge in Queens—it was simply the pleasure of looking that hooked me, even as I discovered that the birds that had seemed so exotic in class were frequently referred to in the guidebook as "common."

At Jamaica Bay—accessible from my apartment by subway—I saw ibises and egrets and snow geese flying against the Manhattan skyline as airplanes from nearby John F. Kennedy Airport took off and landed. I loved that I could see birds against the silhouette of the World Trade Center, incorrectly perceiving this as a poetic juxtaposition of the permanent towers and the evanescent birds. Discovering that you yourself, and the civilization from which you peer out, are as fragile as the birds you are watching is also part of the story—though this was something else I did not realize at the time.

Gradually the strange contradictory elements of birding seeped into me and deepened its rich appeal. Birdwatching, like all great human activities, is full of paradox. You need to be out in nature to do it, but you are dependent on technology—binoculars—and also on the guidebook in your back pocket, which tells you what you're seeing. The challenge of birding has to do with keeping the bird and the book in balance. The book you bring with you draws the birds you see into the library world—a system of names dating from the eighteenth century, when scientists ordered the plant and animal world and labeled them so that anyone in any country would know he was referring to the same bird. But at the same time that you are casting your scientific net over the wild world, the birds are luring you deeper into the woods or the meadow or the swamp. The library world and the wild, nonverbal world meet in the middle when you are birdwatching. We need both sides of this experience to feel whole, being half wild ourselves. Birdwatching is all about the balance.

I should be outside right now. It's a crisp, brilliant day in mid-

September and fall migration is in full swing. Central Park, one of the great places in North America to watch birds, is two blocks from my house. Yet here I am, hunched over my computer.

My father, who was a professor of German literature, was very fond of Kafka's parable about Poseidon, the king of the sea, who has never actually *seen* the ocean because he is so busy with the paperwork required for administering it. He eagerly awaits the end of the world so he can go out and have a look. What was true for Poseidon and the sea is true for us and the air, or the earth. In his own life, Kafka—whose name, he was amused to note, was the Czech word for "jackdaw," a crowlike bird of ill omen—dreamed of being a "red Indian" galloping across the American plain. Instead, he spent his brief tubercular life working in an insurance office in Prague or chained to his writing desk. This is a writer's dilemma—you're drawn to experience but need to be stationary to make sense of it. But writing, like birdwatching, has universal human application. Most people live in cities or suburbs but pine, at some deep level, for the wild world that produced us long ago and that our ancestors, with animal fury, worked so hard to subdue. This is why birding, though it can seem like a token activity, an eccentric pastime, is so central to modern life.

There's a phrase I learned from birding—"binocular vision"— that sounds like it should describe the act of birdwatching itself, but that actually means the ability to see the same thing through both eyes at the same time. Because each image will be slightly different, it gives the looker the capacity for depth perception. If you don't have binocular vision, things need to be in motion for you to notice them, and catch them. The *Tyrannosaurus rex* in *Jurassic Park* (though not necessarily in life) lacked binocular vision, and so if you stayed very still—like the children in *Jurassic Park*—you could avoid detection. The velociraptors had binocular vision, so if you didn't hide, you'd get eaten.

Most birds have some binocular vision—we may have evolved ours leaping from tree to tree and catching food up in the branches, and birds needed their eyes even more—but birds, especially vulnerable ones, have other needs, like seeing what's swooping down or sneaking up on them, and so they sacrifice a large area of overlapping vision for astonishing peripheral vision. The eyes of woodcocks are spaced so far apart, they see behind them better than in front and can look up with their bills stuck in the mud. A pigeon can see 300 degrees, but needs to bob its head to get a sense of depth. Predators tend to have better binocular vision than prey; owls have eyes on the same plane, like us, which makes them master hunters.

We, needless to say, have binocular vision even without binoculars, but I often think of the phrase in a metaphorical way, to mean the sort of double vision that birding requires. One of the best descriptions of this double vision was provided by the writer Harold Brodkey in his memoir about dying of AIDS:

> At one time I was interested in bird-watching, and I noticed that when I saw a bird for the first time I couldn't really see it, because I had no formal arrangement, no sense of pattern, for it. I couldn't remember it clearly, either. But once I identified the bird, the drawings in bird books and my own sense of order arranged the image and made it clearer to me, and I never forgot it. From then on I could see the bird in two ways—as the fresh, unpatterned vision and the patterned one. Well, seeing death nearby is very like the first way of seeing.

I love this passage because it captures the weird conundrum of birding—that until we know what a bird is, it's hard to recognize it properly when we see it for the first time, but until we've seen it for the first time, it's hard to know what it is. For Brodkey, death, that ultimate undiscovered country, could never be seen properly because he'd never been there before. And yet, in his book, he does see it, and lets us see it, too. We are looking for life when we bird, but that very formulation implies the presence of death.

DARWIN BEGAN BY simply looking, accumulating beetles, birds, and eggs as a schoolboy. Sailing around the world on the *Beagle* as an energetic twenty-one-year-old, he gathered anything he could drop in alcohol, shoot, or press between pages. It was only after his five-year collecting trip was over that this acquisitiveness gave way to deep thought, and the great melancholy theory we all still grapple with today. But things, even when you don't think about their meaning, still hint at meaning.

The first thing we're told Sherlock Holmes has banished from his brain is Copernicus's discovery that the earth revolves around the sun. Who needs such gloomy knowledge weighing down your thoughts?—though as a homicide detective Holmes is everywhere presented with evidence of our imperfect nature and doesn't really need to know that our planet is not the center of the universe. In the same way, birding, an exhilarating diversion, is nevertheless freighted with the burden of natural history. Tennyson's 1850 poem "In Memoriam" saw "Nature, red in tooth and claw" nine years before the publication of *The Origin of Species*, with its grim definition of evolution as an endless bloody struggle for survival. Tennyson got there simply by longing for a dead friend and looking at the world around him.

But the lessons we divine looking at nature aren't always gloomy ones. Looking at birds, I feel, for lack of a better word, whole. I had grown up believing that if you could not articulate something it did not really exist. This law was contradicted for me by birding. There was something wonderful about seeing birds going dumbly about their business, without reflection or articulation. They did not seem diminished because of this, they did not seem like lesser animals. They seemed fully alive and complete in themselves. And some of this feeling of completeness rubbed off on me, in the same way that having children later on altered my way of being in the world. Having children is, partly, a biological delight—those moments when you are all lying on the big bed, maybe you are talking or singing and maybe you are quiet, but there is a kind of lounging, monkey-troop delight that always makes me think of those moments in a nature film when the chimps are grooming each other, chasing each other around a tree, fishing calmly for termites. They seem to possess something that transcends happiness or sadness—they simply are. Birding gives me a little of that, a glimpse of rightness that may not be something I can articulate but that I know is there and that reduces the sting of my intellectual anxieties about evolution.

The title of this book comes from a prose poem by D. H. Lawrence that he put at the beginning of the bird section of his poetry collection *Birds, Beasts and Flowers*. Lawrence declares that "birds are the life of the skies, and when they fly, they reveal the thoughts of the skies." For many years I used to quote that line incorrectly—I thought it was "when they sing, they reveal the thoughts of the sky." I was very happy when I realized I was wrong. Birds can't articulate meaning with their voices, much as we may love their song. It is their bodies that speak the truth. Nerdy, wordy birding isn't an intellectual activity. The bird is either there or it isn't.

In his poem "Of Mere Being," Wallace Stevens describes a "palm at the end of the mind." This tree grows "beyond the last thought"—maybe death, and maybe something beyond even death. In that tree, of course, there is a bird:

A gold-feathered bird
Sings in the palm, without human meaning,
Without human feeling, a foreign song.

The fact that the bird is not singing for the benefit of the human listener is oddly not disheartening; it's proof that something new and strange is there. The yearning hero of Saul Bellow's novel *Humboldt's Gift* attempts a spiritual exercise in which you remind yourself, whenever you hear a dog bark, that the bark is not for you. It is a sound coming out of a creature separate from you, with its own mysterious life. This exercise is intended to break the solipsistic manner in which we often go through the world. To let real outside otherness penetrate our bubble of self-absorption. This is how I felt when I went birdwatching those first few times. The strange fact that the birds were there brought home the strange fact that I was there.

What Stevens captures so well in his weird poem is the essence of the title, the sense "of mere being":

You know then that it is not the reason
That makes us happy or unhappy.
The bird sings. Its feathers shine.

The bird is simply there—alien, but the fact that it is alien is oddly a sign of hope, because even though it is in our minds, it is not of our minds. It is something else. It is reality—though maybe a very unfamiliar reality. It is not "the reason" that makes us happy or sad. Being happy or sad is separate from this reality.

Stevens conjures, in a very cerebral poem, the opposite of thought. Just as he creates, despite the weird chilliness of the poem, a kind of comfort. The sort of comfort that comes from encountering reality—even harsh reality, even death.

Spinoza said it is necessary to love God without in any way expecting God to love you back. This was the sort of thing that helped get Spinoza excommunicated in seventeenth-century Amsterdam, but for me it is a perfectly understandable and oddly consoling assertion. Just as I love watching birds, knowing full well they couldn't care less about me. Their existence is still bound up with mine, we share a secret, though I am hard-pressed to tell you what it is. I hope, though, that this book touches on that secret in some way.

In *Consilience*, a stirring book suggesting that all knowledge is governed by a handful of laws, Edward O. Wilson writes: "Neither science nor the arts can be complete without combining their separate strengths. Science needs the intuition and metaphorical power of the arts, and the arts need the fresh blood of science." Wilson seems to anticipate grand new godless sagas spun out of evolutionary knowledge that will perhaps replace works like the Bible, whose relevance has waned in a rationalist world. I am too wedded to my own inherited saga to go along with him—birds may not have been created on the fifth day, as the Bible tells us, but that doesn't mean that they aren't, like us, in some sense descended from a divine act of creation. Nevertheless, I am deeply inspired by a great deal of Wilson's writing and I see in birding a fulfillment of some of his observations.

Birds shuttle between what is urban in us and what is wild. They knit these things together in our soul. Birding surrounds us with our evolutionary history, but it also connects us to that word, "soul," which—however much it seems an embarrassment in contemporary culture—nevertheless is as hard to kill off as our animal heritage. I can't think of any activity that more fully captures what it means to be human in the modern world than watching birds.

Wilson writes: "Interpretation will be the more powerful when braided together from history, biography, personal confession—and science." That has certainly been a guiding principle in this book. Birding for me is a kind of intermediate term, a place where poets and naturalists, scientific seekers and religious seekers, converge.

Can religion and science meet somewhere in the middle? And what about science and art? Can we stitch earth and sky together again, in a single fabric of meaning? In "Ode to a Nightingale," Keats tells his nightingale he will fly to him on "viewless wings of Poesy." That phrase doesn't inspire today— "poesy" being as dead as the dodo. Wallace Stevens captures this sad fact in a poem of his own, "Autumn Refrain," where, clearly thinking of Keats, he says the nightingale is

> *. . . not a bird for me*
> *But the name of a bird and the name of a nameless air*
> *I have never—shall never hear.*

But the impulse behind Keats's great ode—to close the gap between us and the natural world—is still there, and more urgent than ever.

This book offers no grand synthesis. It is a book about birds, the impulse to watch them, the impulse to capture them in poetry and in stories. It is a book unified only by my own experience, enriched by my reading and the stories and experiences of others. But I do feel that birding, a great and fulfilling pastime, and by the way a lot of fun, is more than merely that. Birdwatching is intimately connected to the journey we all make to find a place for ourselves in a post-Darwinian world. This book is my journey.

PART I

BACKYARD BIRDS

If I ever go looking for my heart's desire again, I won't look any further than my own back yard. Because if it isn't there, I never really lost it to begin with. Is that right?

—DOROTHY, in *The Wizard of Oz*

1

THE GHOST BIRD

I'm gonna go to Slidell and look for my joy
Go to Slidell and look for my joy
Maybe in Slidell I'll find my joy
Maybe in Slidell I'll find my joy

—LUCINDA WILLIAMS,
"Joy," from *Car Wheels on a Gravel Road*

As a rule I tend to avoid activities that require snake-proof boots. But when I learned about a possible sighting of an ivory-billed woodpecker I knew at once that I would be going down to the Louisiana swamp where the bird was reportedly seen in the Pearl River Wildlife Management Area. This was in the fall of 2000, before September 11 darkened and diverted my vision, before Hurricane Katrina virtually destroyed the Pearl River refuge, before a purported 2004 sighting of the woodpecker in Arkansas became national news, before my second child was born. In short, a lifetime ago.

I had been birdwatching only about five years at that point, and though I was quite devoted, I wasn't then and am not now a die-hard "lister," the sort of person who rushes off, binoculars in hand, whenever a rare bird is spotted. (The British call such people "twitchers," as if birdwatching were a disease of the central nervous system.) I was and am a simple birdwatcher, a much more comprehensive and to me appealing term that makes room for King Solomon, Roger Tory Peterson, and millions of people with backyards and bird feeders. But though I am no twitcher, news of an ivory-billed woodpecker sighting did make me jump, and that is because the ivory-billed woodpecker wasn't a rare bird. It was extinct.

That, at least, was the verdict of many experts who had been pronouncing the bird gone since 1944. Consulting guidebooks in preparation for my trip in 2000, I discovered that the American Bird Conservancy's field guide, *All the Birds of North America*, listed the ivory-bill, alongside the passenger pigeon, the great auk, and the Carolina parakeet, in its "Extinct Birds" section. There was no mention of the bird at all in the recently published *Sibley Guide to Birds* or in Kenn Kaufman's new *Birds of North America*. My National Geographic guide more circumspectly referred to the bird as "on the brink of extinction," and my Peterson guidebook dutifully described the bird, but then added, cagily, "very close to extinction, if indeed, it still exists."

Extinction. The finality of the word sends a shiver down the spine. "You take away all a man has and all he'll ever have," says Clint Eastwood as a hard-bitten, philosophical killer in *Unforgiven*. But extinction is worse—the death not merely of an individual but of all the individuals—past, present, and potential—that collectively make up a species. Once gone there is no retrieval, and the bird will have more in common with *Triceratops* than with the American robin. This despite the fact that there are photographs of the ivory-bill, recordings of its voice, and even a silent movie of its nesting habits, made in the 1930s, when the bird was studied in one of its last redoubts—an area of old-growth forest in Louisiana that was, despite a fight waged by conservationists, ultimately felled for timber.

Certainly the thrilling possibility of seeing a bird considered extinct for sixty years was one reason I went looking for the ivory-billed woodpecker. But though a rarefied thrill, a sort of "extreme birding" that elevated the nerdiness of the daily pursuit, it was not so different, really, from the thrill of ordinary birdwatching, which this book is primarily concerned with. Even birds we take for granted today, like the Eastern bluebird and the bald eagle, have had their brush with danger and disappearance. Others may yet wind up endangered or missing in action—their fate is not necessarily in our hands but in the hands of governments who control remote rain forests and mountain regions where birds we consider "ours" during migration spend the winter.

And even birds my guidebook calls "common," like the gorgeous scarlet tanager or the Baltimore oriole, can be hard to spot as they flit in and out of the leaves. They require patience and a pair of binoculars. And warblers, the jewels in the crown of spring migration, are only a few inches in length. Looking for songbirds in spring has a special urgency because migration tends to pick up just as the trees are leafing out and there is a sort of race between the birds and spring itself. The deeper into spring, the more birds—and the harder it is to see them. Every day the balance shifts; it's like a chess match where the players keep smacking the clock after every move—just when things get really interesting, you run out of time.

But the ivory-bill has been flitting in and out of history, in and out of extinction, for a hundred years. Looking for it takes what is implicit in birding—the precariousness of the natural world, the urge to recover, to collect, to conquer, and yet to preserve—and makes it explicit. From the moment I learned about it, the bird had a haunting hold on my imagination.

I was not alone. The ivory-bill in particular has what environ-

mentalists refer to as "charisma," a sort
of magical aura that has affected birdwatchers since they started noticing
the bird. For one thing, the ivory-
bill is—or was—very big. At twenty
inches, the bird was America's largest
woodpecker and the third-biggest
woodpecker in the world after the now
(presumably) extinct imperial woodpecker, which lived in Mexico, and the
Magellanic woodpecker, which still
hangs on in South America.

The ivory-bill also has a reputation for unconquerable defi-
ance that, along with its great size, earned it the name King of
the Woodpeckers. The habitat of the ivory-bill was old-growth
forest, trees that had lived for hundreds of years, and the bird
carries with it an aspect of the forest it lived in. It is a sort of untamed emblem of the now-vanished American wilderness. The
white bill of the bird has been discovered in Native American
graves. It continues to have an almost totemic force for birders
today.

Never common, the bird had an indomitable spirit that may
well be what doomed it. That at least is the prevailing fantasy: it
simply could not stand the encroachments of man. Alexander
Wilson, the Scottish-born father of American ornithology, who
died in 1813, offered an account of an ivory-bill that he had shot
and captured in Wilmington, North Carolina. His description
offers as good a report as any of a wild creature fighting to the last.

Wilson brought his wounded bird to a hotel room where he
left it alone for an hour; when he returned, he discovered that
the bird had hammered its way through the wall nearly to free-

dom: "The bed was covered with large pieces of plaster; the lath was exposed for at least fifteen inches square, and a hole, large enough to admit the fist, opened to the weather-boards; so that, in less than another hour, he would certainly have succeeded in making his way through."

Wilson then tied the bird to a table and left again to find it some food. This time when he returned he discovered that the bird had "almost entirely ruined the mahogany table to which he was fastened, and on which he had wreaked his whole vengeance." While he was drawing the bird (which was Wilson's object in capturing it), the ivory-bill managed to attack and cut Wilson in several places, and "on the whole he displayed such a noble and unconquerable spirit that I was frequently tempted to restore him to his native woods." Wilson resisted the temptation and watched "with regret" as the bird, which refused all food, died after three days.

But the bird was not only tough, it was beautiful—boldly patterned black and white, with an ivory-white bill that, from base to tip, measured three inches. The male had a brilliant, blood-red crest. John James Audubon saw the woodpecker as somehow already existing in the realm of art. In his *Ornithological Biography* Audubon wrote:

> I have always imagined, that in the plumage of the beautiful Ivory-billed Woodpecker, there is something very closely allied to the style of colouring of the great Vandyke. The broad extent of its dark glossy body and tail, the large and well-defined white markings of its wings, neck, and bill, relieved by the rich carmine of the pendent crest of the male, and the brilliant yellow of its eye, have never failed to remind me of some of the boldest and no-

blest productions of that inimitable artist's pencil. So strongly indeed have these thoughts become ingrafted in my mind, as I gradually obtained a more intimate acquaintance with the Ivory-billed Woodpecker, that whenever I have observed one of these birds flying from one tree to another, I have mentally exclaimed, "There goes a Vandyke!"

I find Audubon's fanciful description poignant because it comes out of a world so different from my own. Audubon was born in 1785 and died in 1851, before the frontier had been closed and when there were still American birds that had not been named. I require imagination to see the ivory-bill *not* as a painting—artistic representations of the bird are all I know.

Likening the bird, as Audubon did, to a work of art while it still haunted the forests of the South is charming; imagining that the bird is nothing but a work of art is overwhelmingly depressing. Art is long and life is short. I wanted to rediscover the bird as part of the wild world Audubon took for granted. The bird's scientific name, despite its alien Latin, does more than Audubon's poetic flight to put the ivory-bill back into nature: *Campephilus principalis*—"the princely eater of grubs," though I have also seen the translation "principally, an eater of grubs."

Ideally, birdwatching gives you both the symbol and the living bird. You get the Van Dyck painting that eats grubs. Birdwatching is an exercise in balance. It has a built-in acknowledgment that nature is finite: you don't shoot the bird, you look at it. You bring along a guidebook, emblem of the library world, even as you wander out into nature in pursuit of something wild. You get the thrill of seeing an untamed creature, but immediately you cage it in its common or scientific name and link the bird, and yourself, to a Linnaean system of nomenclature that harks back to an Enlightenment notion that nature can be ordered. And behind Linnaeus lurks the biblical belief that, like Adam, we name the animals. It is simply our job.

Looking for an ivory-bill today takes the mediating nature of birdwatching to an even higher level, because in this case the quarry is a kind of ghost bird, a creature that does and does not exist. Birds have always been emblems that shuttled between the natural world and the man-made world, between science and poetry, between earth and sky. But the ivory-bill is even more of an in-between figure—flying between the world of the living and the world of the dead, between the American wilderness and the modern wasteland, between faith and doubt, survival and extinction. No wonder the bird has taken on a sort of mystical character. Its physical prowess made it king of the woodpeckers. But is it a once and future king?

Enter David Kullivan, a twenty-two-year-old forestry student at Louisiana State University. In the spring of 1999, Kullivan was out turkey hunting in southeastern Louisiana in an area called the Pearl River Wildlife Management Area. He was alone, it was early morning, and he was wearing camouflage pants, shirt, and cap. He was sitting on a tree stump holding his 12-gauge shotgun and waiting for a turkey to call when he suddenly saw a pair of very large birds that settled about twenty yards from him.

Though not a birdwatcher, Kullivan has a woodsman's sense of the local birdlife and he knew that he had never seen these birds before. They were larger than pileated woodpeckers, which are, after the ivory-bill, America's largest woodpecker. The birds Kullivan saw were black and white, like pileated woodpeckers, but they had more white on the wing and the bills were larger and whiter. One of the birds had a red crest. The other had a black crest. They flew to a water oak about ten yards from where Kullivan was sitting. He had what birders would call a very good look. He had brought a camera with him, in the hope of recording the turkey he planned to shoot, but it was zipped into his turkey vest and he decided it was better to study the birds as carefully as possible rather than risk taking his eye off them.

The bird with the red crest, which Kullivan decided was the male, began to call. Kullivan described the sound as a "loud, nasal *kent.*" After a few minutes the birds flew off, but Kullivan continued to hear the call for some fifteen minutes after the birds were gone. He abandoned his turkey hunt and spent the rest of the day chasing the birds through the woods, but he never got another decent look.

Unfortunately, only a photograph would have given Kullivan's sighting authority. Adding to his difficulties was the fact that it was April Fools' Day—not an auspicious time to announce the appearance of an extinct bird. Kullivan admits he was afraid to go public, but he never doubted it was the right thing to do. When spring break was over that Monday, he went to see his professor of zoology, Vernon Wright.

Wright was in many ways already a believer in the continued existence of ivory-billed woodpeckers. He'd been fielding reports of sightings for twenty years, and though he himself had never seen the bird, he firmly believed it was out there. It was Wright who had told his class about the ivory-bill, along with several other animal species presumed extinct but still rumored to live in the heart of the swamps and forests of Louisiana. In some sense, he had prepared his students for a sighting by telling them the bird was still out there, which, depending on your point of view, increased the likelihood of a credible sighting or diminished it by planting the image of the bird already in his students' minds.

Almost nobody sees an apparition of the Virgin Mary without first having a mental image of what she might look like. On the other hand, a great deal of birding is based on knowledge acquired before you go into the field. This paradox is amplified a thousand times when birding for extinct birds.

Wright took Kullivan to see James Van Remsen, an ornithologist at Louisiana State University and curator of birds at the university museum. Though an expert in South American birds, Remsen, like Wright, had been fielding ivory-bill reports for years and knows a great deal about the woodpeckers and their habits. Remsen examined Kullivan—asking minute questions about the bird. Kullivan had noticed details that do not appear in guidebooks—like the way the crest of the female curls forward. Remsen came away convinced—if not 100 percent that the bird was out there, then at least that Kullivan hadn't fabricated his account. "It was," he told me, "the most credible report I've heard in twenty years on the job."

Remsen helped persuade Louisiana Wildlife and Fisheries to halt logging in the region of the Pearl River Wildlife Management Area, where the bird was reportedly seen. That winter, when the leaves had fallen off the trees and the snakes had gone into hibernation, several teams composed of members of Wildlife and Fisheries, as well as local—and visiting—birders, searched the area. They found nothing conclusive, but not seeing a bird is almost never proof that it isn't out there. Websites sprouted up and hundreds of birders went down—some in the hope of adding a new bird to their life lists that they had never dreamed of adding. For others there was a more mystical sense of cosmic correction—a chance to reverse history, to undo a crime for which human beings are in large part responsible.

Kullivan, too, became obsessed, to a degree, with finding the bird—in part to vindicate himself, in part because, having once seen it, he was not about to give up the quest. He continued to search for the bird during the summer months when the temperature exceeded 100 degrees and the leaves on the cypress and sweet gums reduced visibility and the snakes and mosquitoes reclaimed the swamp.

It was to meet Kullivan and go looking myself that I went down in the fall of 2000. I'd also gotten an assignment from *The New Yorker* magazine to look for the bird—I was getting paid to go birdwatching! The swamp, though I had pictured a vast region of uncharted wilderness, was only forty minutes east of New Orleans on Route I-10. There is literally a "swamp exit." It is right near a town called Slidell that I knew as a line in a song by Lucinda Williams. I kept chanting the line to myself—"I'm gonna go to Slidell and look for my joy"—amused to find myself in Lucinda's Southern Gothic landscape, where love and heartache hang like Spanish moss.

There are always personal motivations for every quest, however joined it may be to noble public purpose. At the time of my first trip to look for the ivory-billed woodpecker—and I was to make several more—my father was losing his mind to dementia. In some half-conscious way this quickened my desire to find something, to recover something, just as it may have fueled my larger passion for birding itself, which seems at times like a kind of antidote to memory loss.

I was still new enough in my pursuit to relish the burgeoning vocabulary of birding, whether of new bird names or the world of descriptive words that came with them—"buff" as a warm yellow color, as in "buff-breasted sandpiper"; "rufous" for rusty red, as in "rufous-sided towhee" (since renamed "Eastern towhee"). There was a specialized vocabulary for body parts, words like "auriculars" for ear patches, or "lores" for the tiny region above the bill of a bird. There was even a smattering of

Latin, a language my father had learned as a boy; in English the yellow-rumped warbler may be known by the colorful patch on its ass, but in Latin *Dendroica coronata* boasts a crown.

All these new words now hung like bright stars against the darkness of forgetfulness. And the ivory-bill was literally in danger of falling from the sky—I did not want the bird to be erased from biological consciousness, and extinction is a form of zoological memory loss. I wanted this one species to remain lodged in the mind of the world. And I wanted it to be more than a mere memory. What is all that greedy looking that birdwatching induces, a kind of gobbling need to know and see and marvel, but a hunger for life? And life, as John Ruskin beautifully said, echoing the Hebrew Bible, is the only wealth. Birdwatching is all about looking for life.

My father was in a nursing home in Manhattan on 106th Street near Central Park; 106th Street was the original northern border of the park when Olmstead and Vaux began work in 1853. The park was later expanded north to 110th, and the northern end still has a wilder feel than the parts near my apartment—the rocks seem more abrupt and exposed, the trees less tamed. There is a tree-ringed body of water at 101st Street called The Pool, out of which a stream flows through dark stone tunnels, where it is possible to be the only person on a weekday morning.

It is a very good place for birds, and I would often bring my binoculars when I went to visit my father, birding before and after my visit, as if shoring up all those particles of life against my father's collapse would fend off a collapse of my own.

As someone who could get lost in his own apartment, I suddenly valued the unfolding knowledge of geography—totally ignored in my 1970s public school education—that birding gave me. Now I wanted to know why the blackpoll was usually the last warbler I saw in Central Park at the end of spring migration, like Santa Claus bringing up the rear of the Thanksgiving Day parade, and I was led to the wintering ground of the bird in far-off southern Brazil. I looked at maps more and more. Suddenly it mattered where Louisiana was and where the Mississippi Delta was and where Slidell was.

But before I go to Slidell, I need to go backward a bit. Because birdwatching doesn't just unfold outward into space. It carries its own history with it and carries the looker backward in time—to his own animal origins, and also to cultural origins that are bound up with the challenges of life in the modern world.

The ivory-bill is, like birding itself, a perfect emblem of our own paradoxical relationship to the American wilderness, of what is lost and what can be recovered, and of our own divided impulses. While carrying the ivory-bill to his hotel room back in the eighteenth century, Wilson noted the wounded creature's cries, "exactly resembling the violent crying of a young child." And with the bird hidden beneath his coat, Wilson asked the innkeeper for a room "for myself and my baby." His joke has painful meaning. Wilson shot a bird he longed to liberate and pretended a wild animal he was in the process of killing was his own child.

The urge to kill and the urge to conserve live side by side;

they are our heritage, and the ivory-bill somehow carries our double burden on its black-and-white back. But so does bird-watching itself. My forays into Central Park are, as much as my trip to a Louisiana swamp to look for a possibly vanished bird, part of a larger journey the country itself has been making since its earliest days with increasing urgency. All this no doubt sounds grandiose, but then, birding isn't trainspotting.

2.

AUDUBON'S PARROT

[The monkey] certainly showed his supremacy in strength
over the denizen of the air, for, walking deliberately and
uprightly toward the poor bird, he at once killed it, with
unnatural composure.

—JOHN JAMES AUDUBON,
Myself

If this were a history of birdwatching, it would have been hard to know where to begin. The ancient mists of Neolithic life, when birds were totemic powers turning up on cave walls and in burial mounds as well as on the dinner table? Or the modern period that began roughly a hundred years ago, when binoculars replaced the shotgun and birdwatching became its own pursuit, unconnected to hunting? Both approaches would be valid, the way one might begin a history of Zionism with Abraham moving from Ur to Haran four thousand years ago, or with Theodor Herzl deciding, in the 1890s, that Jews ought to have a modern nation-state like the ones that Germany and Italy had created twenty years earlier.

Since I'm not a historian, I tend to believe in the advice Freud gave his patients—wherever you start is the right beginning. But if I *were* writing a history of birdwatching, my impulse would be to begin with Audubon, who exhibits elements of the modern and the mythic together and who was a sort of transitional figure, very different from the champion of bird preservation his name now conjures and yet in many ways anticipatory of that world.

There are traces of Audubon everywhere, but just as I began birding with the birds that throng through Central Park during spring and fall migration, so I am drawn to the Audubon who lives in my own backyard.

Stand in front of the grand Central Park West entrance of the American Museum of Natural History in Manhattan, so instrumental in the rise of modern birdwatching, and look up. All the way up, past the great bronze statue of Theodore Roosevelt mounted on his horse, attended by two proud—but subjugated—figures, an Indian and an African. Past the pigeon sitting on Roosevelt's head. Past the President and the pigeon and the long flight of stone steps and the great banners—announcing the butterfly conservatory or the exhibit devoted to chocolate—attempting to disguise the fact that the museum is primarily a giant mausoleum.

Keep looking up. Perched at the top of the building's façade you will see four figures made of stone—Meriwether Lewis, William Clark, Daniel Boone, and John James Audubon. They are like the four evangelists on the façade of a cathedral. These men, all born in the eighteenth century, hover over the modern era of birdwatching the way they preside over Roosevelt's statue. Roosevelt, whom I will write about later, was to some degree playacting a drama that these men lived. They hail from the time when categories were more fluid—when exploration, soldiering, science, and sport were often hard to tell apart. Even Audubon, the only artist in this group of adventurers, and the man whose name is synonymous today with birdwatching and bird conservation, is leaning on a gun.

Audubon was born in 1785, grew up in France, and didn't arrive in America until 1803, when he was eighteen years old. It was the year of the Louisiana Purchase, when the size of the United States had suddenly doubled. At the time, Thomas Jefferson—who dispatched Lewis and Clark to the West—was President. Audubon experienced a country where the wild and the tame were still neighbors, where Kentucky was frontier, and where the passenger pigeon, now extinct, accounted for 30 to 40 percent of the breeding bird population of the United States; it was possible to watch the birds flock overhead in a sky-blackening mass that took three days to pass and that may have contained upward of one billion birds. (The population of the United States at the time was between 5 and 6 million people.)

No descriptions of the great flight of passenger pigeons, and the slaughter they inspired, are more riveting than Audubon's own. He described one frenzied bird massacre like this:

The sun was lost to our view, yet not a Pigeon had arrived. Every thing was ready, and all eyes were gazing on the clear sky, which appeared in glimpses amidst the tall trees. Suddenly there burst forth a general cry of "Here they come!" The noise which they made, though yet distant, reminded me of a hard gale at sea, passing through the rigging of a close-reefed vessel. As the birds arrived and passed over me, I felt a current of air that surprised me. Thousands were soon knocked down by the polemen. The birds continued to pour in. The fires were lighted [to asphyxiate them], and a magnificent, as well as wonderful and almost terrifying, sight presented itself. The Pigeons, arriving by thousands, alighted everywhere, one above another, until solid masses as large as hogsheads were formed on the branches all round. Here and there the perches gave way under the weight with a crash, and, falling to the ground, destroyed hundreds of the birds beneath, forcing down the dense groups with which every stick was loaded. It was a scene of uproar and confusion. I found it quite useless to speak, or even to shout to those persons who were nearest to me. Even the reports of the guns were seldom heard, and I was made aware of the firing only by seeing the shooters reloading.

This was the sort of slaughter that led to the birds' extinction, of course—it continued, as Richard Rhodes points out in his excellent biography of Audubon, until "comparable but sustainable commercial slaughter commenced in the twentieth century of domestic fowl." An important point that should keep us from judging Audubon's generation too harshly—if the birds we eat today flew overhead on the way to slaughter, we might never see the sun.

Though he has come down to us in the guise of a backwoodsman, Audubon was an exhilarating mixture of elements. He self-consciously posed in buckskin, sporting a rifle, which is how he appears atop the museum—but he was also a dandified European who danced, fenced, and played the violin and the flageolet—a kind of recorder that he brought into the wilderness with him. He sang, knew how to plait a woman's hair, flirted with the ladies, and generally charmed the pants off everyone.

Installed by his French father on an estate in Pennsylvania, he married the girl next door—the prosperous daughter of an English gentleman—moved west to run a dry-goods store in Missouri, prospered, faltered, and failed, and then decided, against all odds, to abandon business in order to become a full-time painter—not of people or landscapes, but of birds. Thanks to his enormous ambition, and his wife's willingness to find employment on various Southern plantations and raise their children while he was off hunting, painting, and self-promoting, he managed to fulfill his dream of painting every known American bird in life size and getting them reproduced by master printers and bound into gigantic volumes that he sold to museums and royalty and institutions of higher learning at home and abroad. This at a time when neither artist nor naturalist was considered in any way a viable profession. Astonishingly, he put two half professions together, created something altogether new, and in the process became an international celebrity. (He died demented in Manhattan, oblivious to his family's declining fortunes, but that's another story.)

Like his approximate contemporary and fellow Frenchman Alexis de Tocqueville, Audubon created a portrait of America—not by canvassing its political gatherings or examining its prison system, but by painting its avian inhabitants. His birds are weirdly anthropomorphic (his white pelican looks as if it might consult a pocket watch before flying) and yet they are preternaturally realistic. They look like people who have been turned into birds and might turn back at any enchanted moment, but they have the simultaneous effect of returning their viewers to the wilderness.

There is something potentially quaint about this anthropomorphism, but there is also something prescient about it. Audubon had finished his best work by the time Darwin was a young man poking around the Galápagos, but the two naturalists intuited similar things about the connection between people and the wild world around them. Audubon may have made his birds look at times like people, but the lingering effect is to make people feel like birds, an irrefutable part of nature.

Audubon is a weirdly prophetic figure. Despite the scientific lapses in his work—for dramatic effect he had no problem showing rattlesnakes and mockingbirds doing battle high in a tree where no self-respecting rattlesnake would have slithered—and despite various artistic flaws that give even his most sophisticated work a sort of folk aura, he continues to feel like a contemporary. His primitivism is our own.

Alexander Wilson, the man who caught an ivory-bill and locked it in his hotel room, had actually arrived on the scene first. The Scottish-born Wilson, who died in 1813 in the middle of Volume 8 of his *American Ornithology*, was half the artist Audubon was, though he may have been twice the scientist and is probably the true father of American ornithology. But Audubon, blurring art and science as he did, and creating a mythological persona in the process, is more truly the father of birdwatching and all it has come to mean.

The two men actually met, in 1810, when Audubon was living in Louisville, Kentucky—trying, and failing, to make a go of things as a dry-goods salesman. Wilson came into his store looking for subscribers to *American Ornithology*, having heard that the young Frenchman liked birds. After looking at Wilson's work, Audubon went and fetched his own, already far superior, though he assured Wilson that he had no plans to publish. Meeting Wilson may in fact have given him the idea of a grand comprehensive group portrait of American birds, but there is something else about Audubon, beyond his encyclopedic enterprise, that makes him still so central and emblematic.

Perhaps this is because Audubon's awakening to the avian world, much like modern birdwatching itself, grows out of murder, loss, and longing. On the first page of *Myself*, his memoir addressed to his children, Audubon writes that when he was a little boy, a monkey killed his favorite parrot. Audubon tells his children that he has thought of this violent episode thousands of times, remembers it as if it had happened "this very day," and that it's possible the event led him to love birds and study them with infinite pleasure. The story is a parable about men and birds as much as it is a true-life narrative. It's a weird story and yet em-blematic in so many ways that it is worth looking at in detail.

"My mother," Audubon writes, "had several beautiful parrots and some monkeys; one of the latter was a full-grown male of a very large species." One morning, the servants were arranging little Audubon's room when "Pretty Polly," the parrot, asked for her breakfast as usual: "*Du pain au lait pour le perroquet Migonne.*'" For some reason the monkey, whom Audubon refers to as "the man of the woods," seemed to grow offended at "the bird presuming upon his rights in the scale of nature." Whatever the cause, the monkey "certainly showed his supremacy in strength over the denizen of the air, for, walking deliberately and uprightly toward the poor bird, he at once killed it, with unnat-ural composure."

That's the way it is with birds; they represent life, but they're always dying. I remember the woman leading that first birding field trip I went on, mentioning, almost casually, that 50 percent of migrating birds die on the journey. I was in the first flush of my newfound passion, scribbling unfamiliar names in a notebook—black-throated blue, prairie warbler, brown thrasher—pointing my cheap binoculars in every direction, thinking, Oh, baby, where have you been all my life? and feeling young and alive de-spite the slow white-haired ladies who kept getting in my way.

The realization that these birds, hidden from me by my own blindness for so long, were a remnant gave the whole pursuit a human ache, just when it was the energizing, alien animal life I was delighting in. And then of course I got the larger news that the places they spend the winter, the rain forests of South and Central America, are shrinking or disappearing, and that not merely individual birds but whole species live on the brink.

The website of the Rainforest Foundation informed me that in the time it will take to read this sentence, 2.47 acres of rain forest will be destroyed (assuming you read a sentence per second). Other websites offered similarly harrowing statistics. I leave it to others to track these statistics to their source, untangle the thicket of political and cultural disputation surrounding them, and clarify the combination of need and greed and poverty and wealth that go into the destruction of a vast natural resource where indigenous people and corporate powers and desperate governments and environmental demands all collide. But however you parse it, the news is bad. Suddenly, I felt like the Tin Man in *The Wizard of Oz*—*Now I know I have a heart, because it's breaking.* It took me until the age of thirty to shatter my urban shell and wake up to the natural world. No sooner had I discovered birds and that beating place in myself that craved and needed nature than I discovered how precarious the wild world is.

From the beginning, Audubon's bird killing was tied to an opposite impulse to preserve and restore. Our greatest bird artist, Audubon loved birds, shot them by the hundreds, and then delicately impaled them on wires attached to a special board of his own devising that allowed him to pose them and paint them in lifelike attitudes, rather than in the inert, flightless isolation that had dominated bird art till then. The impulse to kill and then resurrect is everywhere evident in Audubon's paintings. He was obsessed with bringing the creatures he shot back to life; it is the key to all his work. This connects him to modern-day birdwatchers. It also gives his work a quasi-religious component.

Harold Bloom has observed that the true American religion isn't Christianity but a faith in which each citizen sees himself as the risen Jesus. Audubon's birds are icons of an emerging American religion. This makes it fitting that his name is now inseparable from bird conservation, and that it was at the New

York City chapter of the Audubon Society that I first learned about birds. Audubon's birds, perched between life and death, are, like all birds, great mediators. Audubon had one foot in the world of art and one foot in the world of science, and his paintings occupy a special place—half ornithological and half works of the imagination. They are incredibly detailed and accu-

rate—usually—but they possess something extra, a human dimension that gives them their uncanny appeal.

If you look at Audubon's painting of Carolina parakeets, you feel in it the story he told in his memoir. One bird looks straight at us, making the sort of eye contact we usually see in portraits of human beings. (When Audubon's dry-goods business failed, he supported himself as a portrait painter while devoting his greatest energies to painting what really mattered to him, birds.) Audubon has imbued the Carolina parakeet with a sort of human curiosity, a wariness and deep regard that makes our knowledge of the impending death of the bird all the more acute.

This is why photographs of birds can often seem oddly inert and why Audubon's paintings have such enduring life. Audubon wasn't a birdwatcher in the modern sense, but he epitomizes the birdwatcher's spirit. He didn't just put the watcher into the bird, he also saw how much of the bird was in him—and so it is hard to tell if his birds look like people or if people resemble birds in certain ways that Audubon was uncannily attuned to. That killing the birds he painted helped him achieve this intimacy is part of the strangeness of art, and human nature. The urge to kill and the urge to preserve seem equally great in us, and are often inextricably linked. The double identity applies to all of us and goes to the heart of our ambivalent relationship to nature, and to ourselves—a relationship that haunts birdwatching whether we know it or not.

In Audubon's painting, the "man of the woods" is about to do in "Pretty Polly" and Audubon's sympathies are with the bird, even though he *is* the man of the woods. Audubon's painting tells a story as human as it is avian. And it raises in us a question that hangs over modern civilization—can the talking parrot in us survive the killer primate?

Birdwatching holds out the possibility of a hopeful answer. In 1900, Frank Chapman created the first Christmas Bird Count as a way of transforming the traditional Christmas Day hunt into something bloodless. Though it began in New York City, the count has now become a fixture throughout the country. In some sense, Chapman is a child of Audubon. He gave up a promising banking career to pursue his love of birds in the days before ornithology quite existed as a profession. But in 1888 he landed a job at the American Museum of Natural History, where he worked for many years, helping to make the museum one of the great centers of ornithological study.

Chapman knew personally the killer instincts the Christmas Bird Count tried to sublimate. In his fine history of American ornithology, *A Passion for Birds*, Mark V. Barrow, Jr., tells the story of Chapman shooting Carolina parakeets in Florida in 1889, when hardly any of the birds remained. Though an early advocate of bird protection, Chapman could not resist the chance to collect some rare specimens, and when he heard a flock had been found, he grabbed his gun with great excitement. When he finally gets his prize, he is overtaken with remorse:

> I admired them to my heart's content, counted them backwards and forwards[,] troubled over them generally, all the time almost doubting whether it was all true—for now we have nine specimens and I shall make no further attempt to secure others, for we have almost exterminated two of the three small flocks which occur here, and far be it from me to deal the final blows. Good luck to you poor doomed creatures, may you live to see many generations of your kind.

Despite this touching vow, Chapman can't help himself when he finds another little cluster of birds: "Good resolutions like many other things are much easier to plan than to practice. [T]he parakeets tempted me and I fell; they also fell, six more of them making our total fifteen." Twenty-nine years later, having already vanished from the wild, the last known Carolina parakeet died in the Cincinnati Zoo and the species became extinct.

Thanks to binoculars, as well as laws protecting migratory birds, birdwatching is no longer conducted with a shotgun, but it is still related to hunting. The urge to stalk and kill are murmuring silently in the blood even while you are pursuing what is often parodied as a dainty egghead pastime. Looking and listening are restored to active, not passive, functioning, as they must have been when we lived in the woods and our lives depended on them. I felt it the very first day I went birding, an almost sick excitement of anticipation, as if what I was doing were dangerous, a life-and-death matter. The group I was in may have looked as if it were taking a tour of a college campus, but plodding and unaerobic as we seemed, I felt stirring in me every childhood dream of being an Indian, becoming part of nature so that you can stand up at the last minute and shed your buffalo skin and take aim.

Not everybody shares this conviction. I remember once, in Central Park, craning after a Blackburnian warbler, a tiny bird with a blazing orange throat. In exasperation I said to the woman next to me, "You can see why they used to shoot them." I was met with a look of horror and revulsion. Now, I have no plans to go hunting with a gun, and it has been—appropriately—illegal to kill songbirds since the migratory bird act of 1918. But certainly one of the things that makes us part of the natural world, instead of merely tourists in it, is our killer urges.

Which makes the story of how Audubon came to love birds, with its French-speaking parrot and murderous monkey, not just the story of his own origins. Audubon was a true child of the eighteenth century, caught up in the great rational, classifying urge born of the Enlightenment that gave rise to so much modern science. But he also lived through the failure of the Enlightenment; his family suffered through the Reign of Terror, and Audubon even attributed his flowing locks to memories of the French citizens barbered for the guillotine.

In Europe, the age of reason gave rise to the orderly system of nomenclature, the elegant classification of every living thing and the belief that science and rationality could save us from our baser instincts. But the conviction that ultimate truth was knowable by science, and that animals might be ordered by those with superior knowledge, is related in disturbing ways to the belief that human beings, too, must fit into a system. The French Enlightenment contained the seeds of its own overthrow because of its very absolutism. The conviction that society might be engineered along scientific lines that were best for the species in the long run undid it.

It was this world that Audubon was fleeing in 1803, when his father sent him to America to avoid conscription in Napoleon's army. But the parrot and the monkey, those mythic forces, followed him to America, because they lived inside him, just as they live inside us all.

By the time Audubon died, on January 27, 1851, the world around him had radically altered. No longer a backwoodsman—which he only half was, anyway—he had retired to Manhattan and built himself an estate on the Hudson called Minnie's Land. He lived long enough to feel keenly the changes in his adopted country that made the subjects of his paintings objects of exoticism, not simply because they had wings and lived in hard-to-reach places, but because they were starting to disappear. It was from Audubon's house in Manhattan that his friend Samuel Morse, inventor of the telegraph, sent the first electronic message from New York to Philadelphia, shrinking the world a little more. But then America had been shrinking even before it was done expanding; Daniel Boone, Audubon's companion in stone, had, even before Audubon's arrival in America, fled Kentucky for parts farther west because, according to legend, he felt he was running out of "elbow room." As it happens, it was Boone himself who had blazed Kentucky's Wilderness Road in 1775 and helped settle the region in the first place.

3

LOVE AND DEATH

A quiet passion burns, not for total control but for the sensation of constant advance.

—EDWARD O. WILSON,
Biophilia

n New Orleans in 1821, in love with birds and pursuing his dream at last, Audubon met a beautiful young woman who asked him to paint her nude. He'd been supporting his bird art by doing speedy portraits of the faces of local citizens at twenty-five dollars a pop, but this woman, of European birth, wanted her whole self captured in paint as a gift to her lover. She had paints and brushes for him, soft lighting, and a sheet of "elephant paper," the same giant paper Audubon would use for the life-sized portraits in *Birds of America*. She swore him to secrecy, stepped behind a curtain, and when, at her instructions, he drew the curtains, he found her arranged on a sofa, naked as a blue jay.

Audubon's version of the story, which he sent his wife—who was back in Cincinnati with their children—has him trembling so much at the first encounter that he needed a shot of cognac and an hour to compose himself. But he managed, over several days and many hours, to paint her as she wished (though the woman, a painter herself, did a fair amount of retouching). For his pains and his discretion, the mystery woman gave Audubon a gun, which she inscribed with the words "Do not refuse this gift from a friend who is in your debt; may its goodness equal yours." He used it often to kill the birds he painted.

He had the gun with him not long afterward when a giant flock of golden plovers passed through the area. It was one of those vast flocks from those years of avian abundance that takes a full day to pass, and Audubon noted the crowds of hunters who took up positions with dogs to fetch the dead and who, with expert imitations, called to the birds so that they would lower their flight to shotgun range. For the duration of the day men fired without rest until, by Audubon's estimate, forty-eight thousand birds had been killed.

I met no nude women and shot no birds on my trip to New Orleans when I went south in 2000 to look for the ivory-billed woodpecker, but consulting Audubon's diary to get a feel for his time in the area, I felt the twin pull of those stories and their weird relationship to each other, and to bird hunting conducted with or without a gun. The two stories braided together—each is for Audubon an aspect of his search for the birds of America—and put me in mind of a poem by Elizabeth Bishop called "Brazil, January 1, 1502." Despite the wintry date of the title—which marks the arrival of the conquistadors—it is eternal summer in the poem, and literal summer in the Southern Hemisphere. The poet is looking at rich jungle vegetation, seeing it like the painting of Eden the conquistadors saw, "every square inch filling with foliage." Everything is rich and symbolic; the landscape has a sexual allure, a female lizard holds "her wicked tail straight up and over, / red as a red-hot wire." And somewhere beyond the foliage, women are hidden deep in the jungle.

Bishop, who grew up bereft in Nova Scotia and chilly New England—her father dead before she was one, her mother committed to an asylum by the time she was five—settled in Brazil in 1951. She herself had fallen in love with the jungle landscape and with a woman in Brazil, where she lived for many years, happy for the first time until her lover became ill and eventually committed suicide. In her poem, desire and violence and violation enter all at once with an image of the conquistadors. Having discovered a "brand-new pleasure," they race in armor through the jungle:

> *they ripped away into the hanging fabric,*
> *each out to catch an Indian for himself—*
> *those maddening little women who kept calling,*
> *calling to each other (or had the birds waked up?)*
> *and retreating, always retreating, behind it.*

In this poem, which reads at times like the description of a painting, the jungle itself becomes a painting, the armed men ripping away "into the hanging fabric." Or is it a painting that has turned into jungle? It's hard to tell, just as it is hard to tell if it is our stories of the natural world that shape our encounter with it or vice versa. Audubon, after all, called the ivory-bill, which he painted with great vitality, the Van Dyck bird. The interplay of art and nature, the erotic urge and the conquering urge, the strange interchangeability of people and birds in Audubon's work, haunts me deeply.

I think many birdwatchers carry an unspoken hope in the heart: not to be in a world where everything is preserved, but to be in a world where nothing needs to be preserved. To feel that watching birds is not an artificial pursuit but a natural one. Because for so many eons of our evolutionary history, nothing in nature had to be preserved. It was our own preservation that we spent all our time and energy on, not the preservation of the world around us. It took all we had just to dent the wilderness a little.

All that changed not so very long ago, so can we be blamed

for still harboring dreams born from that earlier time? Edward
O. Wilson expresses it beautifully in *Biophilia*:

> Now to the very heart of wonder. Because species diversity
> was created prior to humanity, and because we evolved
> within it, we have never fathomed its limits. As a conse-
> quence, the living world is the natural domain of the most
> restless and paradoxical part of the human spirit. Our sense
> of wonder grows exponentially: the greater the knowledge,
> the deeper the mystery and the more we seek knowledge to
> create new mystery. This catalytic reaction, seemingly an
> inborn human trait, draws us perpetually forward in a
> search for new places and new life. Nature is to be mastered,
> but (we hope) never completely. A quiet passion burns, not
> for total control but for the sensation of constant advance.

This is an ancient longing, one which "pulled human populations like a living sheet over the world during the ice ages."

It was this urge, Wilson notes, that was called up by the
American frontier; he experiences a version of it himself visiting
an Arawak village in Suriname in 1961. There he allows himself
a sort of conquistador fantasy, a dream of ever-receding wilderness to be ever conquered by his explorations:

> My mind maneuvered through an unending world suited
> to the naturalist. I looked in reverie down the path
> through the savanna woodland and imagined walking to
> the Saramacca River and beyond, over the horizon, into a
> timeless reconnaissance through virgin forests to the land
> of magical names, Yekwana, Jivaro, Siriono, Tapirape,
> Siona-Secoya, Yumana, back and forth, never to run out
> of fresh jungle paths and glades.

But Wilson's dream of "fresh jungle paths and glades" is just that, a dream. We have run out, though the urge to subdue still remains. Our rate of technological advance, growing exponentially since the Industrial Revolution, has changed everything. Wilson readily acknowledges the paradox of his own dream, since without technology, the plane that got him to Suriname and that will get him out, or the malaria pills, gamma globulin shots, netting, and rubber boots that keep him from turning into food for parasites, he wouldn't have come at all. It's only because we have so thoroughly achieved victory that we can dream so romantically about the unknown.

Certainly my head was full of romantic dreams when I went down to the Pearl River Wildlife Management Area to search for the ivory-bill in early October 2000, a year and a half after Kullivan's original sighting. Logging was still suspended in the region, though hunting continued unabated. I was there a few days before the start of squirrel season. There were also seasons for deer, feral hog, rabbit, turkey, and woodcock. Blackbirds, cowbirds, grackles, and crows could be killed at any time of year, as could raccoon and opossum. Trapping was permitted for mink, bobcat, raccoon, beaver, and something called nutria, which sounded to me like a vitamin supplement but which turned out to be a large, aquatic, ratlike rodent whose fur is highly prized. I realized with a shock that "wildlife management" basically means the area is maintained to facilitate hunting.

Bow hunting (for deer) was already under way, and Bill Vermillion, my guide from Wildlife and Fisheries, handed me a bright orange vest and an orange cap that read: *Support National Hunting and Fishing Day.*

"That hat'll be popular in Central Park," Bill said slyly. But I did not feel betrayed by my cap or its legend. I had begun to recognize the deep link between hunting and birding. It seemed to me entirely appropriate that the last man who might have seen an ivory-billed woodpecker, and who had reawakened the drive to save it, was actually in the woods in order to kill a large bird.

Since then I've only grown more aware of the role of hunters and fishermen—who helped create the wildlife refuge system in which the ivory-bill might have survived. It was a shock to discover that wildlife management areas were managed so that people could shoot the wildlife. But it was bracing and somehow liberating, because it offered a definition of human nature that seemed truer, if less flattering, than the one I was used to.

At the moment, I wished I were a hunter, if only to have better gear. I had failed to purchase snakeproof boots and was concerned about highly venomous water moccasins, locally referred to as "cotton mouths" because of the white you see when they open their jaws. I was wearing only ankle-high hiking boots. I mentioned this to my guide, whose boots came up to his knees. "I'd give a look down for every look you take up," Bill said laconically.

Bill had the quiet, watchful intelligence of someone who spends part of each day walking alone in the woods. His attitude to the ivory-bill seemed one of agnostic optimism. Like me, he brought along a camera, just in case. "Every time I don't see the bird, it takes the wind out of me," he told me before we set out.

For the next six hours we tromped across scraggy underbrush, cane and blackberry brambles, passing through thick stands of water oak, tupelo, and sweet gum. I was looking down for snakes and up for birds. I also kept an eye out for the enormous webs of "banana spiders" that stretched several yards from tree to tree. Bill, who went first, cleared the webs out of the way by delicately pinching a few anchoring filaments between thumb and forefinger and then tearing across—he looked as if he were unlatching and then opening a gate. The spiders themselves, several inches long, black with yellow underbellies, occasionally wound up riding on his back. I flicked them off for him with a stick.

There were clouds of mosquitoes, though we had both doused ourselves in Cutter's. I remembered something I'd learned from a documentary about Indonesian tribes who simply decide they will "share" their blood with insects the way one might decide to give a quarter to every panhandler rather than feeling assaulted, guilty, and resentful. I failed at this approach and stopped frequently to apply more Cutter's, which I felt sifting through my skin and into my bones.

What with the mosquitoes, my fear of snakes, the physical exertion of walking through pathless woods, and my inward efforts not to scream whenever I stepped out of line and felt the velvety slap of a spiderweb on my face and the tickle of arachnid legs, I did not make a particularly effective searcher. Still, there were a lot of birds—we heard red-bellied woodpeckers and white-eyed vireos and indigo buntings—and the bird life of the upper canopy carried with it the hope that a more unusual bird might be lurking there as well.

The swamp is a stirring place. It was easy to see how both birds and myths about birds could survive there. An armadillo ran across our path, still dressed for a prehistoric age. The very mosquitoes suggested something fertile about the swamp, even with fall approaching and the days growing short.

But the sound of the highway followed us into the woods. I was, at various times, aware of the report of rifles from a shooting range operated by Wildlife and Fisheries, and the churning of trucks from nearby gravel pits.

In *Tristes Tropiques*, the great anthropologist Claude Lévi-Strauss recalls his search in remote areas of Brazil for the last tribes to have remained isolated from contact with Western man. On one of these forays into the rain forest, Lévi-Strauss describes his disappointment when he realizes that he can't get a particular passage of a Chopin nocturne out of his head. Here he is looking for the most primitive tribes on earth and he is being pursued into the jungle by piano music. It is one of those moments when the narrator realizes how much of an illusion the desire to step beyond the reach of Western civilization is; if it isn't strewn about us, then we bring inner reminders of it in our heads.

This, I suppose, is the flip side of the hunting urge nestled in the scientist's curiosity. Perhaps we cannot rid ourselves of civilization any more than we can abandon our animal natures. Birding, for me, is where the two impulses meet. And searching for the ivory-bill, an almost mythical creature of the primeval forest, as well as a poor last survivor of our vanquished natural world, brings disparate elements together even more. I'd have liked my search to be a kind of Ahabian pursuit of my own white whale, but if this is *Moby-Dick*, it is a quest with a difference, because finding the bird will lead, ideally, to the bird's salvation.

Still, once I was inside the area, it was easy to feel very far away indeed, and had it not been for a drought, much of the region would have been impassable without a boat. The area had the feel of a place that was ordinarily buried, hidden from view. Even with the drought, the black, reflective waters of various bayous cut through the woods. The beautiful silver-barked cypress trees had an otherworldly presence, swollen at the base as a natural buttress against flooding water that, because of the drought, had failed to come that year. Surrounding the cypress trees, like a brood of children, were cypress "knees," knobby protuberances between one and three feet high that help the trees "breathe" underwater and that help keep them anchored in shifting, sodden soil. They were also nakedly exposed because of the drought. Dry earth and rotting stumps had been plowed up in patches by the snouts of wild hogs. Everywhere I smelled what Robert Frost calls "the slow smokeless burning of decay."

We covered only a tiny fragment of the thirty-five thousand acres of the Pearl River Wildlife Management Area, but we were in the general vicinity of Kullivan's sighting. Bill had a Global Positioning System set for one particularly large tree of the sort favored by ivory-bills, but the signal kept bouncing off the surrounding trees, making his readings inaccurate. Several times we lost our way, but Bill had a compass and a topographical map and we blundered back to familiar ground eventually, though we never did find the giant tree.

Big trees play an important role in the life of ivory-bills. James T. Tanner, who studied the last significant population of the birds between 1937 and 1939, noted that they fed on the grubs that attacked recently dead trees. The birds scaled off the bark with their massive bills to get to the bugs beneath. To have a steady supply of dying trees, the birds required the sort of old-growth forests in which trees are mature enough to die on a regular basis, and they needed an area warm and moist enough to promote fast decay. The bottomlands of the Mississippi Delta were ideal, as were parts of East Texas and the Florida panhandle. Tanner's birds were in a region of Louisiana known today as the Tensas River National Wildlife Refuge but that Tanner refers to as the "Singer Tract," because the land was then owned by the Singer Sewing Machine Company, which, despite protests, leased the land to loggers who clear-cut it in 1944.

The ivory-bill's highly particular feeding requirements are a perfect example of specialization—a restricted habitat that nevertheless eliminates the competition of other birds. The price a species pays for specializing, though, is vulnerability to a change in the environment. The Kirtland's warbler, which breeds in a single spot of northern Michigan, will nest only in jack pine trees five to six years old—*if* there are sufficient clearings as well. Such finicky behavior has nearly cost the species its life. Fewer forest fires over the years meant fewer young pine trees sprouting up, and what has kept the bird going is a human determination to artificially plant new trees and fire the old ones. But it is easier to create small trees than to conjure up huge ones. When the last stands of virgin forest were logged out of existence in the Deep South, the fate of the ivory-bill may have been sealed.

Christopher Cokinos quotes the last official observer of an ivory-billed woodpecker in his excellent book *Hope Is the Thing with Feathers*. This was Don Eckelberry, a nature artist who in 1944 went to the Singer Tract while the area was being logged. After much searching, Eckelberry found the lone female reported to still be in the area. She was sitting near her roosting tree and, despite the encroachments of tractors, refusing to fly to remaining areas of the forest.

From Eckelberry's description one gets the feeling that the bird was simply waiting for its doom. As another eyewitness put it, there may have been "psychological factors" involved in the bird's demise. In other words, the bird's defiant character was its fate—this is a tragic, romantic view of the ivory-bill as a creature so wedded to its habitat that, like the self-starving bird Alexander Wilson captured, it would rather die than compromise.

Reading descriptions of the last ivory-bill in 1944, a lone female that refused to fly from its perch as the tractors moved in, I often thought of the moment in *Moby-Dick* when, at the end of the novel, the native American harpooner Tashtego hammers a flag to the mast. As the ship sinks, the hammer catches the wing of a "sky-hawk": "So the bird of heaven, with archangelic shrieks, and his imperial beak thrust upwards, and his whole captive form folded in the flag of Ahab, went down with his ship, which, like Satan, would not sink to hell till she had dragged a living part of heaven along with her."

But the ivory-bill may not have gone down with the forest. There are ornithologists, like Remsen at LSU, who speculate that ivory-bills can live in recently dead trees that are only a hundred years old—instead of the five- or six- or seven-hundred-year-old virgin timber they were known to favor. If that is true, then there are many areas where logging stopped some fifty or sixty years ago—including the Singer Tract, which, after its demise, was put under the "protection" of the Louisiana state government—that are once again producing trees capable of supporting ivory-bill habits. There are also areas, like the Pearl, where, because of the region's frequent inaccessibility, enough large trees may have been left uncut to give the birds a place to roost and breed.

Provided that the birds are still around. This, of course, is *the* question, and it divides ornithologists and naturalists and bird-watchers. It is notoriously difficult to prove the absence of something. The birds have a life expectancy of about twenty years, and many ornithologists, even doubtful ones, concede that a few renegades might have dodged detection, like those Japanese soldiers who refused to surrender and were gradually forgotten. A few geriatric survivors could never reconstitute a breeding population. This would add a tragic dimension to Kullivan's sighting—we might only find the bird in time to give it a proper burial and label it the last of its kind.

I will never forget the melancholy sight of two Micronesian kingfishers, big-headed birds with blue-green wing patches living behind glass at Brookfield Zoo in Chicago. Their species had thrived on Guam until, in the 1940s, human beings inadvertently introduced brown tree snakes from other islands; by the 1980s, the birds were extinct in the wild.

But there is still hope for the kingfishers, which were gathered up by zoos just as they were disappearing from the wild and which breed in captivity. There are now more than fifty birds—

not many, but enough to give scientists hope that they might someday end their exile, if not by returning to Guam, then at least on a nearby island free of snakes. They may yet avoid the fate of Martha, the last passenger pigeon, who died in the Cincinnati Zoo in 1914, and Incas, the last Carolina parakeet, who also lived at the Cincinnati Zoo and flew into oblivion in 1918. (Once you are given a human first name, your species is usually in trouble.)

As for the ivory-bills, it is still possible that the birds were more adaptable than anyone imagined and that they are quietly reproducing in remote regions. Kullivan, after all, claims he saw *a pair*. It has only been fifty years since the last authenticated sighting, and there have been numerous unauthenticated ones, many delivered years after the bird was seen by locals who were afraid of having private land confiscated by the "government" if an endangered bird were found nesting there. Remsen told me he was shown photographs from the 1970s—that he found credible—of nesting ivory-bills. The man who showed him the photographs had not wanted to lose his land. Kullivan told me a local adage—"There's no such thing as an endangered species on private property." As for why birdwatchers never seem to be the ones reporting ivory-bill sightings—it is often observed that birders do not, like hunters, stray far from marked paths. Even many hunters do not go far. And the birds do fly.

It is this possibility that inspires the faithful and may make Kullivan's sighting more than a novelty. It is what keeps Bill Vermillion and David Kullivan and a host of other people—including me—looking up. And what makes areas like the Pearl so exciting to visit. There are many lofty ways of putting the desire to find a bird that may be gone, but I like what Bill Vermillion said when I asked him why he wanted to find the bird: "It would mean that maybe we didn't screw things up that badly."

In the course of our six-hour trek, something strange happened to me. A vague longing to see an ivory-bill turned into an unexpected powerful ache. I cared less and less about spiderwebs and snakes. I really wanted to see my bird. And just when I had lost faith, a noisy shadow stirred above me, a large slow black flapping, and my heart began to beat faster.

I tried to remember where I put my camera and wondered if Bill could reach his in time. I thought of Mary Scott, a fine nature photographer who maintains an ivory-bill website. Scott traveled with the first wave of searchers the winter after Kullivan's sighting and believes she may have seen one of the birds—she was so moved by the experience that her eyes filled up with tears and she flubbed the photo.

As it turned out, what I had just seen was a pileated woodpecker. I had seen the bird before and had always been—until that moment—grateful for the view. It is a large and beautiful woodpecker, though I'd read on Mary Scott's website that locals refer to it as the "jackass bird" because of its raucous call. Less specialized than its cousin (it can eat more than the grubs that grow in big decaying trees), the pileated has thrived and turns up not merely in the swamps of the South but in suburban areas of the Northeast as well, where, without dignity, it will even visit suet feeders.

If the pileated woodpecker were considered extinct, it would cease to be a jackass and become enchanted, transformed by the kiss of death into something fine and mystical. We would have to dig up its nobler common names, and if none could be found, we would meditate on the word "pileated," a reference to the bird's crest, derived from the Latin word *pileus*, which describes a brimless felt cap. The cap was donned by liberated Roman slaves, and so served in antiquity as an emblem of freedom itself. The bird would become a figure for liberty lost, and we would compose fitting elegies. I tried to remind myself of this as the great bird launched itself again and vanished noisily into the swamp.

4

WHITMAN'S MOCKINGBIRD

Now in a moment I know what I am for . . .

—WALT WHITMAN,
"Out of the Cradle Endlessly Rocking"

In 1819, the year of the economic panic that drove Audubon out of business and set him on his bird-painting path for good, Walt Whitman was born on Long Island. The country itself was only forty-three years old, and Long Island, settled by the British from the east and by the Dutch from the west, was a patchwork of farms and fields and tiny towns, still imprinted with traces of Native American life. Hard times drove Whitman's family to Brooklyn, where he spent much of his childhood, but he continued to visit his grandparents' houses on Long Island and to spend his summers there.

During one of those visits, when Whitman was still a boy, he got out of bed in the middle of the night and went down to the beach, barefoot and alone. There he heard a mockingbird singing. The boy had been watching this bird and its mate for days as they guarded their nest, but suddenly the bird's mate vanished. And the male bird, as if in mourning, began to sing all night. The boy went out into the darkness to hear the bird and was transformed forever.

Some activities are important, even life changing, without

obvious danger or bloodshed. In that regard, birdwatching is like poetry. The poem that Whitman wrote based on this little episode, "Out of the Cradle Endlessly Rocking," is one of the great poems in the English language. In its fusion of the human and the animal, and in its depiction of an entire country through animal symbols, it is a kind of poetic extension of Audubon's paintings—but it takes the combination of the small and specific, and the cosmically ambitious, to a new level.

"It is difficult to get the news from poems," William Carlos Williams wrote, "yet men die miserably every day for lack of what is found there." That's the quote I chose for my high school yearbook, and for a long time I could not read those words, or contemplate the bespectacled, pretentious, frightened face above them, without loathing. The quote I'd wanted to choose was from Thoreau—"What demon possessed me that I behaved so well?"—but I was too well behaved to choose it and so I stuck with the news about poetry.

It's one thing for a doctor-poet like Williams, who knew death in its bodily as well as its spiritual form, to write such words. But not a high school student who seldom left the house. I was all talking parrot and no killer primate—I think that's what made me ashamed in later years. Williams wasn't lying, but I was. Now, however, after the loss of people I love and after the birth of people I love, after the grim discovery of politics and history, not to mention the humble business of earning a living, I find that I'd choose those words all over again. I've come full circle. And I'd add that what Williams said about poetry is true for birdwatching, too, a modest, mediating activity alive in the modern world but with roots planted deep in ancient magic.

Poetry, it should be said, can be bad for the environment. The most famous example of this is the release of sixty European starlings in Central Park in 1890 simply because they were mentioned, once, in a Shakespeare play. They roosted first in the eaves of the American Museum of Natural History, where their acid droppings quickly began eroding the masonry. They have since spread to all forty-eight continental states (Alaska and Hawaii appear to be safe), driving the bluebird out of the Northeast and so ticking off farmers that in 2004 two million birds were killed by the U.S. government as part of a pest control project.

Nevertheless, poetry is also necessary for the environment. John Burroughs, the hugely influential nineteenth-century naturalist and literary critic, observed that "all the great ornithologists—original namers and biographers of the birds—have been poets in deed if not in word." He used Audubon, of whom he wrote a biography, as a case in point, noting that "if he had not the tongue or the pen of the poet, certainly had the eye and ear and heart." And Burroughs implied that the opposite is also true, that poets are really ornithologists of a sort, with a special relationship to birds.

Burroughs is hardly known today, but in the nineteenth century he was perhaps the most famous nature writer there was. His first nature book, *Wake-Robin*, a collection of essays about birds published in 1871, sold over a million copies (compared to the five hundred copies of *Walden* sold in Thoreau's lifetime). This parenthetical fact doesn't make Burroughs better than Thoreau, of course, but it did make him more influential, and he had a huge impact on the men and women who went on to create the conservation movement at the turn of the century and beyond. He wrote at a time when industrialization was already at a full roar and sentimental longing for the world that was vanishing was at its peak.

Burroughs, as it happens, was an early champion of Walt Whitman. He defended Whitman tirelessly and in 1867 wrote the first biography of him, *Notes on Walt Whitman, As Poet and*

Person. In his collection of essays, *Birds and Poets*, he says, accurately, of "Out of the Cradle Endlessly Rocking," that though it is "not at all ornithological," yet it offers an unmatched representation of a bird translated into words.

Whitman took up his pen around the time that Audubon dropped his brush. The world he depicted, with its teeming, varied multitudes, is much closer to our own, but Whitman had been touched in his childhood by Audubon's pre-industrial world and never forgot it. In fact, much of his poetry is about bridging these different worlds.

By 1859, when "Out of the Cradle" was written, Audubon had been dead for eight years and the world that formed him was gone. Whitman had spent much of his life in Brooklyn, which had gone from a population of less than 12,000 in 1822, around the time he arrived, to a population of 280,000 in 1859, making it the fourth-largest city in America. Civil war was on the horizon, and the unified country implicit in Audubon's *Birds of America* was about to fall apart.

Which may explain Whitman's obsession with the world of childhood—his mockingbird poem was first published with the less romantic title "A Child's Reminiscence." The title he later chose, "Out of the Cradle Endlessly Rocking," gives the news of poetry in just a few words. It is a phrase of such haunting beauty that you can chant it to yourself in times of trouble or confusion and take comfort from it, because it says the child in us is still alive, and we are still alive, and maybe we are still children rocked by an invisible hand. It says that our adulthood is also a kind of childhood, and the whole world is really a cradle, and perhaps we will grow up someday into something more, and in any event, the mysteries of childhood are still close at hand and still unanswerable, so why pretend otherwise?

The poem begins with the mature Whitman revisiting the

Long Island beach he knew as a boy. It is the middle of the century and Whitman is in the middle of his life. Overcome with emotion, he rolls in the sand and weeps, and in weeping he becomes again the child he once was, and we are suddenly transported with him to his boyhood, when you could slip away undetected in the night and open a door on the infinite.

But the boy sees with a scientific as well as a poetic eye. With the precision Burroughs admired, Whitman recalls:

> *Two feather'd guests from Alabama, two together,*
> *And their nest, and four light-green eggs spotted with brown,*
> *And every day the he-bird to and fro near at hand,*
> *And every day the she-bird crouch'd on her nest, silent, with*
>   *bright eyes,*
> *And every day I, a curious boy, never too close, never disturbing*
>   *them,*
> *Cautiously peering, absorbing, translating.*

The child in the poem is a good observer of birds, almost modern in his birdwatching impulse: "never too close, never disturbing them." After the Civil War, when America became far more industrialized, tokens of the natural world would cry out for collection, and a boy like Whitman might well have helped himself to one or two or all of the eggs. He might have helped himself to one or both of the birds. But the boy Whitman is content simply to look and listen.

And just as he notices with great accuracy the eggs "spotted with brown," he notices the way a mockingbird really does sing, which is to say everything two or three times:

> *Shine! shine! shine!*
> *Pour down your warmth, great sun!*

While we bask, we two together.
Two together!

The birds are a poetic fantasy, singing their love song to each other and the world and the boy, but they are also real birds. Whitman represents poetry touched by science. His catalogs of himself are wild and fanciful, but also part of an encyclopedic world that attempted to make lists, that believed in knowledge. In the Middle Ages people must have seen the world in perspective, but they didn't draw it in perspective because, for some strange reason, they had forgotten how, which is another way of saying they didn't care. The symbolic way of seeing meant more to them than the literal. Whitman is holding these worlds in balance. His birds have symbolic meaning, but they are also actual birds.

Today I do not believe that Burroughs's observation is still true—that ornithologists are really poets and poets are a species of ornithologist. Perhaps science and art will make friends again, but for now some link has been severed. But in the nineteenth century it still held true. The decision Audubon made, meticulous though he was, to paint his mockingbirds battling a snake high in a tree clearly owes something to his own identification with the bird. Rattlesnakes don't climb trees, but if the laws of nature are broken in Audubon's painting, it is because some deeper mythic element as old as the Garden of Eden is being reinforced. This admittedly makes Audubon more an artist than an ornithologist.

Although the boy in Whitman's poem isn't a killer, death enters his world as well:

> *Till of a sudden,*
> *May-be kill'd, unknown to her mate,*
> *One forenoon the she-bird crouch'd not on the nest,*
> *Nor return'd that afternoon, nor the next,*
> *Nor ever appear'd again.*

The lone surviving mockingbird begins to sing all night long. This, too, is accurate—mockingbirds, when they have no mate, do not, like most birds, sing only in daytime to attract a female, but sing all night as well.

This also makes Whitman's poem, like Audubon's paintings, an act of cultural assertiveness. Just like Wallace Stevens, who in the twentieth century declared that the nightingale was "not a bird for me," Whitman needs an American bird to do what so many European poets like Keats and Coleridge loved about the nightingale. He needs a bird to sing all night, out of the darkness. As Burroughs points out in his essay, the mockingbird is America's nightingale, adding, with the chauvinism that often tinged nineteenth-century nature writing, that it sings more beautifully. (Even in the eighteenth century, Abigail Adams wrote to John: "Do you know that European birds have not half the melody of ours?") In Whitman's poem, the bird is downright operatic—Whitman loved opera—but it also retains the rhythms of a real bird:

Here I am! here!
With this just-sustain'd note I announce myself to you,
This gentle call is for you my love, for you.

Every night the boy comes out to hear this lone bird sing. And the boy does what birdwatchers still do—standing very still, he watches and listens, "Silent, avoiding the moonbeams, blending myself with the shadows." He sees the bird perched "on the prong of a moss-scalloped stake," almost touching the waves, singing and singing.

And now strange things begin to happen. The boy becomes the lone singing bird and he becomes the missing mate, hearing the song of the bird. A boy and a bird, married, and out of this union the boy is reborn as something new. He becomes a poet.

Is it indeed toward your mate you sing? or is it really to me?
For I, that was a child, my tongue's use sleeping, now I have
*   heard you,*
Now in a moment I know what I am for, I awake,
And already a thousand singers, a thousand songs, clearer,
*   louder and more sorrowful than yours,*
A thousand warbling echoes have started to life within me,
*   never to die.*

Just as the death of Audubon's parrot made him, or so he claimed, a bird lover and artist, so the death of the mockingbird makes Whitman a poet, in particular a poet of death and resurrection. Our greatest American poet was born, in his own fantastic phrase, "out of the mockingbird's throat." And what better bird for a poet to spring from than one that imitates the songs and calls of other birds and whose Latin name is *Mimus polyglottos*? This is especially true for Whitman, who wanted to absorb all the songs of America and sing them back transformed to the country.

Whitman's dream of marriage to a bird, or at least of sympathetic harmony with the natural world, is not restricted to poets. Thomas Jefferson kept a mockingbird named Dick in the White House, which he often allowed to fly free. It hopped up the stairs after him, traveled on his shoulder, and even pecked food from his lips at the dinner table. But Jefferson lived inside a pastoral dream of America that was breaking down by the middle of the nineteenth century.

The year of the poem's composition, 1859, was a dark time in Whitman's life—he had completely failed to achieve the popularity he dreamed of—and it was a dark time in the life of America. The "feather'd guests from Alabama" are birds, but they come up North from a Southern world about to be severed from the democratic union Whitman cherished. Birds don't know boundaries, but humans are obsessed with them. Whitman's poetic project had been to sing all of America, just as Audubon had been intent on painting every known American bird. But fragmentation was coming.

It wasn't only America that faced disunion in the middle of the nineteenth century. Eighteen fifty-nine was the year of the publication of *On the Origin of Species by Means of Natural Selection*, which, like the firing on Fort Sumter, leveled a blow against a bastion of religious certitude, a dream of wholeness that had been alive for more than four thousand years. Darwin represented not the death of faith but the transformation of it, and we are still coming to terms with how. Although *The Descent of Man* wouldn't be published until 1871, Darwin lifted a mirror to millions who cherished the notion that they were made in God's image, and showed them a very different face. As Darwin wrote in *The Descent of Man*:

We must, however, acknowledge, as it seems to me, that man with all his noble qualities, with sympathy which feels for the most debased, with benevolence which extends not only to other men, but to the humblest living creature, with his god-like intellect which has penetrated into the movements and constitution of the solar system—with all these exalted powers—Man still bears in his bodily frame the indelible stamp of his lowly origin.

The endlessly rocking cradle from which we emerged is adrift in a new way now in the human imagination. Or it is perhaps the sea itself, from which we really did emerge. In Whitman's work, prophetically, the sea is a powerful voice, and indeed has the last word in the whole poem.

And what does the sea say? It whispers the "low and delicious word death." Singing to his nightingale, Keats is "half in love with easeful death," but in Whitman's poem, death is half in love with him:

Hissing melodious, neither like the bird nor like my arous'd
    child's heart,
But edging near as privately for me, rustling at my feet,
Creeping thence steadily up to my ears and laving me softly all
    over,
Death, death, death, death, death.

Death is implicit in the notion of evolution. There are more extinct species than living ones—we ourselves stand on the bones of superceded primates. In our own lives, psychologically, we know that to change is to kill and cast off a self, and that it's difficult to part even with the selves we wish to leave behind— the dependent child, the unhappy lover, the fearful worrier. And if we contemplate our potential future as a species, can we really face leaving behind parts of ourselves—the violent parts, the irrational parts—which we pretend to hate and may denounce publicly, but that we secretly know are aspects of our core identity? These are unanswerable, speculative questions, but they are part of any discussion of evolution, whether we articulate them or not. Whitman understood these questions intuitively.

What has all this to do with birds? Birds say *life life life*, but something right alongside them is always whispering *death death death*. More than the blue sky, death is the backdrop against which the birdwatcher sees the bird. We go to look at them while they are still here to be seen and while we ourselves are still here to see them. During spring migration, every day I fail to take my binoculars and go to the park I feel a sense of deep loss, and recall Hemingway saying that every day he failed to write was a day closer to death. My wife has often heard me moan, when I'm overwhelmed with work and responsibility, "I'm missing migration!" as if I were somehow part of the flock. When I do make it outside and lose myself in looking, I don't think any of the thoughts I'm giving voice to now, but I know they're there, somewhere. I may know the names of the birds I see, but not the nature of my relationship to them, not how much of my own fate to read into theirs. And not what will happen when, as Yeats said in one of the great metaphors for death, "I awake some day / To find they have flown away." Against this fear of encroaching darkness, the birds stand out like stars.

We've lost more than affordable beachfront property since Whitman's day. We've lost Whitman's easy sense that the poetic imagination has an essential role, his deep awareness that life and death are intertwined. Whitman understood, and wrote against, our own dislocation. The post–Civil War world that ultimately recognized and embraced Whitman lived on the far side of a collapse that made his vision of a single but polyphonic America all the more essential. Like Audubon, Whitman is an artist of death and resurrection.

Born out of the mouth of a bird, flying between childhood and adulthood, between rural and urban, between simple and complex, Whitman is, for me, the birdwatching poet of the nineteenth century. Though "Out of the Cradle" is one of his only poems about birds, I keep returning to his self-description in "Song of Myself"—"Both in and out of the game and watching and wondering at it"—as a sort of birdwatcher's motto.

Set where the sea meets the land, "Out of the Cradle" represents a turning point, a moment when the world of Whitman's childhood was breaking apart, though its memory, transformed by art, was strengthened and offered up as national inspiration to the divided world that would come after. More and more, birds have come to represent the shards of a broken world that Americans have become increasingly intent on gathering up. We have been liberated—by the train, and the automobile and the airplane—to find the birds of America for ourselves, even as these inventions have contributed to the fragmentation that endangers the very things we seek. This paradoxical interaction is bound up with the essence of birdwatching.

By the Civil War, the Audubon family had fallen on hard times, and in 1862, Audubon's wife, Lucy, sold the original watercolors for *Birds of America* to the New-York Historical Society for $2,000. Years later, nostalgia for the world that Audubon lived in would make those paintings priceless and elevate Audubon into a kind of national sainthood. But in 1865 Lucy was sufficiently desperate that she sold, as well, the copper engravings of those watercolors that Audubon had carefully brought back from Europe. The firm she sold them to, unable to resell them as artifacts, decided to have them melted down in

1871. But as this was happening, the fourteen-year-old son of the plant manager recognized the bird images and, enlisting his mother's help, managed to save about eighty plates. I like to think that this boy, a child of industrial America, was a budding birdwatcher. In any event, he had enough poetry in his soul to recognize and rescue those doomed birds from the fire.

5

BEAR NECESSITIES

*To him, they were going not to hunt bear and deer but to
keep yearly rendezvous with the bear which they did not
even intend to kill.*

—WILLIAM FAULKNER,
"The Bear"

Two days after my first outing with Bill Vermillion I
found myself in the swamp again, this time with David
Kullivan himself, his zoology professor, Vernon Wright,
and another forestry student and friend of Kullivan's named
Chris Hurst. Hurst's family owned a hunting store and he described all the ways people like to hunt deer I hadn't thought
about—old-fashioned muzzle-loading guns, bow and arrow. He
described watching a deer shot with an arrow from a compound
bow—the deer seemed not to know it had been shot; it kept
grazing for a second before falling over "graveyard dead."

Kullivan was wearing blue jeans, knee-high Wellingtons, a
camouflage shirt, and the "turkey vest" he had on the day he saw
the bird. A hunter since the age of nine, he at the time was
spending his summers working for the National Rifle Association. He had close-cropped blond hair and an air of casual confidence, respectful but self-assured. He looked like a young
platoon captain ready to reconnoiter.

I found Kullivan, from the time I first spoke with him, enormously credible. He was a polite and serious young man, a practicing Catholic, modest but firm in his claims. "I would never," he had told me earlier, "risk becoming a pariah in my own chosen field." When I asked him if he viewed himself as someone mystically elected to see the bird, someone to whom the bird revealed itself, he would have none of it, referring to his sighting only as a piece of strange good fortune. "It was a lagniappe," he said, using a Louisiana word meaning an unexpected gift.

His professor, Vernon Wright, had put it to me succinctly: "He's not a hot dog." Wright had much more of an air of certitude, heaping scorn on the doubters and on Kullivan's critics. "It pisses me off the way they've gone after him," he told me forcefully. Finding the bird, for Wright, "isn't a matter of 'if,' it's a matter of 'when.'"

A bluff middle-aged man with a white mustache and an encyclopedic knowledge of the fauna of Louisiana, he has two Ph.D.s—one in statistics and one in zoology. I was impressed by his outdoorsman's energy, and by the way he sprayed Off! into his camouflage hat and then onto what remained of his white hair, like hairspray. He was wearing jeans and tennis sneakers and was obviously not afraid of snakes. Wright had brought along a tape recorder, not to play a recording of the bird and so attract it, but to record an ivory-bill if it should call. I couldn't help finding such confidence infectious. Clearly, I was among the believers.

This was a more serious operation, in some sense, than my excursion with Bill Vermillion. For one thing, I was asked to shed my orange hunting hat. The whole point was to disappear into the woods, not to be seen. Everyone, including Wright, was a hunter, and they smiled at my fear that a stray arrow might find my head.

We arrived at the wildlife management area before first light.

It was 5:00 A.M. and pitch black. The first half-hour of hiking was done by flashlight. We were looking for an old pig trap that Kullivan used as a landmark to help him find the spot where he saw the birds. When we got there, he suggested that we split up and meet back at the trap in an hour.

How they thought I would be able to find my way back to them was a mystery. I delicately inquired. Kullivan handed me a compass, as if this would solve the problem. If he had given me a sextant or an astrolabe I'd have felt equally lost. I held the item in my hand, utterly ashamed.

I knew the needle pointed north, of course. I even knew that the great molten core of the earth generated a magnetic field that surrounded the whole earth and made the compass work. I knew the Chinese had first developed a version of the compass, though they used the swinging needle not for navigation but for divination, which is a little like inventing the wheel and then using it as a lazy Susan. I knew that the rocks in Central Park are so magnetic a compass will not work there—as if this explained my incapacity. I knew—false consolation of literature—that in Faulkner's great story "The Bear," set in a Mississippi swamp not so different from the place where we were, the boy at the center of the story is granted a glimpse of the elusive bear only after he has laid down his gun and hung his compass on a tree, divesting himself of the trappings of civilization so that he can meet the wild animal on equal terms. I knew all this and more, but nothing disguised the fact that I had never used a compass before—which is to say, I knew nothing at all.

I confessed my ignorance as a man might confess illiteracy to his reading group, and vowed that I was going to learn—but not in a swamp in the dark. My counterproposal, that we go in groups of two, was accepted. I joined Wright, the bluff zoology professor, who struck off into the swamp and stopped when we reached a clearing where we could sit on the ground in the enlarging glow and wait.

We turned off our flashlights and spent half an hour simply listening while the woods went from black to gray to green. It was utterly silent, but suddenly there was life everywhere. The sounds reminded me of nothing so much as the stirrings my daughter made in her crib before she was fully awake. Wright turned on his tape recorder in case he heard the double taps of the woodpecker's drumming or the loud, nasal notes of its call.

I tried to picture the bird in my mind. It was easier since I had visited Louisiana State University in Baton Rouge the day before, where Remsen allowed me to examine the ivory-bills in the university's collection. Remsen, a lively talker with a great-horned owl mounted over the door of his office—wings spread, talons bared—had an ornithologist's air of being both bookish and outdoorsy. He slid open one of the museum's specimen drawers—the place was a kind of bird morgue—and there, folded like portable umbrellas, were the bodies of six ivory-bills.

I picked one up, more than a foot and a half long, stiff and light. The feathers had the dry, oily softness they might have had in life. The eerie realization that this was perhaps the only time I would ever see an ivory-billed woodpecker, certainly the only time I would see one so close, was overwhelming. "It's a cosmic moment," Remsen said, as I held the bird in my hand.

The bird I examined had a tag tied to one clenched foot—it was "collected" in Florida in 1899. Looking down, I realized why those early hunter-naturalists knew birds so well. It was possible to take in every detail—the frazzled, unkempt sweep of the male's red crest, the slicked-down, recurved black crest of the female, pointed as if the feathers had gel in them. Every detail was there—except, of course, that the flight had gone out if it and it wasn't a bird anymore at all. But the manner in which the black on the

back gave way abruptly to white, the full-moon luster of the bill compared to the tarnished beak of a pileated woodpecker—which I also examined—was fixed forever in my mind. Moved by a sudden impulse, I took out my camera and photographed the inert ivory-bills, lying beside their smaller pileated cousins.

I conjured a mental picture of the birds as I tramped through the woods with Wright and his two students. It took a little work to animate the birds on the tray and turn them into the wild creatures I knew from numerous descriptions. Kullivan, at least, was looking for something he had already found, or so he believed. The rest of us were looking for something we had never seen. It was a strange and exhilarating quest, but it was also a melancholy one.

KULLIVAN TOOK US to where he believed he had seen the wood-peckers and also to a spruce pine that might have served as a roost for ivory-bills at some point—it was old enough and tall enough and had several large holes bored about twenty-five feet up. But if the birds had been there once, they were not there now. Exhausted, we called it quits and dined at a nearby Wendy's, where the young men swapped preferred methods of killing fire ants. (Flooding them till they linked together to form a living raft and then pouring gasoline on them and setting them on fire sticks out in my mind.)

I felt strangely excited by the day's outing and the talk, a link to something I craved, though what exactly I wasn't quite sure. I'd read about fire ants in Edward O. Wilson's memoir *Naturalist*. At the age of thirteen, the precocious entomologist had discovered a colony of fire ants in Alabama, the first record in the United States of the flesh-chomping species that marched north from Brazil and Argentina in the middle of the last century.

But it wasn't just the ants. And it wasn't just the woods. Perhaps it was something Southern as well as wild—since the South, where the ivory-bill lived, hung on to its relationship to the woods longer than the North did, having lost everything else. Or, untouched for longer by industrialization, hung on to some sense of the land that still had a mystical component to it. Faulkner's story "The Bear" really does capture this, and perhaps it isn't surprising that an ivory-billed woodpecker actually turns up in the story. Here is a description of the bayou from "The Bear"—listen for the ivory-bill at the end:

> With the gun which was too big for him, the breech-loader which did not even belong to him but to Major de Spain and which he had fired only once, at a stump on the first day to learn the recoil and how to reload it with the paper shells, he stood against a big gum tree beside a

little bayou whose black still water crept without motion out of a cane-brake, across a small clearing and into the cane again, where, invisible, a bird, the big woodpecker called Lord-to-God by Negroes, clattered at a dead trunk.

The ivory-bill is not an incidental character here either, brief though its appearance is. In Faulkner's story, hunting gives way to watching. The boy knows the great, mysterious, powerful bear, which has survived bear traps and bullets, is nearby because the bird stops its tapping.

> He only heard the drumming of the woodpecker stop short off, and knew that the bear was looking at him. He never saw it. He did not know whether it was facing him from the cane or behind him. He did not move, holding the useless gun which he knew now he would never fire at it, now or ever, tasting in his saliva that taint of brass which he had smelled in the huddled dogs when he peered under the kitchen.
>
> Then it was gone. As abruptly as it had stopped, the woodpecker's dry hammering set up again.

Somehow, the bear and the bird become fused in that moment. The boy knows the bear is there because the bird stops what it's doing. He doesn't see the bear. He doesn't even see the bird. He doesn't even hear the bird, but its silence speaks to him and communicates to him something out of the depth of the swamp that taints his saliva with the thrilling taste of fear, but also something much greater than fear, some animal presence that he is seeking and that hunting is only an excuse for. The way Faulkner describes the bear, which is a simultaneous description of the swamp and the land itself, might serve perfectly for the ivory-bill today:

> an anachronism indomitable and invincible out of an old, dead time, a phantom, epitome and apotheosis of the old, wild life which the little puny humans swarmed and hacked at in a fury of abhorrence and fear, like pygmies about the ankles of a drowsing elephant.

In my little token jaunt to look for the ivory-bill I got to feel a part of the world of Faulkner's bear—not a cheap literary thrill, I think, but something still alive in the woods. And with it the paradoxical knowledge that the woods lasted longest in the South because the South was totally vanquished and therefore was ignored by the capitalist energies of the rest of the country. The giant trees supporting the last ivory-bill seen in Louisiana weren't cut until the 1940s—like the brownstones on the Upper West Side of Manhattan that were often best preserved when they were in poor pockets of the neighborhood, lived in by people with no means or inclination to renovate, so the tin-print ceilings and brass sconces were simply left in place.

Faulkner's story carries with it all the tangled, tragic complexity of land in America. The boy who hunts the bear has grown up hearing "the best of all talking. It was of the wilderness, the big woods, bigger and older than any recorded document:—of white man fatuous enough to believe he had bought any fragment of it, of Indian ruthless enough to pretend that any fragment of it had been his to convey."

And there is the deeper, stranger knowledge of the historical complexity of America, too, in the casual aside that it is "Negroes" who have their special, semidivine name for the ivory-bill, who call it the "Lord-to-God" bird. "The Bear" appears in *Go*

Down, Moses, published in 1940 and dedicated to Caroline Barr, Faulkner's "mammy," the black servant who was a sort of second mother to him, a woman he felt in many ways gave him his soul.

Caroline Barr was born in slavery and died one hundred years later, the year the book was published. *Go Down, Moses* is one big meditation on the complex relationship of the land and people, stained with blood and bad history, but also something that transcends human folly and even human history. The ivory-bill, a black-and-white Southern bird, flies through Faulkner and takes on these added meanings, too, becoming a reminder that with the swamp and bayou and Southern vegetation comes a cultural legacy as well. It was a shock when I learned that Audubon, in his briefly prosperous years as a Kentucky dry-goods salesman, had, between 1813 and 1819, owned nine slaves—boys, men, and women.

Audubon was a contradictory figure living in a contradictory time. He seems to personify American liberty and yet was at one time a slaveholder, and though that period didn't last long, his wife supported the family, and enabled Audubon's art, by teaching on slave-owning plantations in Louisiana. Like Thomas Jefferson, who was President when Audubon arrived in this country, Audubon became an emblem of an ideal freedom much larger than the limitations of his own life. The Old South preserves the paradoxes of America—a fierce devotion to the land, which inspired many Southern soldiers in the Civil War who didn't own slaves at all to take up arms and fight for one freedom, even though it meant fighting against another. Among its gifts to us, the ivory-bill can help us see ourselves as we really are, torn between our own desire to be free—to shoot and develop and cut down and expand—and the desire to live among free things that can survive only if we are less free. With the double vision of birders, we still can recognize ourselves as the wild children of American fantasy, but also as the far less romantic, but equally biblical, stewards of the earth.

A MONTH AFTER I returned from Louisiana I got my roll of film developed. Most of the pictures were of my daughter's first birthday party. But at the beginning of the roll there were several shots of dead ivory-bills, lying on their trays in orderly rows. Seeing these birds for the first time may have constituted a "cosmic moment," but in the photographs they seemed to me doubly dead. It was disconcerting to see the cotton stuffing where their eyes had been, the specimen tags tied to their feet.

The longer I am a birder, the more I feel there is a link between the bird at the beginning of the roll and my daughter at the end of it. I can't help thinking that Alexander Wilson's weird charade back in the eighteenth century, when he brought a wounded ivory-bill to a hotel and pretended that it was in fact his child, was an unconscious acknowledgment of what we owe the natural world. At the very least, I owe my daughter—who does not yet know what we have done to the environment—a world where a bird logged and hunted to near-extinction can be coaxed back from the brink by human concern.

The ivory-bill has come back from the dead before. In 1924 a nesting pair was found in Florida after several years during which naturalists considered the bird gone forever. And when the Florida birds were shot and stuffed by hunters, an ivory-bill turned up in the Okefenokee swamp in Georgia in 1932. Then came Tanner's find in Louisiana in 1937. In this regard, the ivory-bill is already a once and future bird, a symbol not only of what is gone but of what is possible.

Hope isn't the thing with feathers, as Emily Dickinson said—it's a strictly human affair. The sense of urgency I felt in the swamp invaded my local birding. I would find myself in Central Park, alive with the thrill of possibility, as if the bird might at any moment fly like a ghost out of a maple tree and dip for a second into view. The trick was to remind myself that whatever I saw—even a downy woodpecker, smallest of American woodpeckers—shared something with the largest American woodpecker lurking, perhaps, a thousand miles to the south. And that is as it should be—since birding collapses the space between what is far away and what is close, not simply through the use of binoculars, but through some other powerful but invisible mechanism. All birding is global, given the borderless world birds live in, but it is also, like politics, always local. And some of its greatest philosophers—yes, birdwatching has philosophers—hardly left home at all.

6

THOREAU'S SPYGLASS

One world at a time.

—THOREAU,
on his deathbed, asked by a clergyman if he could see Paradise

In March of 1845, a young man borrowed an ax and built himself a cabin. He built it on borrowed land a mile and a half south of Concord, a town that was itself just twelve miles west of Boston. He built his cabin to have a place to write and to have something to write about. He did this unnatural thing in order to be close to nature.

Henry David Thoreau lived in his cabin, with interruptions—including a trip to Maine and a night in jail—for two years and two months, though the book he wrote about his experience, *Walden*, takes the shape of a single year and follows the seasons from summer to spring. It takes a lot of artifice to give something man-made, like a book, the shape of something natural, like a year. But Thoreau was a genius and he pulled it off. We might even be tempted to believe him when he tells us that he moved into his cabin on the Fourth of July by sheer accident, despite knowing that this man, desperate for freedom, was self-consciously writing his own declaration of independence.

I think of Thoreau when I hear the refrain of "The Cuckoo," a folk song famous from the *Harry Smith Anthology*—though later recorded by everyone from Janis Joplin to Bob Dylan. Smith went around, like Audubon, gathering up American folk music in the 1950s, and he included a 1929 recording of the song by Clarence Ashley, who accompanies himself on a haunting banjo. "The Cuckoo" seems to have come over from England in the seventeenth century, but got caught, preserved, and Americanized in the Blue Ridge Mountains, where Harry Smith found it:

Oh the cuckoo is a pretty bird
She wobbles as she flies
She'll never holler "cuckoo"
Till the fourth day of July.

Thoreau didn't drink or gamble like the man in the other verses of the song—in fact, he drank only water—but he seemed like a cuckoo to many of his neighbors in his own day, especially after he burned down the Concord woods while cooking lunch for himself. Most people didn't think about him at all. *A Week on the Concord and Merrimack Rivers*, which he wrote while living at Walden, sold three hundred copies.

The cuckoo gets its reputation for laziness—and for changeling strangeness—because the European cuckoo practices what is called "brood parasitism"—it doesn't raise its own young but lays its eggs in the nests of other bird species and trusts that they will bring them up. (This is also why the bird is an emblem of infidelity and the origin of the word "cuckold.") Thoreau was patriotically lazy, idle in the service of a radical idea of freedom. This seductive and unsettling notion still nests in the American mind, pecking away at the Protestant work ethic. For years I drew inspiration from this passage in *Walden*, summoning me like a trumpet to sublime inactivity:

There were times when I could not afford to sacrifice the bloom of the present moment to any work, whether of the head or hands. I love a broad margin to my life. Sometimes, in a summer morning, having taken my accustomed bath, I sat in my sunny doorway from sunrise till noon, rapt in a revery, amidst the pines and hickories and sumachs, in undisturbed solitude and stillness, while the birds sang around or flitted noiseless through the house, until by the sun falling in at my west window, or the noise of some traveller's wagon on the distant highway, I was reminded of the lapse of time.

Thoreau was for decades the best-kept secret of the nineteenth century, a footnote to his famous friends, like Emerson—who lent him the land—and a host of poets like Longfellow and Lowell who were giants in their day. But the giants have shrunk while Thoreau gets bigger and bigger and has finally assumed his rightful place: he is the patron saint of backyard birdwatchers. It took a long time for Thoreau to achieve this eminence because, when he started, there weren't any birdwatchers. That is the price of being ahead of your time.

"Backyard birding" is not a notion that quickens the heart. It's like "weekend warrior" or "armchair mountain climber," somehow belittling, if not downright humiliating. The difference is that armchair mountain climbers aren't climbing and weekend warriors aren't fighting, but backyard birders really are birding. Nearly 42 million of those 47.8 million American birdwatchers told the Fish and Wildlife Service that they watch birds in their backyards. Travel is always involved in birdwatching, but in backyard birding it is the birds who do it.

Thoreau somehow realized as far back as 1845, when he moved to Walden Pond, that token activities can have the mythic grandeur of death-defying adventures. That's why he declares in his essay "Walking" that the word "saunter" is "beautifully derived" from the phrase *à la Sainte Terre*—to the Holy Land. This is because there were "'idle people who roved about the country, in the middle ages, and asked charity, under pretence of going *à la Sainte Terre*,' to the Holy Land, till the children exclaimed, 'There goes a *Sainte-Terrer*,' a Saunterer—a Holy-Lander." Thoreau goes on to denounce those who only pretended to go, but that's incidental—he has already planted the notion that sauntering is a holy calling and utterly confused the conventional categories of what is idleness and what is activity of the highest order. This helps me explain why I never think of birdwatching as a mere pastime. Like writing itself, it is one of those activities that seems simultaneously marginal and utterly central to the business of being human and of figuring out what it means to be human.

Thoreau's idea that his own age could be as great as any mythic age before it, his own quiet life as heroic as any hero's from mythology, had a geographical analog. The woods close by could, and do, house nature as wild and eternal and full of mystery as any wilderness. What was an experiment for Thoreau is a necessity for us today. In my dreams I climb mountains and travel to the ocean floor. In reality, I watch birds.

There was still a wild frontier in Thoreau's day. There were herds of buffalo, undefeated Indians, the Oregon Trail, the great swamps of the South. But he understood something in the middle of the nineteenth century about the future shape of the country that makes him feel, for all his weirdness, like a contemporary. I wonder if we would still read *Walden* as we do if he had gone to some remote outpost where the wolves howled at night, instead of to a spot five hundred yards from the railroad tracks, where the whistle of the train mingled with the hooting of owls.

In the great second chapter of *Walden*—"Where I Lived, and What I Lived For," which comes as a relief after the taxing first chapter, "Economy"—Thoreau makes this observation about his new home:

> The Harivansa says, "An abode without birds is like a meat without seasoning." Such was not my abode, for I found myself suddenly neighbor to the birds; not by having imprisoned one, but having caged myself near them. I was not only nearer to some of those which commonly frequent the garden and the orchard, but to those wilder and more thrilling songsters of the forest which never, or rarely, serenade a villager—the wood thrush, the veery, the scarlet tanager, the field sparrow, the whip-poor-will, and many others.

It may seem unfair to call this backyard birding, since Thoreau makes a point of telling us that the birds he heard at Walden were not the same as the ones in the village. But he is only a mile and a half away from the village, and his cabin is his home. He's merely done what Americans have done ever since—find a place a little farther away from everyone else where the illusion of true country is a little easier to preserve.

When I first read the passage, I somehow assumed the Harivansa were an Indian tribe, but I had the wrong Indians. It refers to a portion of the *Mahabharata*, the 2,500-year-old epic about the genealogy of Vishnu. Thoreau needs an epic to account for his backyard birding because to him it is epic. As local a writer as there is, Thoreau doesn't feel any need to stay in America imaginatively. He cared about Native American culture and subcontinental Indian culture, too. True to the spirit of birding, he liked to find things that were far away and bring them near to home.

In 1853, still revising and refining *Walden*, Thoreau bought a spyglass to bring the world closer. Binoculars had not yet been invented or he'd have no doubt bought a pair. But he had already intuited that however much you "simplify, simplify, simplify," as he exhorted in *Walden*, you still need technology to encounter nature more fully. On June 10, Thoreau recorded the use of his spyglass in his journal:

> By the way, I amused myself yesterday afternoon with looking from my window, through a spyglass, at the tops of the woods in the horizon. It was pleasant to bring them so near and individualize the trees, to examine in detail the tree-tops which before you had beheld only in the mass as the woods in the horizon. It was an exceedingly rich border, seen thus against, and the imperfections in a particular tree-top more than two miles off were quite apparent. I could easily have seen a hawk sailing over the top of the wood, and possibly his nest in some higher tree. Thus to contemplate, from my attic in the village, the hawks circling about their nests above some dense forest or swamp miles away, almost as if they were flies on my own premises!

What I especially like about this passage is that Thoreau isn't even outside. He's in his room, looking out the window. And though he crows that his new toy brings faraway birds to him as if they were "flies on my own premises," he actually hasn't even seen any birds in this passage. He could, he realizes, easily have seen a hawk, if there was one. But there isn't. But that doesn't stop him. He imagines what it might be like to see hawks circling above their nests, he knows he could see them, and this makes him happy.

In a sense, there is a hawk in the picture, and it is Thoreau himself. He now has hawk eyes, thanks to his telescope. Robinson Crusoe has become the bionic man. Perched in his attic room, he can see like a bird of prey. Thanks to his imagination, and a bit of technological innovation, he grows wilder, not tamer. A bookish man who loved the outdoors, a writer of great artifice who continually sought the "natural," a man of solitude who craved connection, Thoreau appreciated all the paradoxes of birding before it properly existed.

The fact that he wasn't all that good at it is also inspiring. John Burroughs wrote of Thoreau that "to the last, his ornithology was not quite sure, not quite trustworthy." In his journal in 1856, Emerson described Thoreau, in a passage later reprinted in a memorial essay, endlessly hunting for a bird Thoreau called the "night warbler." The bird was always diving into the bushes before Thoreau could get a good look. This bird fascinated Thoreau because, like Whitman's mockingbird, it sang day and night. "What short work a naturalist would have made of his night-warbler," Burroughs wrote disparagingly, speculating that Thoreau was "looking too intently for a bird behind the bird" to settle accurately on the real thing.

But Thoreau was striking a balance between the mythic and the real. It was Emerson who, in his journal, recalled telling Thoreau that finding things was overrated. Regarding the night-warbler, Emerson "told [Thoreau] he must beware of finding and booking it, lest life should have nothing more to show him." To which Thoreau responded, sounding almost like Kafka, "What you seek in vain for, half your life, one day you come full upon, all the family at dinner. You seek it like a dream, and as soon as you find it you become its prey." Thoreau knew that looking at nature was bound up with a primal quest for knowledge and therefore contained exalted pleasures and terrors.

I need Thoreau and his example to keep the gloom away when I am birding in Central Park, not hunting for exotic birds in a swamp or flying great distances to see what lives on the far side of the Rocky Mountains. Central Park is also borrowed land—I borrow it every time I go there. It is fully mine and fully everyone else's, so in that sense it's better than borrowing land from Emerson and anticipates the national parks that Theodore Roosevelt and those who came after him would create. And the truth is that, in the middle of Manhattan, two blocks from my apartment, I can see or hear all the birds Thoreau listened to at Walden, even "those wilder and more thrilling songsters of the forest which never, or rarely, serenade a villager." I hear and see wood thrushes and veeries, and scarlet tanagers and field sparrows. I have even seen a whippoorwill hunched in perfect camouflage in the fork of a tree. Central Park is, for better or worse, my Walden Pond.

IN 1853, the year Thoreau bought his spyglass, the New York legislature voted to apply eminent domain to set aside 848 acres in

Manhattan, stretching from Fifty-ninth Street to 106th Street, between Fifth and Eighth Avenues, for the creation of a park. Work began in 1858, and New York needed to borrow more than an ax. It needed to import 4 million trees and plants and shrubs to go with the 500,000 cubic feet of topsoil hauled in from New Jersey. It needed to haul out 10 million cartloads of earth and rock. And it needed to kick out 1,600 people—with compensation—who were living on the land, including the inhabitants of Seneca Village, a primarily African-American community with three churches that stretched from West Eighty-second Street to Eighty-ninth Street.

Is Central Park real or man-made? In some way, it is like Marianne Moore's definition of what a poem should be—an "imaginary garden with real toads in it." It's a collaboration, and one might say the same about much of America—the Great Plains transformed into farmland, the Florida Everglades now sustained by pumps and sluices created by the Army Corps of Engineers to undo all the damage it did a hundred years ago. The swamp I visited in Louisiana when I looked for the ivory-billed woodpecker, deforested by loggers but now regrown into something new. And everywhere there are the ghostly traces of the Native American life that once was present and is now gone—Thoreau was always picking up arrowheads and gleaning remnants of Indian life that reminded him that Walden Pond was in its own way man-made—its population altered by human transformations. Central Park harbors the troubling memory of the inhabitants of Seneca Village, whose relatively prosperous community of free blacks lacked the political clout to divert the legislature's plan for a park. This was also true for the Irish and Italian immigrants who lived alongside the blacks—boiling bones in the "piggery" and farming sheep in the Sheep Meadow. All were displaced.

Of course, one could ask the same question about human beings—are we natural or man-made? Even if I hadn't been circumcised on my eighth day of life, altered by a traditional idea of how men ought to be, I would have a hard time saying what sort of state I inhabit. The tools I require—starting with my glasses—not to mention clothing, language, fire—confuse the question hopelessly. At the beginning of "Walking," Thoreau may write that he intends to "regard man as an inhabitant, or a part and parcel of Nature, rather than a member of society," but in practice he gets no further than Whitman, declaring that he is both in and out of the game, and watching and wondering at it.

I don't know that Thoreau would have appreciated my sense that Central Park is Walden. He didn't like New York very much. He came here not for nature but for commerce—to try to sell articles and establish himself as a published writer with a broader readership than Brahmin Boston. In 1843, two years before he built his Walden cabin, he went to live on Staten Island as tutor to the son of Emerson's brother. Staten Island was rural enough, and Thoreau even discovered the ocean, but it was trips to Manhattan that mattered, where he could meet editors and other writers, though his hopes of finding paying outlets evaporated pretty fast.

He came again for the same purpose in 1856, two years after Walden had been published, and he even went to P. T. Barnum's museum, where he was fascinated by a stuffed cougar whose body had been found years before floating in the Hudson. That same visit he took the ferry from Manhattan to Brooklyn and shlepped up to Walt Whitman's attic bedroom. Whitman was like the cougar found floating in the Hudson, the embodiment of something wild and unexpectedly urban. Though Thoreau himself embodied that mixture of ferocity and civility, too, and the men clearly felt a kinship, Thoreau found some of Whitman's poetry too "sensual" at times, just as Whitman found Thoreau a little too morbid. Nevertheless, Thoreau carried his copy of *Leaves of Grass* around Concord like "a red flag," as Emerson later reported to Whitman.

In their way, both were avatars of the same thing, which we surely need and crave even more today. Both were trying to keep a wild, individual spark alive as the mechanical, commercial weight of the growing country bore down with exponential force. They do what birds themselves do for me when I walk around the Central Park reservoir—now named for Jacqueline Kennedy Onassis but once possessed of the Whitmanian name "Lake Manahatta"—and look in winter at ruddy ducks and Northern shovelers, and grebes and coots and the occasional ring-necked duck or hooded merganser.

Central Park is a better place to see birds than most suburban backyards—and than Walden Pond—precisely because it is in the middle of a big city; migrating birds have fewer choices about where to land as they stop to rest on their migratory journeys. When Thoreau lived there, Walden was a natural spot that the artificial world was encroaching on. Central Park is an artificial spot that is visited by elements of the natural world that more and more transform it, turning it into something new.

This is certainly hopeful, but it is hopeful only to a point. There are times when the birdlife in the park can seem like the bloom of a magnolia tree in a cemetery, its very intensity suggesting a sort of graveyard profusion that undermines the feeling of exaltation. The owl of Athena flies at dusk. Never have I better understood the meaning of Hegel's observation, which essentially means that insight arrives when the end is near, or that cultures peak as they are about to die, than when I started birding. Birds cluster in patches of green because they have fewer places to go on their journey. There is a reason why birdwatching is an urban invention and a modern—perhaps the quintessentially modern—activity.

Reading *Walden* I think of a story told about the Baal Shem Tov, the eighteenth-century Jewish mystical master. It's a story about how each generation has a little less than the one before, but how each generation finds a way to come up with its own magic. Here is the story as told in Gershom Scholem's *Major Trends in Jewish Mysticism*.

> When the Baal Shem, the Master of the Name, as the founder of Hasidism was called, had a difficult task, he would go to a certain place in the woods, light a fire and meditate in prayer—and what he had set out to perform was done. When a generation later, the Maggid of Meseritz was faced with the same task, he would go to the same place in the woods and say: " We can no longer light the fire, but we can still speak the prayers"—and what he wanted done became reality. Again a generation later Rabbi Moshe Leib of Sassov had to perform this task. And he, too, went into the woods and said: "We can no longer light a fire, nor do we know the secret meditations belonging to the prayer, but we do know the place in the woods where it all belongs—and that must be sufficient," and sufficient it was. But when another generation had passed and Rabbi Israel of Rishin was called upon to perform the task, he sat down in his golden chair in his castle and said: "We cannot light the fire, we cannot speak the prayers, we do not know the place, but we can tell the story of how it was done." And, the storyteller adds, the story which he told had the same effect as the actions of the other three.

Thoreau is not like the Baal Shem Tov—he was already doing something late in the day. He was finding his own place in the woods, declaring it sacred simply because he went there, and then telling the story so that other people could do the same wherever they might be. There is nothing sacred about Walden Pond.

And there isn't any such thing as a single forest. Every birder knows that the migratory birds of Central Park need the forests of Central and South America to winter in, and the woods and fields of North America, or regions farther north, to nest in. The birds of Walden, local as they seemed to Thoreau, might have flown a thousand miles or more to get there. They are like a story told by one part of the world about another part of the world. Which is why backyard birding is a kind of misnomer, after all.

Birds are like those castles in the air that Thoreau said we must now put foundations under. This is how birdwatching, which grows out of books but can never be satisfied with books, creates environmentalists. If we don't shore up the earth, the sky will be empty.

7.

SAILING TO GONDWANALAND

The scientists say
It'll all wash away
But we don't believe any more.

—GRAM PARSONS and CHRIS HILLMAN,
"Sin City"

When I got back from Louisiana, I took a behind-the-scenes tour of the ornithology collection of the American Museum of Natural History, hoping, among other things, to see an ivory-bill, though halfheartedly, because what good would a glimpse of a dead bird in New York do me? As it turned out, I didn't see one, though I did learn, among other things, that the museum uses a colony of flesh-eating beetles to strip skeletons clean before assembly and display. The museum, which has one of the great collections of bird skins in the world, still needs skeletons, because in the heyday of bird collecting, in the nineteenth and early twentieth centuries, the custom was to keep the colorful wrapping of a bird and chuck the rest as worthless filler. As it turns out, skeletons contain important morphological clues to species evolution; thus, there is still a need for fresh birds—and a need for beetles. They didn't show us the beetles, though I'd love to have seen them, but I learned that double rows of sticky tape guard the threshold of the room where the beetles are kept—if they were to escape, they would reduce much of the museum's collection, and the lovingly created animal dioramas, to a pile of bones.

The tour in general had a macabre cast. We were taken to an upstairs storage room lined with metal cabinets whose shallow sliding drawers contained row after row of dead, eyeless birds, little ID tags tied around their ankles giving the date and location of their death. The color tends to drain out of the feathers of dead birds, the same way fall leaves lose their color after a few months, and many of these birds were a hundred years old.

Still, these were the famous bird skins that schooled generations of ornithologists and bird artists whose books, or whose students' books, I use today. This was the great collection that made the American Museum of Natural History one of the places where ornithology and birdwatching evolved in the early part of the twentieth century. The curator obligingly fetched a stuffed great auk for us so that we could see an extinct bird.

All these dead birds engendered a vague feeling of melancholy in me, an urge to escape to the woods. It was winter and we were wearing our coats, despite the indoor warmth. Only the curator looked comfortable. He was a handsome young man in a T-shirt, tanned from a collecting trip he'd just made to Vietnam (despite the international migratory bird treaty of 1918, it is possible for scientists to get permission to collect—that is, kill—certain endangered birds if a scientific need can be established).

I envied him his tan, his T-shirt, his earring, and his aura of adventure. He was full of information about the museum's collection, but at that moment I didn't really care. I wanted to *be* the curator of birds, not a shleppy tourist demoted from birdwatching to the even geekier activity of gazing at the labeled dead. Still, I knew these birds were bound invisibly to the live ones I watch. The bird guides I carry with me, books that lead millions of people outdoors, grew out of an ornithological world that needed specimens on which to build its authority, the subtle distinctions in taxonomy that determine what is a new species, what is a subspecies, what is a mingling of subspecies hybridizing their way to something new. In some sense, modern birdwatching is built on the bones, or at least the skins, of these dead birds. Set up in a corner of the room were drawing materials and a sketch of some tanagers—even now an artist was turning the dead into a guide to the living.

I recognized the artist's name—Steve Quinn, a curator who worked at the museum and led excellent bird walks. I had also taken an "animal drawing" class with him. This met after hours in the museum; we sat sketching in the Aikley Hall of African Mammals, the room full of glassed-in dioramas of stuffed wildebeests, kudu, rhinos, lions. In the thrilling silence of the empty museum, the lights of the great hall dimmed, the animals woke to eerie life against magnificent realistic backdrops of their habitats, a novelty in the twenties, when the hall was constructed. Many of these animals had been shot by Theodore Roosevelt himself, others by Carl Akeley, for whom the hall is named.

The first day we went in there to sketch, I had parked myself in front of the mountain gorilla diorama, which I remembered vividly from childhood, with its big silverback pounding on his chest. My drawing looked like a racist caricature of a hairy pregnant woman covering her breasts in horror. I was, to begin with, the worst artist in the class, but Steve kindly explained that gorillas are particularly difficult to draw because they suggest people in certain ways—arms, head, chest, belly—but the proportions are all off. It's harder, it seems, to give a true picture of something that's like us, but different, than something that's simply different, like an elephant, to which I soon turned my attention. Strange that I had chosen the gorilla, really, since I had taken the class in the hope of learning how to draw birds, but it is hard to shake the urge to find traces of the human in the world around you and I had made my gorilla a kind of ape person, a missing link of some sort, though in real life we seem to be doing the opposite and erasing living evidence of our primate past; I've since learned that the lush area depicted in the gorilla diorama is now farmland and that only six hundred mountain gorillas remain.

The ornithology tour gave me an occasion to go back to the museum after hours, with a chance to look at nothing but birds birds birds, but somehow the old gorilla gloom came over me. My gloom increased as we descended to the off-limits, windowless basement of the museum, where a pale technician who looked as if he had never been outside in his life showed us how he prepares bird specimens before turning them over to the beetles for final cleaning. While he passed around the wing of an osprey—astonishingly light, since birds have hollow bones—he pointed to a defrosting penguin on the table, which I had already gotten a whiff of. Sea World in Florida, he informed us, sends all its dead penguins to the museum, packed in ice. He had once tasted one of the penguins and found it "fishy."

He then led us into a cabinet-lined catacomb where, as a special treat, he offered to show us some of the "larger birds." We gathered around as he opened an enormous metal tub the size of a sarcophagus. Peering down I saw, floating in an amnion of formaldehyde, a tangle of giant bird bodies, their long limp necks seething like snakes. They turned out to be a rhea and a cassowary, flightless birds as tall as a person, that had been preserved decades before.

It was fiendishly hot in the basement. A wave of slow-moving formaldehyde washed over me and completed what heat and claustrophobia had begun. My head began spinning and I felt myself turning into supper for the flesh-eating beetles. I slipped away, found an exit, and headed out into the cold winter air. I revived at once, but I couldn't shake a vague sense of failure, as if, despite wishing to be a doctor, I had just fled the cadaver in my gross anatomy class. But it was living birds I wanted, and I was happy to encounter the lowly sparrows that even in winter are visible on every street corner of Manhattan, popping in and out of the hollow metal crossbars supporting traffic lights.

In my zeal for birdwatching I had wanted to take a behind-the-scenes tour that I imagined would lead me closer to birds. I hadn't wanted to be like those collectors who had thrown out the actual bird bodies, settling for the bright exterior of birds at the expense of other considerations. I thought the museum might bring me closer to birds, but I felt farther away—not over the rainbow, but under it. It was animal drawing all over again.

Still, I tried to make up for my flight from the flightless birds—doubly flightless, if you think about it—by doing a little research. Birding is about seeing and also about knowing, and I couldn't help wondering about certain things. Why, for example, was a cassowary, a bird found only in Australia and New Guinea, rooming with a rhea, a bird found only in the wilds of South America?

Well, for one thing they both belong to the group of birds called ratites. (I admit to loving all the new words you learn from birdwatching.) The word "ratite" comes from the Latin word for raft; the breastbone of flying birds has a kind of keel on it that gives the flight muscles something to hold on to, but in flightless birds there is no such keel. All flightless birds have an unkeeled sternum, a sort of flat-bottomed structure, like a raft.

I also learned that in a strange way these birds were neighbors even before they wound up sharing a tub. All flightless birds— all ratites—hail from Gondwana. Gondwana, or Gondwanaland, as it is sometimes called, no longer exists, but turns out to have been arguably the most important geological structure in the last billion years. Six hundred and fifty million years ago, Gondwanaland was a supercontinent made up of what are now the continents of Australia, India, South America, and Africa, all smooshed together. Even Florida and parts of southern Europe joined in (which is why prehistoric camel bones have been found in Florida). This supercontinent didn't break up until around 130 million years ago, connecting these landmasses (and their inhabitants) for something like 520 million years.

These numbers, of course, are more than difficult to fathom. They're something you can learn, and know, and take on faith, but not really something you can feel. And perhaps if we could feel them they would annihilate us with our own littleness—although such numbers make me think of the mysteriously comforting Keats poem "When I have fears that I may cease to be," about the poet's fear that he will die before he is able to do all the work that is in him, before he will be recognized for his talents, before he will be able to marry the woman he loves. (Dead of tuberculosis at twenty-six, Keats was certainly justified in his fears.) The last lines of Keats's poem are:

> *. . . then on the shore*
> *Of the wide world I stand alone, and think*
> *Till love and fame to nothingness do sink.*

Try standing on the shore of Gondwanaland—wider than anything we can imagine, and older, too, older than people or even proto-people—and see how fast everything sinks. Though a sense of wonder certainly rises up, too, because, well, here we are.

Knowing the giant numbers of geography, and knowing the names of things, and having a system for putting what we know in its proper place, takes the chill edge off the presence of unfathomable things, which is perhaps a fancy way of saying death. After Adam eats the apple, he gets to keep his knowledge, even if he loses immortality and his comfortable place in the world and becomes a permanent wanderer, no matter how settled he seems to be. We follow in his footsteps. The names of constellations give us a handle for the stars whose ultimate origin, Big Bang or no Big Bang, is simply beyond our ken. Once it's been explained by science that all matter in the universe was once contained in something the size of a single seed, you know that science, without myth or story or imagination to accompany it, will always fail to persuade us of anything ultimate.

But that doesn't mean that I didn't find a kind of comfort from my research, and from having those names—rhea, cassowary, ratite, Gondwanaland—and all those big numbers, too, under my belt. I enjoy the detective work that comes with birding, and after untangling those bird bodies for myself a little, I felt better—but only a little. Armchair birding is an oxymoron, even if your mental flight takes you to New Guinea and Argentina and Gondwanaland.

In the end, no matter how long I had managed to stand over that ratite soup, I hadn't "seen" the birds in the birding sense. I could never check them off my world list, and though I'm not a real "lister," I do appreciate the almost mystical nature of a list, which isn't called a "life list" for nothing. It isn't just your life— it's the bird's life. (The standard is actually higher than that; if I saw a cassowary in a zoo—and there's one in the Australia Zoo in Brisbane called Stomp because it keeps trying to kill people— I still couldn't count it. It must be seen in the wild.) Suddenly I really wanted to see those birds alive and realized I would in fact have to put Patagonia and the Australian rain forest on my list of places to go after all. And that I would have to hurry—there are only two thousand cassowaries left in Australia.

In real life a cassowary, which can stand up to five and a half feet tall, is an impressive sight. It has a blue neck, from which twin red wattles hang down, and a bony helmet on its head—the only helmeted bird we have—a core of cartilage covered with hard skin, called a casque, which helps when it runs headfirst through the rain forest, its neck parallel to the ground. Its name was determined by Linnaeus in 1758—he took it from "cassuary," the Papuan New Guinea name, which is made up of the word for horn and the word for head. The bird is shy but aggressive and can kill a person—it jumps feet first to attack, and the nails of its inner toes are five inches long.

Its cousin, the rhea, is less colorful—its neck is gray—but it is almost as tall and nearly as dramatic. I recalled the story of young Charles Darwin, during his voyage on the *Beagle*, encountering rheas for the first time in southern Argentina. Darwin had been particularly struck by the great communal nests he saw in the ground—pits dug by the male, who then rounds up females, all of whom lay their eggs in the common nest. The young are then raised by the male bird. Occasionally Darwin would notice a lone, orphaned egg simply lying on the ground—when the females did not find a mate, they abandoned their eggs.

Darwin hunted rheas with gauchos near the Rio Negro. The Argentine cowboys swung metal balls tied to ropes over their heads and then flung these *ballos*, tripping the big flightless birds. Darwin, despite being an excellent horseman, succeeded in

tripping only his own horse. But he managed, being a good shot, to get his hands on plenty of the birds.

What Darwin really wanted, though, was a rare "lesser rhea." This bird was one-third smaller than the common rhea that he had hunted with gauchos. The lesser rhea kept eluding him until, one day in Patagonia in 1833, Darwin was eating supper when he suddenly realized that he was in fact feasting on a lesser rhea and that he and the crew had already eaten two-thirds of the bird. Here is the literal enactment of Thoreau's notion that "what you seek in vain for, half your life, one day you come full upon, all the family at dinner." Fortunately, the head, neck, legs, wings, much of the skin, and some feathers had been saved and these remnants were shipped off to London, where the reconstructed bird was put on display and dubbed a new species by the British bird artist and taxonomist John Gould, who called the bird *Rhea darwinii*, after the bird's "discoverer." (It later turned out the bird already had a Latin name, though it is still sometimes referred to as Darwin's rhea.)

The name "rhea" was chosen in 1752 by Paul Mohring, a German physician and zoologist who published a book on bird classification that divided all birds into four groups, anticipating aspects of modern bird taxonomy. He seems to have been thinking of Rhea, the Titaness who figures prominently in Greek mythology, though he gave no reason for his choice.

It always fascinates me that scientists reach so often for names from mythology. Perhaps someday, if science truly triumphs over Western religion, there will be interspace probes named Jesus, and planets named Jacob with moons named Rachel and Leah. The sky is where they put you when you're dead but, like certain stars, still giving light. But for now it is dead religions that lend their mythological force to science.

Rhea is in fact the mother of the Greek gods. She is married to another Titan, Cronus, who is also her brother. Cronus keeps eating their babies—Hera, Poseidon, Hestia, Demeter, and Hades—because of a prophecy that his children, led by Zeus, will overthrow him. When Zeus is born, Rhea tricks Cronus by giving him a rock swaddled in baby clothes, which Cronus, strong but stupid, crams down with the other children. Zeus meanwhile is raised far away, hidden in a cave in Crete. When he matures, he defeats his father with the help of his disgorged siblings, and the reign of the gods begins.

Rhea helps Zeus win the fight, but when she asks for half the universe as payment, he spurns her request, and so she forsakes Olympus, choosing earth instead, where she haunts the hills and forests, riding in a carriage drawn by wild beasts. It seems possible to assume that to Mohring the big earthbound bird seemed worthy of Rhea, who became a sort of earth goddess, especially since even the male of the species exhibits a maternal quality, sitting on those great hordes of eggs deposited in a shallow pit and rearing the young himself.

But how different these birds must have seemed in the eighteenth century, when the world they lived in looked to Westerners as wild and strange as they were. A time when a physician like Mohring might think the specimen before him shared properties with a mythological creature.

I can't help envying Mohring and Linnaeus for living in a

world of unnamed birds and unknown places. And I can't help envying men like Darwin, who were scientists, explorers, and hunters all in one, and who lived in the days when you could have your bird and eat it, too. Even when I'm not spotting birds in a barrel in a museum but am out "in the field," I am conscious of a hankering for more, for closer, for some deeper intimate knowledge of the bird that's never wholly satisfied. Is it that wholeness I crave when I go birding—a wish to go beyond mere looking?

It isn't necessarily something I'd achieve if I took up hunting. It's something more elusive than that—wholeness that is perhaps not possible but that maybe Darwin tasted in Patagonia. In those days, before he had drawn his soul-rattling conclusions about the origin of species, to which birds contributed mightily, he still had his faith in a traditional God and a feeling that the abundance of life forms, even the finches he saw in the Galápagos Islands, were a confirmation of a divine profusion. He was hunting, killing, eating, classifying, exulting all at once. Darwin was in his twenties at the time, and that one exuberant five-year voyage fueled all his later work. Afterward came decades of invalidism from tropical disease, as well as terrible headaches that might have resulted from his intense anxiety, the hemming and hawing over conclusions he knew would shake the world and the upper-middle-class society he lived in so comfortably. But in those heady days on the *Beagle*, neither the birds, nor God, nor the place of man in the universe, were endangered.

What makes our relationship to nature so complicated is that, being part of the natural world ourselves, we are the vanquished as well as the victor. There is something truly Oedipal about our relationship to the natural world in this regard. Freud was right when he recognized that we absorb aspects of our parents into ourselves at crucial stages of our early development, which is why the process of youthful rebellion is so excruciating—we are always rebelling against an aspect of ourselves. And if you reject the psychological component, just think of it biologically—we are the genetic product, in some sense the genetic messengers, of the parents against whom we may struggle for liberation. Our relationship to the wild world is this struggle writ large.

There is a haunting moment in Ernest Jones's biography of Freud in which Jones, also a psychoanalyst, ventures his own interpretation of Hamlet. The prince's problem, for Jones, is that he had a natural Oedipal urge to see his father dead—so far, so normal—but that somebody actually did murder his father, and that is where his nightmare began. His deep, unconscious secret longing fulfilled, Hamlet is paralyzed, because that particular fantasy is not meant to be fulfilled—it is the buried engine, not the overt action, that should drive a man through life. Like Edward O. Wilson's dream of walking down ever-receding forest glades, mastering them but never exhausting them.

AT ITS BEST, birding for me is a way to awaken, but then rechannel, the conquering urge. Which doesn't make the dream of conquest any less forceful. For Wilson it was most powerfully expressed during the colonization of the New World, and he finds it most vividly imagined by the nineteenth-century landscape painters who captured the conquest of the West and the jungles of South America. Wilson's desire as a naturalist is to keep conquering the unknown but to always have more before him.

Our problem comes when there is no "more." Modern birdwatching grows out of this painful knowledge. I have spent splendid hours birding in the Florida Everglades, and they certainly felt wild to me, though I know they live today, like much of the wild world, on life support bestowed by the very people whose conquering ingenuity dealt them a mortal blow.

I sometimes wonder if birdwatching can ever satisfy at the deepest, mythological level of our beings precisely because it is such an intermediate activity. So many of the great primitive stories are about subduing the wild world, killing the threatening beast, holding up a burning torch in the heart of the forest. Can repair have its own romance?

I am in the habit of telling my daughters stories before they go to sleep. I'm always striving for that perfect balance of adventure and comfort, fantasy and reality that will give them a sense of the big world beyond their beds without terrifying them, but that will make them feel safe without stifling them with soft delusions. I never get the balance right, but I keep trying.

Here is a story I would never tell them, but that I tell myself:

Once upon a time there was a king, Cassowary—a fierce warrior with a crown on his head as hard as horn. He took for his queen a princess named Rhea, who had grown up running freely through the wild places of the earth. It was said they were related, like Adam and Eve, and had been created together, though others said that they had sprung from the monsters who had once ruled the earth, and that they came from a faraway place called Gondwanaland that cannot be found on any map.

Rhea and Cassowary had many children, but the strangest of all their descendants walked upright on two legs, like them but different. Like them, they could not fly. In fact, they had no feathers at all, but what they lacked in feathers they made up for with cunning.

For many years, these children were afraid of their wild parents. In the forests they hid from their father, who was particularly fierce and capable of sudden rages. But in the grasslands they hid from Rhea, too, for even Rhea could kill when she was angry.

Gradually, though, the ones without feathers grew stronger, and bolder and more clever.

They would sometimes pull feathers from the great birds. Dressed in these feathers, they confused the other animals, who began to treat them like the true king and queen. Emboldened, the ones without feathers began to steal Rhea's enormous eggs, and soon they were tearing off chunks of flesh from the birds as they galloped by. The featherless ones multiplied and built cities, and to make room for their cities, they destroyed the wild places where the king and queen lived.

Because Rhea and Cassowary were immortal, they could never truly die, but they were seen less and less. Some say that there were those among their children who took pity on them and who carried them away under a spell and hid them together in a special chest in the bottom of a building deep inside a great city. And that one day, when the children gain sufficient wisdom and learn to share their kingdom with their banished parents, they will release Rhea and Cassowary from the box where they are hidden. This can happen only when the wild places are allowed to grow again. Until that day, which some say may never come, the king and queen sleep forever in their prison, dreaming of the wild places they lived in, worrying about their children, and waiting for deliverance.

8.

AUDUBON'S MONKEY

Very few men can speak of nature with any truth.

—HENRY DAVID THOREAU,
Journal, March 13, 1841

aving just invented a story, I feel obliged to return to Audubon briefly to say one more thing about him before moving on to twentieth-century heroes: he was a liar. Not all the time, of course. And almost never about birds (though he did invent a fish "between four and ten feet long," with bulletproof scales, as a joke on a fellow naturalist who unwittingly included it in a history of fish of the Ohio).

For some biographers, Audubon's lies are essentially embellishments, in the tradition of the tall tales that grew spontaneously out of the backwoods of America. And certainly Audubon did tell what Huck Finn called "stretchers," tales of bear wrestling and wild Indians and encounters with runaway slaves in swamps that might or might not have happened. His stories are in some ways like his posed paintings—there's a general veracity, but every now and then he can't help himself and puts a rattlesnake up a tree for artistic effect. Audubon, who was always hustling for subscribers to his grand project, was advertising himself and a romantic version of wild America all at the same time. And since America was quite wild, and Audubon was quite a romantic figure, this hardly violates his larger, serious purpose.

But Audubon also told some flat-out falsehoods, like the statement that he had studied painting with the great eighteenth-century French master Jacques-Louis David, when in fact he was largely self-taught. This, like the myth that somehow circulated that he might really be the dauphin, rightful heir to the French throne, gets closer to the source of disinformation

in Audubon, which had to do with his origins.

In the same memoir that opens with the tale of the parrot and the monkey, Audubon narrates a little of his parents' history. His father, he writes, was a French sea captain who, on a trip to Louisiana (still then in the possession of the French), met and married a rich and beautiful young woman of high birth. He brought her to the French colony of Saint-Domingue, where they had several children, of whom Audubon was the lone survivor. Not long afterward, the slave revolt that turned Saint-Domingue into Haiti erupted, and Audubon's mother was killed in the uprising. His father barely escaped to France with young Audubon, who was raised by a loving stepmother, the woman with the pet parrots and monkeys.

This background gives new meaning to Audubon's assertion that his love of birds began the day his mother's parrot asked for breakfast and the monkey, outraged, killed it. It makes it a kind of parable with racial and historical and political meaning. And racial and political and historical meaning always run under the surface of any consideration of the natural world. Knowing that Thoreau was an abolitionist who helped a runaway slave make it to Canada changes his Walden experiment, his obsession with individual liberty even for those whose chains were invisible. Audubon's life was also touched by slavery, but like Thoreau, making his own journey of auto-emancipation (*Walden* was influenced by Frederick Douglass's slave narrative), Audubon gave slavery metaphorical meaning in his own life story.

Audubon loved the fables of La Fontaine. These moralizing stories of talking animals often accompanied him into the wilderness, and they shaped aspects of his art, however based on true-life observation his paintings primarily were. The story of the parrot and the monkey, the very opening of his autobiography, turns out to be a sort of animal fable as well. In his telling, the delicate, French-speaking bird is destroyed by the powerful primate, just as he would like us to believe that his mother was killed by black slaves turning on their French colonial masters. On the surface it seems that Audubon has fashioned a crude racial parable that his readers would have grasped intuitively.

There's only one problem. Audubon's natural mother wasn't, in fact, killed in the slave uprising. She died of a fever a few months after Audubon's birth. Nor was she a highborn Louisiana lady—she was a chambermaid in Saint-Domingue. Neither was she married to Audubon's father—she was one of the captain's many lovers.

Audubon's father did fear the rising revolution in Saint-Domingue and did send Audubon to France—leaving behind several mixed-race children he had also fathered with black women on the island, on the assumption that they would be spared by the slave revolt because of the color of their skin. Audubon, who never mentions his mixed-race siblings, made up the part about his mother's murder, just as he made up the story of her upper-class birth.

Why so much lying? There is the obvious fact that Audubon was a bastard and afraid of the secret getting out. And there was more than shame involved—there were still laws in Europe that could have deprived him of his inheritance. It was also part of his romantic, self-inventing nature. Audubon was an American immigrant re-creating himself, particularly after his bankruptcy—a lifelong source of shame—even if his business failure freed him to become a bird artist. In America he acquired a new name (he was christened Jean-Jacques Fougère Audubon), a new persona, and, while he was at it, created a new profession—bird artist. Ever since Adam and Eve hid in the bushes, nature has been a good cover for human nakedness as much as it has exposed it.

A book about birdwatching needs a chapter on lying. Not because birdwatchers are particularly dishonest—I actually find the honor system of birding to be fairly universal. I doubt very much that people are padding their "life lists" with unseen birds—though I admit that in my early days I would sometimes say I had seen a bird just to put an end to the solicitous frenzy of the birders around me: "Not the near tree, the far one, not the sweet gum, the oak, at two o'clock, look through the fork of the branch just below that twig . . ." I would sometimes announce "Got it!" just to terminate the paralyzing attention, and because it seemed more polite than "I no longer care, leave me alone," though I would never check the bird off when I got home if it was one I hadn't seen before.

I mean something else when I say "lying," something that grows out of a fantasy about nature itself and how we wish to see it. A sort of selective viewing, perhaps, that constitutes its own subtle, indirect form of dishonesty. I am familiar with it from my own behavior. I remember taking a trip in second grade to

Sturbridge Village, a reconstructed colonial community. I was overwhelmed by the spirit of the place—the perfect white church with its clean steeple, the large-eyed cows in their barn, the woman churning butter, with her period bonnet and long skirts. I had brought a camera and I kept shooing my friends out of the picture—I didn't want mugging, gap-toothed kids in parkas with ski-lift tags still hanging from the zippers waving in front of the church or spoiling my shot of the cow. Years later, after I'd moved away, I would look at those pictures, which I had put in a little album, and wonder where all my friends were, what they looked like. The cow was a cow, the church was a church. They might have been postcards; they were not my actual experience of that outing. In a weird way, the pictures were lying.

A nature filmmaker once confessed to me that his greatest challenge wasn't finding a lion chasing a gazelle but getting a picture of that lion that didn't have a busload of tourists in the back or an airplane overhead. The films he made, like so many I have seen, have a purity at odds with the reality of wild animals in the world today, who by and large live in game parks. His documentaries inform, to be sure, but they also gratify a fantasy of life as it is no longer lived.

Bill McKibben's landmark book *The End of Nature* shocked me when I read it twelve years ago, just as I began birding, because it informed me, at the very moment that I was discovering what I considered "wilderness," and dreaming of the faraway trips I would take, that true wilderness is a thing of the past. That the wild world has more in common with Central Park than I at first understood. Our industrialization of the world has reached a point of no return and we are bound now to use technology to preserve the things that technology has undone. This part of our modern legacy is one that, interestingly, throws us back on an ancient biblical idea that as a secular society we must struggle to accept; that we are tenders of the garden, managers of the natural world. At this point in our technological advancement, the very idea of "nature" separate from human intervention is something of an illusion, a memory of what once was.

Birdwatching, to my mind, has an honesty that comes from the built-in acknowledgment that we must settle for fleeting natural elements that dance in and out of view, and that the human and technological are woven through our encounter with nature.

I have a beautiful edition of Thoreau's *Walden*, filled with lush color photographs of Walden Pond in all four seasons. It was published in 2004 in honor of the 150th anniversary of the book's original publication, and there is something somehow dishonest about it. Not that I don't enjoy big close-ups of lady slippers, or a white birch in the snow. But it is an artificial world of flowers and ferns, without a glimpse of human life in it. It is a lie.

Leo Marx's classic 1964 book *The Machine in the Garden* essentially pointed out the paradox at the heart of American life— the machinery that brings us safely into nature is airbrushed out of the picture we wish to paint. I understand this impulse intimately—it's what drove me to kick my friends out of the snapshot frame years ago when confronted with a farm. And it was a struggle at first when I started birding in Central Park, with eyes only for the birds, trying to ignore the cast-off condoms I occasionally stepped over, the odd crack vial, the men disappearing into the bushes, dog walkers disregarding the leash laws, children wading into the stream where, a minute before, a northern waterthrush had bobbed along the bank.

The park is beautiful; you could fill an album with big blossoming catalpa trees and glacier-scarred rocks. But it bears everywhere the signs of human use. I will never forget the time I was birding in the park and took shelter under a sweet-gum tree because of a sudden downpour. Under the same tree was a transvestite with a Walkman and a man with a briefcase who had been walking through the park after a day at the office. We acknowledged each other with the awkward averted half smiles of people stuck on an elevator. There was a black-throated green warbler, active among the dripping leaves, that I looked at from time to time, but I had a powerful sense that the human scene on the ground was just as remarkable and, more than that, an integral part of my birding.

Gradually admitting these things into my sight became an important part of birding for me, not the enemy of the enterprise. It became another facet of the double sight of birding. Every birder knows that there is fine birding to be done on golf courses or at garbage dumps or sewage-treatment plants. That may be a sign of the degradation of nature, but also of our interconnectedness with it.

I sometimes wonder if one of the reasons that I have a hard time reading "nature writing" is that the writers are unconsciously making birds—or fish or forests—things that keep you from seeing as much as something you see. Even Thoreau, greatest of American nature writers, and so much more than that, is, despite his deep honesty about the nature of his "experiment" in the woods, often guilty of the lie of omission. He has a habit of writing as if ordinary life were somehow something shameful, something to be shooed out of the picture.

The edition I have of *Walden*, with the pictures, is a betrayal of Thoreau, who wrestled with the tension between community and the individual spirit, but it also picks up on an aspect of Thoreau that is part of his legacy. *Walden* is a very great book, but it would have been even greater if Thoreau had told us that that he often went home for dinner. Or that his mother and sisters baked him pies and doughnuts that they sent along to his homemade cabin.

Or that an unanticipated frost put an end to his famous bean field. Or, much more important, if he acknowledged that a man alone is somehow incomplete, instead of making him a paradigm of wholeness. Did he, during his two-year stint at Walden Pond, dream about women? Men? Did he masturbate when he wasn't watching the leaves turn color? Or did he leave his sexuality behind in Concord when he went to build his little house?

Thoreau is authentically revolutionary, a deep contributor to a genuine American religion, and a great writer. But there is also a familiar fundamentalism to his work, a notion that just as Jesus left his family behind to find truth, and just as Paul said don't bother marrying because the end of days is coming, so there is a sort of apocalyptic salvation to be found in "nature" as opposed to the world of people. Apocalyptic because if we lived as Thoreau did, we would not have children, form families, communities, societies. We would live like Shakers in anticipation of some imminent salvation, and we would leave behind only the furniture of our lives. Apocalyptic visions are never really good for the environment in the long run. People, as much as birds, are locked in the cycle of generations for reasons we do not understand. Whether the larger narrative of evolution has a true plot and is moving toward some sort of conclusion or resolution, or whether it is all mere blind perpetual unfolding, is not an answerable question.

But Thoreau encouraged the illusion that the only way to be in nature is to do something unnatural—go off alone, ignore the very natural urges that in fact link us to nature. He promulgated the belief that the only way to be in nature is to be solitary. I am not just talking about his mother's doughnuts. It's the contempt with which he describes the clerks in town—all serving a form of "penance"—or the farmers or laborers he sometimes meets. "Look at the teamster on the highway, wending to market by day or night; does any divinity stir within him? His highest duty to fodder and water his horses!" Leave aside the arrogance of the judgment—a glimpse and he knows they have no soul! The fact is that these hardworking rural men he sees trudging by and that he writes of so derisively, sunk in a world of labor and family, have more in common with the natural world that seems to Thoreau an image of wholeness than Thoreau himself has. Birds, although they sing during mating season, are obsessed with food, with making a nest, procreating, feeding their young, not being eaten. They sing not for our pleasure or their own but for intensely practical reasons.

We want the world to look and be a certain way. As the bird in T. S. Eliot's *Four Quartets* says, "Humankind cannot bear too much reality." Audubon's lie about his mother's "murder" affects me for this reason. Our personal history and our biological history are always threatening to expose us, and instinctively we try to conceal them. I've already lied in this book with the story I told about being at lunch in Manhattan in late March when a man announced the annual arrival of the warblers and I discovered birding. I was at lunch, but it was not a generic gathering. It was Shabbat lunch—the ritual meal following synagogue on Saturday morning. The omission matters, and I'd like to correct it now.

I've told the story of how I began birding before, in *The New York Times Magazine*, in an essay I wrote celebrating my newfound passion. There I described the occasion as "Sunday brunch." Why drag religion, not to mention Jews, into what had become my great bond with the rest of America? Like Audubon lying about his bastard origins, I felt a powerful urge toward concealment, as well as self-invention.

Maybe I'd inherited what ought to be an outmoded prejudice—that the people of the book aren't the people of the body or of the fields and trees. In a famous story called "The Awakening," by Isaac Babel—the great Jewish Soviet writer who was shot on Stalin's orders in 1940—the autobiographical narrator is a boy who, like other Russian Jewish children, is expected to be a violin prodigy but who stinks at the violin and starts cutting his lessons so that he can learn how to swim at the Odessa seashore. An old sailor begins to teach him not only how to swim but how to value the natural world, the trees and the birds and the sky. When his enraged father finds out that he has ditched his violin for pagan joys, he threatens to kill the boy, who locks himself in an outhouse. We last see him spirited to safety by his grandmother:

> It was a long walk. The moonlight froze on unknown shrubs, on nameless trees. An invisible bird whistled once and then was quiet, perhaps it had fallen asleep. What kind of bird was it? What was it called?

In the last line of the story we are told that the child is thinking of running away. The birds are calling.

Babel's childhood spanned the end of the nineteenth century and the start of the twentieth. Though I played the violin badly myself as a child, nobody expected me to shut myself away from birds or trees or my own animal nature. My mother knows the names of many wildflowers, and I remember her stooping with excitement to show me and my sister a lady slipper while we walked around, of all places, Walden Pond. And yet somehow I felt cut off from the wild world, and held my religion responsible. I wanted to be a child of Whitman, who wandered out the door and had a conversation with a mockingbird and the sea. Who famously wrote that he would raise his own barbaric yawp over the rooftops, a cry inspired by the call of the whippoorwill.

Birds are a way to assimilate into the country, and always

have been. Whitman wanted a mockingbird in his poem because it was an American nightingale, the bird of English poetry singing a new song in his own backyard. Audubon the immigrant mastered the avifauna of his adopted country and made himself a national hero. I remember my surprise, and my happiness, discovering that another immigrant, Abraham Cahan, the editor of the Jewish daily *Forverts*, a Yiddish newspaper created in 1897 for the multitude of Yiddish-speaking immigrants streaming into the country, was a birdwatcher, too. I was working at an English-language version of that newspaper in the 1990s, at the very time I discovered birdwatching, though it was years before I learned of Cahan's pastime. In retrospect, it makes sense; his paper was all about assimilating into the New World, and here was Cahan adding a vocabulary of warblers and thrushes to the English he had mastered on his arrival.

Cahan was in Connecticut birdwatching when he learned of the Kishinev pogrom, the brutal Russian massacre in 1903 that left 49 dead, 500 injured, and 2,000 homeless. As a friend noted in a memoir about Cahan, "He immediately rushed, field glasses and bird manual in hand, for a New York train. 'I felt an urge to be among Jews,' he explained." Among other things, this gives you the idea that birdwatching in Connecticut was not an overwhelmingly Jewish pursuit at the beginning of the twentieth century.

But in 1994, in Manhattan, I overheard a rabbi announcing that soon tiny wild birds—"neotropical warblers," he called them—from as far away as Guatemala and Costa Rica and Brazil—would be stopping in the equivalent of my backyard. And somehow it isn't irrelevant that I was at Sabbath lunch with a bunch of Jews when this short, intellectual, nature-loving rabbi gave me a gift that continues to transform my life. Because if you're a real birder (or a real writer, for that matter, and the two are connected), you are eventually forced to recognize that the way to the universal is through the particular. "I should not talk so much about myself if there were anybody else whom I knew as well," Thoreau writes on the first page of *Walden*. If you don't know the name of the bird you're looking at, and don't care, but just write "bird" in your notebook, you're not birding. On the other hand, if you see only a yellow-rumped warbler, say, or a goldfinch, without also seeing something far more general and mysterious binding you to the bird and all birds to each other, you're also not birding.

It isn't only personal origins that people fret over nowadays, but animal origins, too. Whatever racial intent lurks in Audubon's allegory about the slave revolt in Haiti has been undone by Darwinian evolution, which has made monkeys of us all. Indeed, nineteenth- and twentieth-century racism surely intensified out of post-Darwinian anxiety; it was psychologically necessary to split off an aspect of ourselves and pin the unwelcome animality we had learned was our heritage on a discrete group. Blacks were convenient. So were Jews, who in Nazi Germany were often drawn as apes. (T. S. Eliot, pretending to be English, gives a Jewish woman "murderous paws" in one of his poems. He couldn't stand too much reality, either.) Even before Darwin, Audubon, who died in 1851—eight years before the publication of *The Origin of Species*—recognized he had as much in common with the killer primate as he did with the talking bird.

Audubon may have identified himself, or at least his mother, with the French-speaking parrot, but the monkey has his own human attributes, "walking deliberately and uprightly" to kill the bird. Our two signal human attributes—speech and upright carriage—are equally divided between the "denizen of the air" and the "man of the woods." Audubon, champion killer of birds, was at least as much a man of the woods as a spirit of the air, and in his heart he knew it, though by plunging into an account of his mother's "murder" at the hands of slaves he somehow keeps us from dwelling on this recognition.

It is hard, as Thoreau noted, to write honestly about nature. But we must try, which includes welcoming unwelcome paradox into our lives. "At present I am a sojourner in civilized life again," Thoreau says in *Walden*, explaining that he has left his cabin. He is being ironic, but not ironic enough. There is in truth no escape for us from civilization, nor should there be. And the Thoreauvian urge to simplify is more complicated than we can fathom. What drove Thoreau to Walden today drives millions of Americans into the exurbs, slowly turning the once-natural spaces between cities into a vast single homogenized settled region. Thoreau might not have wished to live there, but he could hardly have denied that the people seeking more privacy, more green, more isolation, are his wayward children.

In his study of the ivory-billed woodpecker, James T. Tanner observed that the most common explanation given for the bird's disappearance was that it "could not stand the presence of mankind or association with advancing civilization." In other words, it was a lot like us as we sometimes idealize ourselves. Huckleberry Finn lights out for new territory because the Widow Douglas wants to adopt and "sivilize" him. The paradox is that the thing that seemed to link us to the wild world, our ferocious independence and unrestrained freedom, was the very impulse that endangered the wild places nourishing our national soul. All of which helps to explain why birdwatching—unsentimental, mediating, open-eyed, technologically powered but fueled by ancient longings—is the real national pastime, it just isn't televised.

In fact, though, it is more than the national pastime, because the field of play is the earth itself. We are the players and the spectators. And the outcome—since bird and watcher are intimately connected—is literally a matter of life and death.

9

THE REPUBLIC OF FEATHERS

*One winter morning the President electrified his nervous
Cabinet by bursting into a meeting with, "Gentlemen, do
you know what has happened this morning?" They waited
with bated breath as he announced, "Just now I saw a
Chestnut-sided Warbler and this is only February."*

—CORINNE ROOSEVELT ROBINSON,
on her brother Theodore Roosevelt

Seven years after Audubon's death (he is buried in Trinity
Cemetery at 155th Street and Broadway, not far from
the Audubon Ballroom, where Malcolm X was shot),
Theodore Roosevelt was born in Manhattan. He seems as good
a figure as any for writing about the next great leap toward modern birdwatching. He was the President who presided over
America's entry into the twentieth century—the century in
which human beings developed the power to destroy the entire
world, which, though it gave us life, is now reliant on us, not
metaphorically but literally, for its continued survival.

It is hard enough to grasp geologic time, those unknown
eons that raised valleys into Himalayas, shaved down mountains, and saw the slow, minute mutations that allowed single-
cell organisms to evolve into us. But even American time is
elusive. One way for me to get a handle on it is to see certain

people as human markers along the way. It is helpful for me to realize that in 1803, when Audubon arrived in America, Thomas Jefferson was President. In 1903, Theodore Roosevelt was President, a man who learned taxidermy from one of Audubon's traveling companions.

And though people may change little in one hundred years, the same can't be said for the natural world. The passenger pigeons that Audubon painted, and memorably described blackening the sky like locusts, and breaking branches with the collective weight of their droppings, became extinct in 1914. If his 1907 sighting is to be believed, President Roosevelt was the last person to see passenger pigeons in the wild. (Roosevelt reported the sighting to his friend the naturalist John Burroughs, who was skeptical, though Roosevelt argued that there were mourning doves present at the time, for contrast, and noted that he had seen the birds twenty-five years before and "could not have been mistaken.")

I have a battered bust of Theodore Roosevelt on my desk. I've owned it for over twenty years—I won it in a high school essay competition sponsored by the Theodore Roosevelt Society—but it is only lately that I've come to really value it.

My essay was on Roosevelt's settlement of the anthracite coal miners' strike, a subject I didn't understand particularly well but must have somehow bluffed and cribbed my way through convincingly. I mainly had a sense of callous mine-owning plutocrats facing off against miserable underground men, mostly Slavs, who at great risk worked the mines of Pennsylvania for low pay and no health benefits. Roosevelt himself seemed like an alien figure from a distant American past. When my high school class visited the Roosevelt birthplace, on East Twentieth Street in Manhattan, I felt no kinship with the man who had shot all those lions and elk and bears stuffed and posed around the house. Owing, I suppose, to my tame urban and suburban up-bringing, Roosevelt's compulsive hunting expeditions seemed like macho posturing, a form of eccentricity or madness, though I did envy the gym his father constructed for him to build up his body after childhood asthma and severe bouts of diarrhea might have labeled him a delicate invalid; I was sick a lot myself as a child, and my parents' response was primarily to encourage me to practice the violin.

I didn't know that Roosevelt was a great birdwatcher. It wouldn't have mattered to me if I had—it would have seemed as eccentric and alien as his big game hunting. But it would have taught me something important to realize the way these two pursuits fit together, just as it is important to know that the President who shot the most animals was, perhaps, the President who saved the most as well.

In 1903, President Roosevelt, having heard reports that plume hunters were decimating the bird population of a five-acre mangrove island off the coast of Florida where brown pelicans nested, signed an executive order making Pelican Island a federal bird reserve—the first time that the federal government set aside land for the sake of wildlife, though it was hardly the last. In the course of his presidency, Roosevelt set aside approximately 230 million acres of land for national game and bird preserves, parks and forests—something like 84,000 acres per day.

All this preservation of land and animals by a hunter, if I had thought about it in high school, would no doubt have seemed like an irony, when in fact it was the opposite: Roosevelt wasn't a conservationist in spite of the fact that he was a hunter, but because he was one. He never discounted the human urge to destroy, since he indulged in that urge so zealously himself. Rather, accepting it as a given of human nature, he allowed that knowledge to inform his understanding of the necessity of checks and balances on human rapacity.

I wasn't equipped to appreciate this when I was younger. I came of age during the Vietnam War, when not merely toy guns but somehow the desire to play with them was viewed as evil. (When I was six years old, a girl in my class who loved horses gave me an air rifle that made a satisfying bang and that was immediately hidden high in my parents' closet; I devoted many hours to attempting to retrieve this gun, though years later my parents admitted they'd soon thrown it out and I was in fact hunting for something that wasn't there.) Likewise, the feminism that dominated my childhood was as focused on expunging the piggish urges of masculinity as it was on changing the legal and political climate for women.

What does all this have to do with birdwatching? Well, we all strive to make ourselves as whole as possible as we get older, and birdwatching helped me discover aspects of myself that had somehow been suppressed. It didn't make me a hunter, but it brought me closer to impulses clearly bound up with hunting. It didn't make me more "manly" in the Rooseveltian sense, but by drawing me closer to the animal world, it did set me on a path of biological awareness that made me feel more keenly what it means to be a man—a human primate with a certain animal heritage.

Roosevelt also needed to make himself whole, and birds helped him do it. As a boy, Roosevelt, in addition to being a sickly child, had terrible vision, though he claimed he didn't even know it until shortly before his fourteenth birthday, when his father, a trustee of the American Museum of Natural History, gave him a pair of glasses. At the same time, his father gave him a gun and lessons in stuffing birds. The glasses "immediately opened a new world to me," Roosevelt later recalled, and like all good boys of the period, he set about killing it. These outdoor excursions were part of his road toward robust health, but there is a more literal—and at the same time, more metaphorical—way in which birds saved Roosevelt's life.

It happened like this: One snowy winter day, young Roosevelt was out with his new gun collecting birds along the Hudson River with another friend who shared his newfound passion for them. Many birds had been driven down by the bad weather, and Roosevelt, like all novices, decided everything was a "notable rarity." When he saw a flock of crossbills in a pine tree, he fired at them. As he raced to gather up the birds, a twig snagged his glasses and flipped them from his face. "But dim though my vision was," Roosevelt recalled, "I could still make out the red birds lying on the snow; and to me they were treasures of such importance that I abandoned all thought of my glasses and began a nearsighted hunt for my quarry." The birds secured, Roosevelt went to look for his glasses but failed to find them, and from then on always carried an extra pair in his pocket. Years later, when he was running for a third presidential term as candidate of the Bull Moose Party, he was shot by a man in Milwaukee; it was the case of his extra glasses (which, since rough days as a rancher, Roosevelt had made out of steel) that stopped the bullet.

Roosevelt's salvation is sometimes attributed to the folded manuscript of a long speech, but in an essay called "My Life as a Naturalist," published in 1918 in the *American Museum Journal*, Roosevelt attributes it all to the extra glasses he started carrying after his youthful bird-shooting expedition. Clearly Roosevelt saw his story as a sort of parable in which his glasses, which made him a hunter, were also a kind of shield that saved him when he became hunted. His teenage salvation via the double-barreled gift of glasses and gun allowed the later, literal salvation.

For a man like Roosevelt, glasses and guns went together. His drive toward health and the outdoor world was somehow bound up with his bookishness, since he was exploring a world he'd known intensely only from books before the gift of glasses allowed him to see it clearly. His need to shoot but also to understand (he seriously considered a career in natural history) made Roosevelt a rare but archetypal creature: an outdoor intellectual. Birdwatchers are inheritors of Roosevelt's transformations.

That he turned out to be our greatest conservationist—that the third element of his father's gift, taxidermy, morphed into the preservation of living wildlife—is a vital part of his story and makes it in some ways a birdwatching parable as much as a hunting one. In birding you keep the glasses but lose the gun, but the phantom gun is still somehow there, and important to acknowledge.

The fact that Roosevelt was a New Yorker (our only President born in New York City) is also a key part of the story. It was in cities that ornithology itself, scarcely a career when Roosevelt was young, took professional shape. Birdwatching, ornithology's stepchild, grew up alongside the new profession. The scientific need for great collections of bird skins, for journals that contained serious, verifiable information, for the systematization of knowledge, made New York City one of the cradles of modern birdwatching as well as modern ornithology. Even Audubon had retired to New York City—a place he didn't much like—building himself an estate overlooking the Hudson River, hoping to benefit from proximity to the publishing world he relied on, just as he had needed, as a young man, to spend years in London turning his bird art into high-quality engravings.

The man Roosevelt's father hired to teach his teenage son

taxidermy, John G. Bell, had sailed up the Missouri River with Audubon in 1843, when it was still the "far west." By the time of Roosevelt's childhood in the 1870s, Bell made his home in lower Manhattan and his shop was a gathering place for naturalists, scientists, and bird enthusiasts.

Roosevelt was part of a generation of men who helped mark the transition from the nature-collecting frenzy that followed the Civil War to what we today recognize as birdwatching. Men like Frank Chapman, the man who in 1900 introduced the first Christmas bird count as a way of transforming seasonal bird hunting into bird observation. (It was Chapman—who killed those Carolina parakeets in Chapter 2—who helped persuade Roosevelt, with whom he was friendly, to make Pelican Island a nature reserve in 1903.)

Chapman's protégé at the American Museum of Natural History, Ludlow Griscom, was a patrician New Yorker who, though groomed for the foreign service by his prominent family, had taught himself as a boy to recognize birds in Central Park. As a young man Griscom, using four-power opera glasses, declared he could identify any bird without killing it; challenged by an older birder in Central Park, he identified a tiny bird perched at the top of a tall tree as a female Cape May warbler, not an easy bird to call. The older man brought the bird down with his gun and confirmed the sighting.

Roger Tory Peterson learned many of his birdwatching techniques from Griscom—he called Griscom's *Birds of the New York City Region* his bible. He absorbed Griscom's methods into his own *Field Guide to the Birds*, the book that, when published in 1934, revolutionized modern birdwatching by offering diagnostic "field marks" rather than those features that could be seen only in the hand. These men weren't birdwatchers and ornithologists in spite of their New York connection but because of it.

Peterson is often considered Audubon's heir, and in certain respects he was. But the vastly different worlds they lived in might be expressed by the story Peterson tells about his own awakening to birds. For Audubon, it was witnessing the death of a parrot, but Peterson had the opposite experience. He was about twelve years old and was walking through the woods with a friend. They entered a grove of trees, and there they noticed a flicker on a branch low to the ground. The bird was exhausted from migration, all brown feathers, with its head tucked under its wing. Peterson believed the bird was dead: "I poked it and it burst into color, with the red on the back of its head and the gold on its wing. It was the contrast, you see, between something I thought was dead and something so alive. Like a resurrection. I came to believe birds are the most vivid reflection of life."

Audubon, who lived in a time of superabundance in the natural world, came to consciousness by witnessing the death of a bird. Peterson, modern like us, and living in a time of imminent extinction, was more astonished by the sudden life of a bird. The entire goal of his bird drawings is to make you want to find an actual, living example of the bird that his drawing merely represents. Art becomes mere illustration—its larger aspirations are cast aside to point you toward the living original. Audubon's paintings aspire to *become* the bird. His resurrections take place on the canvas, Peterson's in the real world.

Peterson's drawings, stripped down and one-dimensional, are in this respect the opposite of Audubon's. They're high-lighted with arrows to indicate "diagnostic" features; they as-sume that you yourself will be encountering this bird in the "field." Audubon painted birds for those who might never bother to look for them, and so the burden of resurrection fell to him. His birds are thus more alive, which is why they don't really inspire you to go out and find them in life. Peter-son, coming of age at a time of increasing scarcity, wasn't try-ing to replace the birds with art; he was trying to get you off your butt so you could find them for yourself. His drawings are shadows that make you want to find the body. With Pe-terson we are in the age of modern birdwatching.

Roosevelt became President in 1901, just as America entered the twentieth century, at a time of enormous national transition. Roosevelt was able to settle the anthracite coal strike because he could sympathize with both management and labor and find a middle path between them. He understood that the gross ex-tremes of capital and poverty were only going to widen without government intervention. For all he loved limitless frontiers, he understood the need for curbs.

Birdwatching mediates between the wild world Roosevelt loved and the urban world that produced him, just as it com-bines aspects of the scientific career he dreamed of and the life of action he ultimately chose. It mediates between the urge to kill and the urge to preserve; between an America of unbounded abundance and a country of shrinking resources. There have been other Presidents with a passion for natural history, but Roosevelt, the man famous for killing animals as well as the man

famous for sparing them (we owe the teddy bear to Roosevelt's refusal to kill a scrawny black bear), was, in fact and in spirit, the birdwatching President. He never got the third term he wanted, but he became life president of the republic of feathers, a far more vital post.

WHERE "E" MEETS "S"

My dear lady, this is a list
Of the beauties my master has loved,
A list which I have compiled.
Observe, read along with me.
In Italy, six hundred and forty;
In Germany, two hundred and thirty-one;
A hundred in France; in Turkey, ninety-one;
But, in Spain, one thousand and three!

—LORENZO DA PONTE,
Don Giovanni (translated by William Murray)

Not long ago I read a remarkable, disconcerting book in which it was suggested to me that despite having a wife, two children, and a penis I am, in fact, a girl. Or at least I have a female brain, according to *The Essential Difference: Male and Female Brains and the Truth about Autism.* This brain is also called the "e" brain, for empathy, as opposed to the male brain, or "s" brain, for systematizing. The "e" brain is good at listening, reading other people's emotions, feeling what they are feeling. The "s" brain likes to quantify things, list things, map things, create categories and catalogs and intellectual order. The book also led me to conclude that my wife, who does our taxes and filing, loves Hebrew grammar, and refuses to ask for directions, is a boy. This, at least, explains why we have a happy marriage.

Having just written about Theodore Roosevelt, I feel this is as good a place as any to bring up a question seldom touched on by birdwatching literature: Is birdwatching for girls? Or is it the ultimate manly activity? Or, put more seriously, is it, in some ways, a biologically determined activity, not for the birds, but for us? And does it allow sexual difference to play out?

This of course is an uncomfortable question, even though it's a perfectly natural one that we would apply to any animal besides ourselves. Male birds tend to be brightly colored; female birds tend to be drab. Males sing; females (usually) don't. Male falcons are one-third smaller than female falcons (which is why they are called tiercels). But sex differences among the watchers is another story, I think because we want human equality to mean that everybody is the same, not that everybody has the same opportunity. We may accept that we are products of a Darwinian world where the rules of evolution act on us as on all creatures, but instinctively we still see ourselves as standing beyond and above those rules.

Twenty-five years ago, when Edward O. Wilson ended his book *Sociobiology* by applying to people the principles of genetic determination, he caused an uproar. In his autobiography, *Naturalist*, Wilson sums up his conclusions like this:

> Human beings inherit a propensity to acquire behavior and social structures, a propensity that is shared by enough people to be called human nature. The defining traits include division of labor between the sexes, bonding between parents and children, heightened altruism toward closest kin, incest avoidance, other forms of ethical behavior, suspicion of strangers, tribalism, dominance orders within groups, male dominance overall, and territorial aggression over limiting resources. Although people

have free will, and the choice to turn in many directions, the channels of their psychological development are nevertheless—however much we might wish otherwise—cut more deeply by the genes in certain directions than in others.

What particularly rankled was a phrase like "male dominance overall," but in general it was the notion that we travel along paths cut by our genes, even though we have the ability to go off-road at times and Wilson makes a point of saying we have free will. If you read the passage carefully, Wilson isn't saying that men are or should be in charge, just that there is an inherited propensity for certain behavior.

Wilson's theories were likened to those "which led to establishment of gas chambers in Nazi Germany" in a letter to *The New York Review of Books* signed by a group of scientists that included Wilson's Harvard colleague Stephen Jay Gould. A few years later, at a symposium on sociobiology sponsored by the American Association for the Advancement of Science in Washington, D.C., protesters dumped a pitcher of ice water on Wilson's head.

What was radical when Wilson was articulating sociobiology has become far more commonplace. I don't think anyone will dump ice water on the head of Simon Baron-Cohen, the author of *The Essential Difference*, even though he states quite simply that birdwatching is for boys, or at least boy brains:

The world's leading birdwatcher, according to the *Guinness Book of Records*, was a woman, Phoebe Snetsinger, the American ornithologist. This might appear to contradict the claim that males are more prone to collect things and compile lists of facts. As it turns out, Phoebe was the exception to the rule. Most birdwatchers, trainspotters, and plane-spotters are male.

I don't know what statistics the author is consulting, but anecdotally there may be a certain truth to this. Kenn Kaufman, one of the country's top birders, acknowledges the absence of female birders in his memoir *Kingbird Highway*. Recounting an exchange he had in Texas as a young teenager with another obsessed birder, he asks where the girl birders are. The answer: "In outer space. In a Laundromat in Albania. What are you, nuts? There aren't any girl birders." Of course two young women with binoculars show up the next moment to disprove the rule, though perhaps, like Phoebe Snetsinger, they only reinforce it.

But Kaufman isn't by his own account a birdwatcher at all. He is a subspecies of birdwatcher, a "birder." I've been using the terms interchangeably, but people like Kaufman created a whole new category of birdwatching in the 1970s. Kaufman's book begins with a defiant definition that sets apart what he was doing from the traditional pursuit of looking at birds: "People always called us 'birdwatchers.' But if we had been, there would be no story to tell."

The story he has to tell is of hitchhiking across the country in the early seventies, when he was sixteen years old, in an attempt to see as many species of birds as possible, something that has since become commonplace but in the seventies was an innovation, giving a stodgy pursuit daring, and even a sort of renegade glamour. It also unleashed, in place of actual hunting, naked competitive zeal, which subsequently gave rise to the "World Series of Birding," an annual event in New Jersey in which teams of top-notch birders have twenty-four hours to rack up the greatest total of birds.

Today it is often rich people of leisure who jet around from birding hot spot to birding hot spot, but when Kaufman was a young man, a big year was the obsession of a handful of renegades for whom the embrace of the natural world and the rejection of corporate America went hand in hand. Hitchhiking his way across the continent—he covered eighty thousand miles in one year—Kaufman was engaged in something countercultural, a kind of guerrilla pastime, where bands of local birders would take him in, share their secrets, and point him on his way. Some of them even went by bird names—the two young women Kaufman met turned out to be "Peli"—short for Pelican—and "Grebe." This was a Texas tradition started by a big-time local birder, Edgar Kincaid, who called himself the "World's Oldest Cassowary." In *Kingbird Highway*, Rose Ann, a.k.a. Grebe, explains: "Victor Emanuel is the Hooded Warbler, and if you knew him you'd understand why—he's hyperactive but profound. Ben Feltner is the Brown Jay, because he's big and rambunctious and outgoing. Roger Tory Peterson is the King Penguin. The names have to be chosen with care." These young birders, fitted with their totemic noms de guerre—one is tempted to say "noms de plume"—effected a revolution in birdwatching that was primitively tribal and also quintessentially modern.

"Birding" was the term they employed for this ferocious, competitive world of bird finding and listing that was facilitated by changes in technology—another "male brain" element. As Kaufman explains it: "Improvements in communication and in travel made it possible for people to seek birds from coast to coast, and birding changed from a mild local pastime to a continent-wide craze."

Kaufman is at pains to say that he was not, in those days in the early seventies, birdwatching at all: "We were out to seek, to discover, to chase, to learn, to find as many different kinds of birds as possible—and, in friendly competition, to try to find more of them than the next birder." Though he is telling us he took the road less traveled, he sounds more like Captain Kirk than Robert Frost. In this formulation, birding is the quintessential "s" brain activity. It is a job for men.

In a sense what men like Kaufman were doing was giving birdwatching back the urgency of the hunting and collecting out of which it had originally grown. In this sense something new, facilitated by technology, was in fact a return to something old that had as much in common with the youthful Teddy Roosevelt racing to gather his blasted birds at the expense of his glasses as it did with anything else. Audubon was a fanatical lister—his journal entries are often catalogs of birds seen and birds shot, and his masterwork, *The Birds of America*, is notable, among other reasons, for its ambition to paint every single American bird. One hundred and fifty years before Kenn Kaufman, he was "out to seek, to discover, to chase, to learn, to find as many different kinds of birds as possible."

Still, what happened in the seventies—the years I was growing up oblivious of birds, inside a biology-negating bubble—was a revolution, though like most revolutions, it has now been reabsorbed into the main body to the point where the distinction between "birding" and "birdwatching" today feels like a false one. The birdwatching I discovered was infused with the spirit of "birding," which in turn was a return to the hunting-and-gathering impulses common to men like Audubon and Roosevelt. When the author of *The Essential Difference* refers to birdwatching as a male activity, he is speaking of birdwatching as transformed by the "birders" of the seventies.

Whether or not it is male, there is certainly a lot of "s" brain systematizing going on. Naturalists tend to be listers and classifiers. Spencer Fullerton Baird, who ushered in the modern era of American ornithology with his *History of North American Birds*, a vast collaborative project that first appeared in 1875, and who, as assistant secretary of the Smithsonian Institution, artfully recruited military doctors as ornithological agents, getting them to send him specimens from all over the country, was "apparently born with the urge to make lists," according to Joseph Kastner, who writes about Baird in *A World of Watchers*, his history of American birdwatching. "As a boy in Carlisle, Pennsylvania," writes Kastner, "Baird listed the money he got and spent, the books he lent and borrowed, the ages of the members of his family (he had not been able, he admitted with the scrupulousness that marked him later as a scientist, to obtain the ages of two aunts), and of 'songs that I like to sing.'" Birds were just the logical extension of an inborn predisposition.

Walt Whitman was infused with the spirit of nineteenth-century natural history, offering in his poetry long catalogs of his own body parts and of the body politic he found himself in, "tallying," in his word, all he saw and felt. As he got older, Thoreau actually worried at times in his diaries that he was giving in too completely to the listing impulse, and that he was becoming as much an arranger of the natural world in lists as a writer and that his writing might just become a catalog. He combated this urge, of course, and it is the tension between the poet and the naturalist that makes his work so stirring today.

One of the reasons birding was such a release for me is that I discovered the pleasure of lists and classifications, the world of information and organization. I never could hold sports statistics in my head, I never cared to note the various makes and models of automobiles, or to memorize all the capitals—all the things that turn out to be "boy behavior." I did not exhibit much interest in what Baron-Cohen offers as a definition of what the male brain does: "Systemizing is the drive to analyze, explore, and construct a system. The systemizer intuitively figures out how things work, or extracts the underlying rules that govern the behavior of a system. This is done in order to understand and predict the system, or to invent a new one." But suddenly I was filling my notebook not with thoughts and feelings but with names; and I was poring over guidebooks and trying to learn the taxonomy of the birds— what was a vireo and what was a warbler—so that in the field I could put all these differences together.

It's too much to say that birdwatching made a man of me, but it is true to say that it allowed me to express an aspect of myself deeply ingrained in my biology that for some reason I had suppressed. I grew up in a world where aggression and sex differences were viewed not as neutral things but as negative things, politically corrupting; perhaps this intellectual utopianism, so at odds with the rougher side of human nature, affected me in other ways. In any event, the recovery of my systematizing self made me feel more whole. It was not simply that there was an undercurrent of hidden hunting urges that were released, but that there was a surface pleasure in listing and cataloging that I do not usually indulge in. I'd found an outlet for my "s" brain usually buried under "e" brain emoting. Suddenly I, who could never remember if you take I-91 or I-95, felt the mechanical pleasure of classification.

When I was handed a compass in the woods and didn't know how to use it, it was not just cultural incapacity but a lifetime of personal disinclination that made me feel so flummoxed. I am not a map reader—another attribute of the male brain that Baron-Cohen highlights—but birding somehow tapped into that desire to read a map and a compass. I felt ashamed I couldn't, because I realized suddenly how primal and important it was.

And wasn't I there—in Louisiana—to be one of the first in a generation to see something? To boldly go where no birdwatcher had gone before? Indeed, it was a hunter who had seen the bird, and I wanted to be like him, even if I didn't know how to use a compass.

Of course, you can't be just a systematizer or an empathizer. Indeed Baron-Cohen—who runs the Autism Research Center at Cambridge University—believes that autism is the result of too much male brain, whether in men or women. He believes in general that an increase in "s"—the systematizing brain—suppresses "e"—the empathizing element. This is a sort of biological version of *Men Are from Mars, Women Are from Venus.* If you are a zealous organizer of the world into categories or systems, Baron-Cohen maintains, it is harder to be attuned to other people's emotions, and to experience them inwardly, to feel and to know how others feel.

But "male brain" and "female brain" are misleading terms. There are plenty of women who have "male brains" and men who have "female brains," and a large group in between who exhibit a mixture of both. It is a continuum, not an either/or proposition. Men and women are not cartoon embodiments of one trait or the other. Baron-Cohen uses himself as an example—he is a psychologist who was drawn to a helping profession, and he tells us further that the woman down the hall programs his computer for him because he can't do it himself. My wife, despite her love of grammar, is deeply empathetic and worked as a hospital chaplain for many years. I am not a bowl of quivering empathy.

In a letter, Elizabeth Bishop articulates this combination of elements beautifully, the strange mixture of feeling and order that makes a poet's world, and a human one:

Dreams, works of art (some), glimpses of the always-more-successful surrealism of everyday life, unexpected moments of empathy (is it?), catch a peripheral vision of whatever it is one can never really see full-face but that seems enormously important. I can't believe we are wholly irrational—and I do admire Darwin—But reading Darwin one admires the beautiful solid case being built up out of his endless, heroic observations, almost unconscious or automatic—and then comes a sudden relaxation, a forgetful phrase, and one feels that strangeness of his undertaking, sees the lonely young man, his eyes fixed on facts and minute details, sinking or sliding giddily off into the unknown.

We all need elements of both brains to function fully, and this leads us back to birdwatching. Birdwatching isn't a male or a female activity, it is both. The urge to systematize, and categorize, and accumulate is built into it, but so are the empathizing elements that make conservation integral to birdwatching. We need both elements for our mental health, and we certainly need them both for birdwatching.

Audubon is a good example of the combination of elements pointing the way to birdwatching. He was a fanatical cataloger and reckless in his murderous pursuit of birds, but he pitied the poor golden plovers killed by the thousands in Louisiana. Writing about the killdeer in *Birds of America*, Audubon described the elaborate attempts the birds make to drive away intruders from their nests, informing his readers that if they wished to see the birds' dramatic display, they might "take up their eggs"—but then he adds, "If you be at all so tender-hearted as I would wish you to be, it will be quite unnecessary for me to recommend mercy!" (Despite the jaunty tone, Audubon is in fact echoing a biblical injunction, found in Deuteronomy, not to take eggs from a nest without first shooing away the mother bird.)

Not long after I took up birding, I went on a falconry outing in Vermont. It seemed somehow a logical outgrowth of birding. I would affiliate myself with a killer bird—I would not do the killing myself, but kill by proxy—and I would, even more than I did in birding, find myself bound up in the natural order of things. I have a great deal of respect for falconers, who are responsible for bringing the peregrine falcon back from the brink of extinction. Falconers know how to borrow birds from the wild, raise them without robbing them of their hunting urges, and then turn them loose. They were well suited to caring for peregrines and releasing them once the dangers of DDT, which had driven them from the wild, were reduced.

The falconer I was with was using a pair of beautiful Harris hawks, chocolate-brown birds not native to Vermont but to the American Southwest—I had seen one once in Arizona. We were in a game park stocked with partridge and quail, and as we walked through the field of scrubby grass, the hawks "followed on," flapping lazily from tree to tree or circling briefly as they kept an eye on the dog they instinctively disliked but had learned to associate with quarry. The birds' jesses dangled down, and they had transmitters on their backs in case they vanished into the woods. Even the dog had on a transmitter, which beeped when he stopped moving, to alert the falconer. The blend of the natural and the technological that is easy to ignore in birding is part of the overt thrill of falconry, where mastery and mimicry are points of pride. Dogs, humans, birds of prey all form a complex company presided over by the falconer.

Occasionally the Harris hawks would fly off fifty feet or so and land on the ground, going for voles or mice invisible to the rest of us, standing awkwardly on their long feathered legs like men in riding breeches who had lost their horses. They had to be called back with a piece of meat on the glove or with a lure—a length of wood with glued-on pheasant wings attached to a long rope and swung like a lasso to simulate a flying creature. The hawks landed on this thing as if it were alive, tearing feathers off with their beaks, hunching over it with almost copulatory zeal, until lured off the lure with a small piece of meat.

I was also "following on," moving in that mingled state of excitement and boredom that I think must characterize a lot of hunting. Our progress was slow and reminded me of taking a walk with my then twenty-month-old daughter, who always stopped to pick up tiny sticks or leaves. The dog needed to be whistled out of the woods. The birds kept going after voles.

Suddenly the dog, after bounding along, began creeping forward like a giant cat. Then he went tremulously still, a foreleg pointing into the underbrush at the edge of the field. His beeper went off. The falconer slipped a leash on him; the hawks landed low in nearby trees. Something unseen and alive was in the tall grass. The falconer had a "beating stick" with him and, for my benefit, pointed with it noiselessly in the direction he thought the cornered bird, a partridge, would fly—like a pool player calling a shot.

In a moment he would use the stick to beat the grass, call down the birds with a sharp "Hey hey hey," the partridge would take off like a football with wings, and the hawks would swoop down and get it. I'd already seen several kills—the yellow beaks of the hawks were at this point splashed with red. The falconer would let them eat for only a moment, then bend down like a medic gently taking the pulse of a patient but actually breaking the neck of the bird, which he would pull away from the hawks, diverting them with cubes of meat.

The falconer had not yet made his move, and the partridge was in shadow when I finally noticed it. The bird was beautifully marked with black shadow lines—the whole bird looked like a painted face. The hawks were both ten or so feet up, but they had not yet noticed the partridge. The partridge, however, was aware of the hawks and seemed so frozen with fear I felt I could reach out and pick the bird up with my bare hands. Perhaps I could have. The silhouette of raptors seems to have burned terror into the very genetic code of game birds, so that even captive-raised birds will freeze at the sight of them. In the sixteenth century, hooded falcons were used for "daring"—or dazing—small birds like larks, which would freeze in terror on the ground until men with nets scooped them up. This explains why, even in the twenty-first century, falcons are used effectively for bird control in airports.

Standing with the petrified bird at my feet and the dark raptors above, I felt not the murderous rapture I had hoped to experience in some perverse way but a kind of bored impatience and a certain amount of shame. This was not what I wanted. My sympathy was with the partridge.

Suddenly I heard, from out of a nearby tree, the slow chant of a red-eyed vireo. Its mechanical song is repeated over and over, even in the heat of noon, when other birds are silent. I am not very good at birdcalls, and at the time was even worse, but there was no mistaking the sleepy, repetitive song that bird guides characterize as *Here I am . . . where are you? Here I am . . . where are you?*

The mnemonic devices for remembering birdcalls, like the diagnostic arrows in bird guides, are enormously helpful even as they simultaneously run the risk of reducing the bird to a single salient feature that eclipses the living animal. Once you know that song sparrows say *Maids maids maids, put on your teakettle ettle ettle* and that white-throated sparrows say *Poor Tom Peabody Peabody Peabody*, you will never forget the song, but you may also never really hear it again. (You could say the same, of course, about the stars—that once you know what the Big Dipper looks like, you'll never see the stars that constitute it—but we do see the stars, and the constellations, which is why looking up is a human as well as a natural wonder.)

The red-eyed vireo called to me with deep hypnotic force. I realized that this bird was my real quarry.

I had brought my binoculars, and I felt an overwhelming desire to slip away and find the invisible bird issuing its calm, unsettling challenge: *Here I am . . . where are you? Here I am . . . where are you?*

FROST AT MIDNIGHT

The question that he frames in all but words
Is what to make of a diminished thing.

—ROBERT FROST,
"The Oven Bird"

In the fall of 1900, around the time that Theodore Roosevelt was elected Vice President (a job he would barely
hold, since President McKinley was shot the following
year), Robert Frost moved his family to a farm in Derry, New
Hampshire. Frost, who was twenty-six years old, wanted to be a
poet more than he wanted to be a farmer, but somehow in his
mind, rural life and writing went together, much as Thoreau's
move to Walden, when he was twenty-eight, and his dream of
making himself a writer, were connected.

One of Frost's biographers, Jay Parini, notes that Frost read
Walden while he was at Derry and reread it many times in later
years. He fell in love with the book, which gave him a context for
what he himself was doing—creating an island of natural, poetic
life for himself in a sea of increasing material development and
industrialization. It must have helped make plain to him why he
was drawn toward rural retreat just as the country was poised on
the brink of its world-conquering century.

Unlike Thoreau, Frost was a post-industrial city boy, and so
his journey backward was greater than Thoreau's. (Frost's short

poem "One Step Backward Taken," about a strategic retreat that keeps him from careening off a mountain, basically says it all.) Frost was born in San Francisco in 1874; until the age of eleven he lived among paved streets and trolley cars.

I remember my astonishment discovering a plaque in downtown San Francisco, on the corner of Drumm and Market Streets, honoring Frost, the city's native son. At the time I was a graduate student at the University of California, Berkeley, but though I was studying English literature, I had somehow failed to absorb the fact that Frost was an urban child. In my mind he lived in his poems, and his poems were rooted in New England soil. But contemplating that plaque, I realized it was an urban landscape that informed his innermost dreams, which no doubt gave a keen edge to his waking dream of rural escape. Stony soil, birch trees, wildflowers, orchards, fields of snow, birds—all had been acquired, like a second language.

In those days I was still waking out of my parochial, Northeastern, urban cocoon. I had grown up believing that even in the mid-1980s, East was East and West was West and urban was urban and country was country. I wanted these things to be true, since it made my own trip across the Rocky Mountains, to the shore of another ocean, feel more dramatic. I wanted to feel that I was going out West, just as Teddy Roosevelt had gone out West, even though the buffalo were already gone by the time he got there and I was not exactly living in the badlands of North Dakota. I was not, alas, a birder yet, or I could have discovered the population of wild animals that still live out West in abundance, as they did in the time of the Indians, and learned that Western birds really are different, since the Rocky Mountains are still a barrier for migrating birds, though they have long since ceased to be a barrier for people.

If I had been a birder, I would have considered Frost what birders call a vagrant, a bird that has wandered off course from where it ought to be. Only for me, he had wandered backward off his adult course and gotten lost in someone else's childhood. He ought to have been born in New England. Somehow, half of me still believed that you could only convincingly be what you were born.

Frost's father, a charming, violent, alcoholic newspaperman, died when Frost was eleven; his mother moved the family to the East, where Frost's father had grown up, and Frost spent his adolescence in small towns north of Boston, attending Dartmouth and Harvard fitfully and finally settling on farm life for himself and his young family.

Here was another difference from Thoreau—Frost was a father, with a wife and infant daughter, when he moved to Derry. He was also grieving. In July of 1900, a few months before the move to Derry, his three-and-a-half-year-old son, Elliott, had died of typhoid fever. Frost had consulted a local physician who had misdiagnosed the boy and given him digestive pills. His wife's mother was a Christian Scientist who urged faith in the Lord. Frost was not, but by the time he called in his own physician, it was too late. Frost blamed himself—what father wouldn't?—and the death haunted him for the rest of his life.

Frost famously said that home is where when you have to go there they have to take you in, but the natural world is also a kind of home to which, however estranged, we go in times of trouble (and go, of course, at the end of our lives, whether we want to or not). Might as well make peace beforehand. Nature may ultimately seem the source of all our woes—our frail, imperfect, biological nature, which permits children to die of typhoid—but it offers its own rough consolation as well, bound up as it is with the mystery of origins and endings.

Thoreau was also grieving during his retreat to Walden. A few years before, his brother John, to whom he was very close, had died suddenly of lockjaw after cutting himself with a razor. While at Walden, Thoreau wrote *A Week on the Concord and Merrimack Rivers*, in which he reconstructed a trip he had made with John six years earlier. That book, full of canoe paddling and poetic natural observations, is really a working out of the death of his brother, the ghost companion shadowing Thoreau as he reconstructed their journey along the river. Knowing that soon after their trip John died in Henry's arms makes the book far more compelling for me and changes how I think about *Walden*, too. I sometimes even imagine, though this is pure fantasy on my part, that at Walden Thoreau was grieving not just for his lost brother but for the family he knew he was never going to have. Thoreau attempted to marry nature the way nuns marry God. *Walden* is the child of that simultaneously all-embracing and chilly union.

When I think about Frost, and any quest for contact with the natural world, I often recall one of Thoreau's parables in *Walden*, a strange story that has animals and birds instead of people but that is steeped in human loss:

> I long ago lost a hound, a bay horse, and a turtledove—and am still on their trail. Many are the travellers I have spoken concerning them, describing their tracks and what calls they answered to. I have met one or two who had heard the hound, and the tramp of the horse, and even seen the dove disappear behind a cloud, and they seemed as anxious to recover them as if they had lost them themselves.

Thoreau's biographer Robert Richardson reports that when Thoreau was pressed to explain this parable, he would say, laconically, "I suppose we all have our losses."

We all have our losses. There is a part of birdwatching that for me is always associated with those losses, and with the hunt for something irretrievable. When I started seeing birds for the first time—really seeing them, with binoculars and proper names—I felt a special elation that was tinged with an ache of longing for . . . what? I'm still not wholly sure, but it was partly the sensation of finding something and in finding it realizing that it was lost without your having known it and then recognizing that other things are missing, too, and that this bird is just a tiny piece of what you want. Every bird I see feels like the fulfillment of something that simultaneously stirs a longing for more—deeper knowledge, more contact, stranger sights. Somehow, I associate this feeling with the sensation I've had dreaming of my father after his death—I wake up feeling I have made contact, but that contact fills me with a larger sense of loss, not entirely unpleasant because so emotionally rich, but never wholly satisfying either.

Frost, who lived in Derry until 1911 and laid the foundation of all his poetry there, wrote and lived like a man always looking for a horse or dog or home that he had owned in some previous life, and he was always ready to glimpse a bird about to vanish behind a cloud. In a beautiful late lyric, "Auspex," Frost remembers a time when he was a boy in California on an excursion to the country and an eagle descended toward him:

> *Once in a California Sierra*
> *I was swooped down upon when I was small,*
> *And measured, but not taken after all,*
> *By a great eagle bird in all its terror.*

Frost's poem reminds me of Leonardo da Vinci's encounter with a bird of prey, recorded in one of his notebooks: "The first memory of my childhood is that it seemed to me, when I was in my cradle, that a kite came to me and opened my mouth with its tail, and struck me several times with its tail inside my lips." Freud famously analyzed this passage as evidence of Leonardo's homosexuality; Freud writes of nipples, cow udders and penises, and various associations of the vulture with Egyptian mythology, where, according to Freud, vultures were always female, associated with the mother and believed to be impregnated by the wind—thus addressing the issue of Leonardo's absent father. Unfortunately, Freud had a bad translation, and the bird isn't a vulture but a kite, a relatively common European raptor whose flight pattern Leonardo, ever obsessed with flight, had been studying when he recorded his childhood reminiscence. (Vasari notes that Leonardo used to buy birds in the marketplace for the sole purpose of setting them free.) Leonardo may well have been homosexual, and probably was, but it seems that some strange encounter with a bird, real or imagined, lifted him, as it did Whitman and Frost, into a dream of creative and literal flight.

Frost's poem about the eagle, typical for him, ends with a note of disappointment, ironic but real, that he had been rejected by the great bird, as if for the rest of his life he dreamed the creature would return and carry him away. I think this is what makes me return to his poetry again and again, and what links it to birdwatching, which is the art of simultaneously finding and losing, and of being simultaneously found and lost.

At some point between the years 1906 and 1910, Frost wrote the poem that is for me the birdwatcher's anthem, a poem steeped in diminished expectations and defiant hopes. The poem is a simple sonnet and it is named after a bird, the ovenbird. The name, for someone unfamiliar with the bird, might conjure something magical, like a phoenix, a bird that gets burned up in fire and is reborn out of the ashes, but in fact it refers to the nest the bird makes, on the ground, which is shaped like a Dutch oven. Ovenbirds can and do fly, but they have an earthbound quality, walking along the forest floor looking for bugs, and bobbing their heads almost in the manner of a tiny chicken. They are olive drab on top, with a white breast streaked with black below. On the back of the head there is an orange stripe, bordered by black.

The whole poem is a lament for a world that has lost its wildness, a world in which "the highway dust is over all," but it's the last two lines that jar and stick in the mind. Imagining the meaning of the bird's song, Frost writes:

> *The question that he frames in all but words*
> *Is what to make of a diminished thing.*

These lines came with me when I went to a swamp in Louisiana to look for the ivory-billed woodpecker, and when I went to look for the bird in Arkansas. They have popped into my head numerous times, not simply when I've seen an ovenbird (which is very shy and doesn't stay long in sight), but when I haven't seen the bird. When I've just seen Central Park, which for all I pretend to myself is Walden is really just a big landscaped garden with streams that turn off in winter by elec-

tric switch and a pond full of turtles from people's home aquariums. And I think of it when describing to other people the centrality of birdwatching, an activity that frames the same question as the ovenbird. How do you relate to nature when so much of it is gone? What *do* we make of a diminished thing?

And the line does not just refer to the external world. What do we make of ourselves in our present form? Are we now, after Darwin, diminished things, not created in God's image, but fallen in our minds to a confused biological standing? And are we diminished things for another, almost opposite reason—less divine but less animal now, too—less free, like Audubon, and like Theodore Roosevelt, to live in wild relationship to nature where we could kill it in its abundance, pit ourselves against it, carve a place for ourselves out of unyielding wilderness, and feel both intellectually and spiritually supreme, while also experiencing a kind of animal triumph? Instead, we are bound by our necessary but limiting codes of conduct, wardens in a catch-and-release world of limited resources.

Frost's modest poem about a modest bird reverberates immodestly in my imagination. But here's the whole poem:

There is a singer everyone has heard,
Loud, a mid-summer and a mid-wood bird,
Who makes the solid tree trunks sound again.
He says that leaves are old and that for flowers
Mid-summer is to spring as one to ten.
He says the early petal-fall is past
When pear and cherry bloom went down in showers
On sunny days a moment overcast;
And comes that other fall we name the fall.
He says the highway dust is over all.
The bird would cease and be as other birds

But that he knows in singing not to sing.
The question that he frames in all but words
Is what to make of a diminished thing.

I always assumed, till looking up the poem's history, that "The Oven Bird" was written in the 1950s, that it was not just a mid-wood bird but a mid-century bird, too. It was unsettling to realize that it was written in the first decade of the twentieth century. Ransome Eli Olds mass-produced the first American automobile only in 1901—how could the highway dust be over all a mere five or so years later? But already, for the poet attuned to nature—even one not grieving for a child—the century began in loss.

This is hardly a new theme for poets of nature. In 1798, at the end of an earlier century, Coleridge wrote his great "conversation poem" "Frost at Midnight" about sitting up late in his house in the country, with his sleeping child beside him, watching the fire in the grate and recalling his own miserable, overcrowded London childhood, with nothing natural to look at "but the sky and stars." Coleridge addresses the bulk of the poem to this sleeping baby, promising him (he never says if it's a boy or girl, but we know it's his son Hartley) a different world, where nature, and God, are everywhere apparent. Certainly I've had this own wish for my daughters in my Manhattan apartment, thinking, How will they learn, how will they see?

When Frost moved to his farm in Derry, he was moving against the grain of the country. In 1790, 95 percent of Americans lived in the countryside. By 1890, 35 percent of Americans lived in urban areas, and by 1920, for the first time, there were more Americans living in cities than in rural areas. The country was headed toward this inevitable shift when Frost went the other way.

And his poem captures this contrary existence. How do you embrace the natural world at a time of industrialization and urbanization? Which is connected to the question, How do you write poetry in an unpoetic age?

Like Whitman's mockingbird, driven by the loss of its mate to sing all night, the ovenbird is singing in this poem after it ought to be, after spring is over, after the blossoms have fallen. The song persists, the way birds themselves persist, after we have gone from 50 percent urbanization in 1920 to 75 percent in 1990. They shouldn't be there, but they are.

Frost's poem is all about being late. Frost was a literal late riser—he told stories about the low regard his fellow farmers held him in because he slept the morning away, having stayed up late writing poetry. And he was a metaphorical late riser—writing after the great age of poetry was over. He was not a late bloomer, but the world noticed him late, in part because he embraced a rural mode that was fast going out of poetic fashion, though this was self-conscious choice on his part. I think this is why he seems allied to the birds for me now, and why birdwatching, which used to seem like a quaint and old-fashioned enterprise, almost an affectation, is really a prophetic pursuit, emblematic of our modern age and quietly becoming universal in its popularity.

In college I had scorned Frost for poets like Eliot and Stevens, holding against Frost his very aura of folksy American accessibility (forget that he knew more Greek and Latin than Eliot or Pound), as if a poet who rooted himself in the soil lacked importance. More parochial snobbishness to outgrow! And Frost was the poet to teach me.

Frost doesn't mention it, but birders know that the ovenbird's song has been described—by John Burroughs in Frost's day and Roger Tory Peterson in our own—as a ringing cry of *Teacher! Teacher! Teacher!* My daughter's copy of *The Burgess Bird Book for Children*, published in 1919, refers to "Teacher the Oven Bird."

Frost takes a teacherly tone in the poem. I'm going to show

THE LIFE OF THE SKIES

you this bird and tell you why it's important, emblematic. But first I'm going to teach you what it is. His poem begins almost like a guidebook entry: "There is a singer everyone has heard,/ Loud, a mid-summer and a mid-wood bird . . ."

I felt chastised by the very first line of the poem. "There is a singer everyone has heard." Really? Has everyone heard an ovenbird? I suppose I might have heard one growing up while on vacation somewhere, but I wouldn't go so far as to say that "everyone," or even most people, have heard it. Most people did not live in New Hampshire farm country, even in Frost's day. The bird, not well represented west of the Rockies, isn't likely to be one he heard in his childhood either.

His answer to the problem of writing poetry in an unpoetic age was to be like the ovenbird, who knows "in singing not to sing." So much of Frost's poetry is poetry disguised. Like Coleridge, who wrote "conversation poems," he used what seemed to be ordinary speech to make his lyrics. They are no less poetic for that, just as birds are no less wild for being seen by me in Central Park. My neighbors see me come back to my apartment building with my binoculars on a spring day and I am like the runners with their MP3 players or the parents with their strollers, just another New Yorker back from the park. But how I must look on the sidewalk with my binoculars and how I feel are awkwardly at odds, because as far as I'm concerned, I've been someplace as exotic as Guatemala, where the ovenbird spends his winters.

I suppose I look like someone with a hobby, but that isn't right at all. I've been doing a disguised activity, which is what birdwatching is. It isn't a hobby, any more than I would call raising my daughters a hobby. Or writing. It's a natural, inevitable part of my engagement with the world. It's my way of answering the question of what to make of a diminished thing.

Again I think of the Hasidic story that frames the same question as Frost's ovenbird, about the Baal Shem Tov going into the woods to light his fire and recite his special prayer. And how the next generation would go to the same spot in the woods and say the prayer but could not remember how to light the special fire. And the generation after that no longer knew how to make the fire or say the special prayer but could still go to the place in the forest. And finally the generation after that did not even know the spot in the forest—but when the rabbi, sitting in his golden chair, simply told the story, it was somehow enough.

This is a story about the power of story, and about the way religions change, and about how physical acts that happened long ago become legends without somehow losing their power. But I now find the Hasidic tale a useful parable, not simply about religious evolution, but about human evolution, too. Once, as a species, we were in the forest—it is where we lived, where we evolved before moving out to sweep across the African plain. And of course fire was our great necessary human discovery, that turned night into day and gave us a way to defy the natural order of the world, so that the line between our dreams and our waking thoughts was blurred. It was magic, no doubt, in the early days of its discovery and use. Gradually we civilized our way out of the woods, out of the plain, out of nature itself. We know we are bound up with the forest in some way, but we really can't remember exactly how. And we congratulate ourselves that thinking alone in our chair in our castle is enough; we can dream our way back to our origins without recourse to the forest or the fire. But can we?

The Hasidic parable used to comfort and inspire me—what writer wouldn't find the ultimate triumph of the storyteller inspiring? But stories shouldn't be only the end of something, they should be the beginning—they should lead us back to the woods as well as away from the woods. Nowadays, I want more than a world of words.

Even in token form, we need to find our own place in the forest. We have to leave our golden chair and wander out into the woods. We won't return to the place we came from any more than Adam and Eve could find Eden again, but that doesn't mean we can stop searching. It is clearly part of our nature, part of our need. Birding, for me, represents the search. The story isn't enough—I need my actual eyes and ears, actual trees, and the life that gathers around those trees. This isn't a return to paganism or even nature. It's a return to humanity.

It would be a sentimental fantasy, and much worse, to wish only for wildness, though. The Nazis worshipped nature because they wanted to be like it—unhampered by human morality. They created the Order of the Wolf to symbolize this aspiration—they wanted to be wild animals, to be the "blond beast," and not to live inside the balance between watcher and watched. They created a world totally at odds with people who sat in their chairs and found thinking "enough."

And so the story of the Baal Shem Tov and his disciples reminds me not just of the world lost before that story was told, but afterward, too. It reminds me that we live in a world of much more terrible extremes than Frost knew when he wrote "The Oven Bird." Frost was writing before civilization became as endangered as the rural life he loved, before civilizing culture became a diminished thing as much as the wild world.

When, in 1942, James T. Tanner's study of the ivory-billed woodpecker was published by the Audubon Society—a study of the bird that doubled as a plea to save it in its last little scrap of old-growth forest—the book carried an introduction by Arthur Allen, a professor of ornithology at Cornell who was one of the leading figures in the rediscovery and documentation of the bird. He ends his preface with a plea to save the ivory-bill, not in spite of the fact that World War II was under way, but because it was under way, because he wants us to see the bird almost as a symbol of what America was fighting for. It's worth reprinting his words:

> Today we are measuring our love of freedom in billions of dollars and thousands of lives. The American way of living is worth anything we have to pay to preserve it, and the Ivory-billed Woodpecker is one little guide post on our way of life, a reminder of that pioneering spirit that has made us what we are, a people rich in resourcefulness and powerful to accomplish what is right. The Ivory-bill is a product of the great force of evolution acting on American bird life in ages past, to produce in our southeastern United States the noblest woodpecker of them all—one that inspired Mark Catesby and John James Audubon and Alexander Wilson—one that has lured scores of recent ornithologists to the cypress jungles of South Carolina, Florida, and Louisiana in the ardent hope of but seeing one individual alive. Is it worth ten dollars to save it? Is it worth ten million dollars? It is worth whatever we must pay to preserve it before it is too late.

I am deeply swayed by these words, and I am persuaded by them, but I feel obliged to argue with them, too, because another question has to be asked simultaneously: What price a single human life, a day less of fighting? How many forests would we pay? How many birds?

The Singer Sewing Machine Company, which owned the forest that Allen was trying to save, leased it to a Chicago lumber concern that clear-cut the woods. German prisoners of war were used to do the logging. The wood was used for tea cases for British soldiers, but it was also used to make gasoline tanks for

fighter jets. In *Hope Is the Thing with Feathers* Christopher Cokinos gives way to a false note when he writes, bitterly, "World War
II veterans of the British Army who sipped their tea in barracks or
at the front—perhaps in distant North Africa—can thank the
trees of the Singer Tract." The fight to save the woods and the bird
should never have come down to a single forest. For all the greed
no doubt exhibited by the Singer Company (and it was consider-
able; according to Cokinos, one company executive rebuffed
environmentalists by saying, "We are just money-grubbers"), human needs are not given to nuanced expression in time of crisis—
that is a fact of our nature.

The wood could no doubt have come from some other
source, but its ultimate use—not just tea but gasoline—troubles
my easy agreement with Allen, for all that I count myself a conservationist. It's like knowing that DDT, that great scourge of
American wildlife—which thinned the eggs of eagles and falcons
and threatened both species with extinction—helped eliminate
malaria, a disease that remains the number one killer of humans
in the world, in this and other countries. We are always fighting
multiple wars at once, and it is hard, perhaps impossible, to get
the balance right. In some ways it has never been so hard.

Frost moved to Derry before the unprecedented carnage of
the First World War, the horrors of the Second World War, the
Holocaust, the use of nuclear weapons were dreamed of. Before
human beings had the power, literally, to destroy the whole
world, and to destroy all its inhabitants, too, a turning point in
human development we are still absorbing.

Frost had only to worry about the loss of trees under the ax
of progress, but the ax, in the twentieth century, cut both ways,
mowing down men and women and children as well as forests.
The rabbi in his golden chair doesn't exist anymore. He was
murdered, along with all the other Jews of Eastern Europe, by a

population tired of the distinction between human beings and animals. The Hasidic tale, which to begin with asked what we can make of a diminished thing, now haunts me with even greater terrors of human as well as natural diminishment.

We are perched much more precariously between life and death now than Frost was a hundred years ago. The ovenbird and the faraway forests it is just an echo of represent only two poles in a much more complicated world, a much more tangled balance. It's harder to long for the wildness in ourselves, and in the wider world, when human wildness has proven to be so cataclysmic in the past hundred years. The rabbi dreaming in his golden chair belongs now to a civilization, the Jewish world of Eastern Europe, that was utterly exterminated in my father's lifetime.

How do I balance human loss and environmental loss? The two phrases somehow embarrass each other, but I feel the need to fit together the relationship between them. I've got a natural history and a human history—and a personal history, too—and I need to bring them all together to live an honest life. People aren't separate from nature, nor are they wholly part of nature, either, which is a big reason, I suppose, that I find birdwatching—inglorious, mediating birdwatching, with its killing urges and its bloodless results, with its scientific foundation but its recreational application—so central, so appealing, so necessary.

Arthur Allen begins his introduction to the ivory-bill book by writing, "The greatest tragedy in nature is the extinction of a species." This is only half true as far as I'm concerned. There are many more extinct species than there are extant ones—and if there weren't, we, and most other present life forms, wouldn't be here. We stand on the bones, and the DNA, of superannuated forebears. Species have always become extinct—we marvel at the dinosaurs, but we do not mourn them. I for one am glad I've only got their descendants to contend with on my spring walks.

And what about the disappearance of our ancestors, whose extinction paved the way for our own appearance? (Or perhaps it is more correct to say, whose extinction was hastened by our appearance.) Hard to imagine sharing the earth with *Australopithicus*, say, or Java Man, and imagining what role they might play in our world today—slaves? zoo exhibits? enemies? Hard enough to maintain our belief that all men and women are created equal in a world of a single species of *Homo sapiens*. Extinction is built into evolution, a gloomy but unavoidable fact.

What Arthur Allen seems actually to mean in his invocation of tragedy is species going extinct, not because they have given rise to a more successful, more adapted offshoot of themselves that then beats them at their own game but that goes extinct because we, human beings, are responsible. He means the extinction of species that happens on our watch.

He doesn't call it our watch, of course, but in fact that's what it is. Inherent in his argument, though unarticulated, is that we human beings have a special role in the world, to protect the animal kingdom around us, to be stewards of the earth. This is a religious idea. The world needs to be seen as "creation" for us to feel this way toward it, not merely a random accumulation of stuff. Our appearance on the earth marked a special change in nature—other animals don't worry about the fate of those they displace, and other animals don't have the power to displace so many—all, in fact—though we'd kill ourselves in the process.

Personally, I believe that there is a divine spark in us that binds us to the rest of creation, not merely as fellow creatures but as caretakers, with an earthly responsibility like the one we imagined for God. I'm not saying you can't be a conservationist without this feeling—it's just harder for me to understand what we owe the ivory-billed woodpecker without it.

This is an old-fashioned notion. Coleridge, in "Frost at Midnight," expresses the calm conviction that if his son grows up in nature he will have intimate contact with the divine world, too, and come to know the God that made the world and that is inscribed in its very fabric. Proponents of natural religion, prevalent in the eighteenth century, famously declared that studying the world is like finding a watch in the grass—we can tell from studying the watch that it had a maker, even if the maker is not on hand to take credit.

It's the idea that preceded Darwin, but that doesn't necessarily mean it died with Darwin, however much one accepts Darwin's view that all life is the result of a struggle of blind forces groping toward survival and leaving in its wake a mountain of extinction. Plenty of Darwinians have subscribed to both. Darwin lost his faith in God, not when he discovered his theory of evolution by means of natural selection, but when his beloved daughter died of tuberculosis at the age of ten. He, too, had a personal as well as a natural history to contend with.

Recently my friend Sam, a poet, sent me a letter about Coleridge. Sam and I have been birdwatching together and he knows my passion for birds. In his letter he talked to me about "Frost at Midnight," which ends with Coleridge telling his son that because he will grow up with nature he will grow up with God, and all seasons will be sweet to him, even winter, when drops of water cannot fall from the eaves but when "the secret ministry of frost / Shall hang them up in silent icicles, / Quietly shining to the quiet Moon."

Sam reported that he had just read a biography of Coleridge and that the biographer associated these last lines with one of Coleridge's favorite quotations from Plotinus, who wrote of divine knowledge, "We ought not to pursue it with a view of detecting its secret source, but to watch in quiet till it suddenly shines upon us." My friend Sam wrote, "This made me think of some of your thoughts on birding."

Since then I've been wondering if that is the true secret motivation behind birdwatching. The descendants of the Baal Shem Tov—like the romantic poets, rebels against the Enlightenment—believed that when God created the world something got broken in the process; the vessels intended to hold God's glory shattered, and the world was strewn with holy shards, scattered in the act of creation. In this kabbalistic system, each person has a sacred task to gather up the divine sparks and thus repair the world. This for me is a very beautiful metaphor for birdwatching. Or perhaps birdwatching is a living metaphor for this mystical process.

There is certainly the purely physical thrill of seeing a trembling fall leaf suddenly detach itself and turn into a redstart or a chestnut-sided warbler. But there is the other unspoken longing as well—that the bird itself will give way to something that lives beyond birds. And that the broken puzzle will someday be complete.

PART II

BIRDS OF PARADISE

Thou wast not born for death, immortal Bird!

—**JOHN KEATS**, "Ode to a Nightingale"

MISSING LINKS

*The far East is to me what the
far west is to the Americans.*

—ALFRED RUSSEL WALLACE,
My Life

On March 31, 1862, a tall man with a bushy beard and wire-rimmed glasses arrived in London by train carrying two live birds of paradise in a great cage. The birds—and their human escort—had traveled all the way from Singapore, a journey of many weeks, during which the birds had begun to develop their breeding plumage. It was not every day one saw in a London train station creatures with a yellow head, black face, blue bill, green eyes, chocolate underparts, and long, dangling plumes of creamy yellow and milky white.

Indeed, birds like this—they were in fact the "lesser bird of paradise," *Paradisea papuana*—had never been seen alive in Europe. This may explain why the man, Alfred Russel Wallace, had taken such care with them. In Bombay they had lived on the veranda of his hotel while the ship refueled. In Malta he had stopped his journey for two weeks so he could collect live cockroaches for them at a local bakery. In Egypt he had actually ridden with them in a baggage train across the desert.

These were rare birds, but so was Wallace; his devotion to the natural world was extraordinary, and he is recognized as perhaps

the greatest field biologist of the nineteenth century. He had just spent eight years in the vast chain of islands that was then called the Malay Archipelago and is today Indonesia and parts of New Guinea, a location he had chosen in no small part because it would give him access to the elusive bird of paradise, though he was omnivorously after everything. Enduring dysentery, malaria, swollen feet, poisonous snakes, torrential floods, and a host of other life-threatening hazards, he had systematically shipped back pieces of the tropics—plants, bugs, birds— in staggering profusion to British museums and private collectors. Many were new to science and given his name in tribute. If that was all he had done, he would still be worthy of great attention, but while accomplishing all this, in almost total isolation, Wallace had written a paper outlining the mechanism of evolution by means of natural selection that earned him a place, alongside Darwin, as the theory's discoverer.

This gives poignancy to his arrival in England with birds whose names summoned up the very Edenic myth that Wallace's conceptual work had shattered. But then Wallace is a figure of great paradox, mirroring the paradoxical nature of birdwatching, in which you arrange wild things into scientific patterns even as you are lured deeper into the wild world you are trying to order.

Wallace brought his scientific eye and aspirations to the tropics, but he brought things back from the tropics, both literally and figuratively, that transformed him and that he came to believe, more and more, Western civilization needed. Not just his theory of evolution or samples of tropical organic life, but something more mysterious that was somehow connected to the bird of paradise, its uncanny beauty and its mystical name.

Hunting the bird of paradise, Wallace came into contact with non-Western peoples who were, in some sense, the guardians of those birds. Wallace was a true Victorian and a devoted man of science who had no problem calling those he met "savages," but he also glimpsed in them something else that left a lasting mark. He admired what he saw as their radical social equality, he respected their beliefs in a spirit world, and he felt they had a way of relating to the natural world that contained something people of the West needed in order to remake paradise.

It may seem strange, after progressing from Audubon and Thoreau to Theodore Roosevelt and Robert Frost, to be back in the nineteenth century, standing on a train platform in London. But just as the American Civil War divides America like a mountain range, so what happened in England around the same time, centering on the seismic disruption of evolutionary theory, represents a great divide that still cuts through us and that we are still figuring out the implications of. We are all of us still standing on the platform of a Victorian train station—that symbol of progress and industrialization and imperial power—clutching a cage with a wild bird in it. An exotic bird with a divine name that has somehow made its way into our hands, into our world, into our civilization, and yet that carries traces of a faraway place we still inhabit, if only in our dreams. The specter of Wallace at the train station haunts me, haunts birdwatching, and should rightfully haunt this book.

You have to be careful talking about Wallace and haunting, because Wallace really did believe in ghosts. At the height of his scientific eminence he went to séances, and once even thought he was encountering the bearded, bowing figure of Charles Darwin—who died in 1882—until the form resolved itself into a beloved uncle. Darwin would have died all over again if he'd known to what irrational uses he was being pressed.

Wallace took the double vision necessary for birdwatching and gave it an extra twist—he believed there was a material level and a spirit level in the world, and that it was necessary to be mindful of both. He believed science would eventually allow us to bridge those worlds and so he did not consider his psychic investigations as belonging to the supernatural—he thought they were all part of nature and that this would be proven someday.

I don't expect modern science to resolve the need for faith anytime soon, but I respect Wallace's wish and believe that an aspect of his longing lurks behind birdwatching. I crave birds because they are alive and beautiful and stirring, of course. I love knowing that birds fly at me out of Southern rain forests and the tundra of the Far North. I love knowing that they fly out of the land of dinosaurs—the feathered reptile archaeopteryx lived 150 million years ago in the late Jurassic period. But if I am honest, I must admit to a deeper longing, too. I want a bird to fly at me out of Eden.

I am not an advocate of intelligent design, which holds, in part, that individual organs within species, like the eye, are too complex to have evolved in accordance with the laws of natural selection. Though I am no scientist, I am persuaded that it is bad science and ought not to be taught in schools. But if I am honest, I must say that the religious wish—improperly imposed on a scientific theory—to find evidence of divine intelligence in the world certainly lives in me. Religious thinkers have struggled for centuries with the question of how individuals could have free will in a divinely ordained world. It doesn't seem any harder to my mind to feel that there is a divine origin to the universe and yet believe that God does not intervene in the mechanisms of evolution. Einstein was allowed to say that God does not play dice with the universe. Why can't the rest of us?

When my elder daughter, who is seven, asks me where she was before she was born, I tell her that her body did not yet exist but that her soul was with God. She never asks for evidence—no doubt one day she will—and I don't have any evidence to give her, though for me she herself constitutes evidence of a sort. But though I do not pretend that I am giving her a scientific explanation, I do not think I am telling her a lie, either. I am a little embarrassed confessing this in a book bound up with science and natural history, but since it is what I tell her, and what I believe, it would be truly shameful to ignore it.

My religious beliefs do not keep me from explaining to her about evolution and the mechanism of natural selection. Our local subway station, because we share it with the American Museum of Natural History, has sculptured bas-reliefs of extinct animals on the walls, including archaeopteryx, which we have looked at many times, tracing with our fingers the long tail feather clinging like a fall leaf to a reptile tree. I do not tell her that archaeopteryx drowned in Noah's flood; I tell her that it gave way to more successfully adapted species that replaced it. When she turned seven, I bought her a pair of binoculars so that she could see real birds. But that doesn't mean I want her to lose the gift of second sight, her inborn ability to spot birds of paradise that might suggest a world made by more than blind chance. I would like her to be able to hold both visions in her head.

Since the professionalization of science in the nineteenth century, it has been harder to hold a harmonized vision of the world. When Thoreau was sent a questionnaire in 1853 by the secretary of the Association of the Advancement of Science asking what branch of science he was especially interested in, Thoreau wrote bitterly in his journal that though interested in many branches of science, if he were to express himself fully, he would make himself a laughingstock, "inasmuch as they do not believe in a science which deals with the higher law." The rest of Thoreau's entry for that day has a prophetic echo for Wallace's career: "How absurd that, though I probably stand as near to nature as any of them, and am by constitution as good an observer as most, yet a true account of my relation to nature should excite their ridicule only!"

Much of the first half of this book explored what it means for man to live in a man-diminished world. Birds bring news of this diminishment like nothing else—they are like carrier pigeons with environmental messages tied to their legs. The messages say: The rain forests are disappearing, the climate is changing, fragmentation is spreading, extinction is rising. But there are questions that follow from that information that are more than merely political. Questions that must be raised, even if they can never be answered. Questions that are moral and theological.

The complacency of religious fundamentalists, and the stridency of ultra-Darwinian atheists notwithstanding, we have still failed to settle the true mystery of mysteries. Where do we come from and why? For some there is no "why"—we are an accident, although a very impressive one. For others, we are divine creatures, and ancient scriptures are our operating instructions. But for many, we live in an undefined middle area that Emerson described with simple force in his essay "Experience" when he wrote: "We wake and find ourselves on a stair; there are stairs below us, which we seem to have ascended; there are stairs above us, many a one, which go upward and out of sight." Emerson goes on to note that the spirit who, according to legend, hands out the drink of forgetting when souls depart for earth did his work too well. We don't know where we come from or where we are going.

Since 1844, when that essay was published, science has taught us a lot about where we come from, if not about where we are going. But I'm not sure the confusion Emerson describes has vanished. We may know a great deal about the Big Bang, but nobody knows what happened in the split second before the explosion. And nobody can yet make sense of the astonishing fact that all the mass and energy of the universe were once, as that theory avers, crammed into a space smaller than a mustard seed. With science like that, who needs mysticism?

For me it is that gap—not gaps in the fossil record that some erroneously cling to in order to refute evolution—that provokes my imagination. The evidence bearing out Darwin and Wallace's theory that we evolved from astonishingly simple origins is abundant. But from what ultimate beginning? And to what end? This we still don't know, and it is accommodating ourselves to those uncertainties, it is living in the middle of opposite poles of possibility, that is a key challenge of life and civilization. Birdwatching in its humble way helps me accommodate myself to living between these extremes.

Birdwatching was my door not only into the natural world but by extension into the world of evolution. Anyone who has watched the American Ornithologists' Union split the rufous-sided towhee into the eastern towhee and the spotted towhee gets a contemporary lesson in the fluidity of species. Darwin, noticing that the beaks of finches in the Galápagos were adapted to different ecological niches, came to realize that species were not fixed by God but were mutable things constantly modifying. We ourselves are like the finches—not fixed forever. The consequences of that realization were not taught to me in school, but they hang over many of the battles in our society.

I sometimes wonder how America could have been founded on the notion that "all men are created equal" without the notion that all men—and women—were created in the image of God. What would the founding fathers have written or formulated if they had drafted the Declaration of Independence a hundred years later, in a world in which we were not created at all but evolved, imperfectly and unequally? If Ben Franklin hadn't simply explored electricity but decoded the genome that reveals not only our common biological heritage but evidence as well of how different we can be from each other and how many of those differences are programmed into us at birth? Would they have embraced a useful lie, would they have abandoned the language of radical equality, or would they have decided that a religious truth still lurks beneath our scientific discoveries, much as Francis Collins, who spearheaded the Human Genome Project, has declared unabashedly that the genetic code is the language of God?

We have other reasons for being forced back on theological questions. Thanks to our technological supremacy, human beings now have the power to destroy nature, and by extension life itself. This power is actual, not metaphorical. Since that is so, we must ask with new urgency, What are the reasons for preserving it? Much depends on the answers we come up with. If human beings have replaced God as the Lord of the earth, what sort of Lord will we be? Or is there something divine in us that makes us, for all our power, not Lord but steward? What do we owe the natural world and why?

The old longings, the old beliefs, still lurk inside our lives and our culture. I have a hard time believing that anyone with any regularity actually called the ivory-billed woodpecker the Lord God bird—or, as Faulkner suggested, the Lord-to-God bird—if only because it's such a mouthful. But the zeal with which the name was seized on when the bird was, perhaps, seen again was more than the expediency of headline writers. It was the religious longing that still lives, the hunger for revelation and resurrection that Audubon exhibited in his bird paintings long ago and that birding continually reveals.

But before we return to the ivory-billed woodpecker, it is necessary to spend some time with Wallace, and to revisit the nineteenth century to contemplate certain questions in their original context. And we need to contemplate them, because the tensions these questions give rise to are still alive in the world today.

Wallace went to the tropics to solve what he called the "mystery of mysteries"—the origin of the species—only to discover, once he had succeeded, that for him the mystery still remained. He had also gone to find the elusive bird of paradise. Both these discoveries were of equal importance to him. I believe they should be of equal importance to us as well. We need to understand both of Wallace's cherished discoveries—the theory of evolution by means of natural selection *and* the bird of paradise and all that it meant to him in its literal and metaphorical incarnations. This doesn't take us away from the subject of birdwatching, but perhaps brings us to its very core.

Birdwatching makes us all naturalists again and somehow brings us back to that time in the nineteenth century when amateurs, not professionals, ruled and when science and religion still overlapped. Wallace was at the center of these transformations, and the debates that went with them, which we are still feeling the consequences of.

So back we go to Wallace, and to several of his contemporaries—like Henry Baker Tristram, a clergyman and ornithologist who embraced Darwin early, then shrank from his conclusions and ran off to Palestine to write a natural history of the

Bible. Tristram gets his own chapter, because while his journey was in some ways an evasion of stark evolutionary discoveries, it was also a deep encounter with the natural world that led him back to evolution through a gentler door that did not obliterate his religious life. Following Tristram takes us to Israel, a spectacular place to see birds, but also a place that captures the symbolic longings that still persist in birdwatching.

Birding in Israel even today carries a biblical undertone and makes explicit certain questions that always live inside birdwatching, whether you are in a swamp in Louisiana or in what is left of the Huleh swamp in the Galilee. The collision of the historical and the biblical and the ornithological and the theological and the political also makes that tiny country a place that is powerfully emblematic of all the intersecting elements present in birding wherever it is done.

You cannot write about America without being mindful of the way the idea of a holy land lives underneath the American dream, so that even a swamp in Louisiana becomes a primal place of promise. And behind the idea of a promised land and a holy land is the idea of the Garden of Eden. Darwin did more than anyone since the serpent in Genesis to disturb the feeling that we were safe in a world of sacred guarantees. He went further than the serpent, because he provided a legitimate scientific basis for thinking that there never had been an ordered time, a divine time, a time in which human beings had a special role. Which brings us back to Wallace in the train station, guarding his birds of paradise as if they were his very soul.

13

BIRD OF PARADISE

The bird's fire-fangled feathers dangle down.

—WALLACE STEVENS,
"Of Mere Being"

Wallace's arrival at the train station in 1862 was a moment of great triumph for a self-taught man who began his training in natural history with a pamphlet on plants produced by the Society for the Diffusion of Useful Knowledge. But before we meet him at the train station, we need to travel back a few years further, where we find Wallace in 1858 shivering with fever in the tropics. Wallace had been in the Malay Archipelago for four years and was at that moment based on the island of Ternate, where he had gone in search of the bird of paradise. His hunting halted by a recurrence of the malarial fever he had contracted during an earlier stint in the Amazon, Wallace, between fits, had time to think.

He later recalled waiting for the chills and fever to subside, his mind throbbing with all the reading he had done, including Malthus's *An Essay on the Principle of Population*—that dark assessment of the way disease and famine keep human populations in check—and Charles Lyell's *Principles of Geology*, with its emphasis on the vast age of the earth, in which tiny incremental changes become amplified over eons. These theories were swirling around in a wild speculative atmosphere partly created by popular books like the 1844 bestseller *Vestiges of the Natural History of Creation*, which raised the scandalous notion of "transmutation of species." (Though heretical, evolution was not in itself a new idea—Darwin's grandfather Erasmus had talked about the concept a generation before. It was finding the *mechanism* of evolution that had so far stumped everyone.)

Added to this heady brew was Wallace's own experience as a collector. His expeditions had given him ample opportunity to note that within each species there were often minute variations that—over the sort of geological time Lyell had written about, and exposed to the struggles that Malthus described—might become new species if circumstances were favorable. When the fever and shaking subsided, Wallace had it: the fittest variations would survive, the least fit would perish, and new species would thus come into being. Over the next two days he wrote a short paper called "On the Tendency of Varieties to Depart Indefinitely from the Original Type."

Reading that rather obscure-sounding title, we need to remember that Wallace, like Darwin, had grown up in an age when the greatest scientific minds of the day believed that God had created each species fully formed and placed it in the spot where it was found. The "original type" therefore bore divine fingerprints. Wallace was departing indefinitely from a biblical worldview. *Vestiges*, which blended creationism with evolutionary speculation, had been published anonymously and created the sort of outrage that helped persuade Charles Darwin to keep his mouth shut.

Wallace, who was morally as well as physically fearless—and who as a poor outsider with no formal schooling past the age of fourteen didn't really give a damn—felt no need to hide his discovery from the world. He mailed the paper to Darwin, who, unbeknownst to Wallace, had been hugging an identical insight to his breast for twenty years in private dread, gathering up massive evidence to build a watertight case for a theory he knew would shake the foundations of an order in which he held a comfortable place.

Darwin had not been especially impressed with a paper Wallace had sent him from the tropics two years earlier—he had written "nothing new" in the margin. That was not his reaction when he received a package from Ternate containing Wallace's latest paper. That very day he wrote to his good friend, the great geologist Lyell, expressing his shock: "I never saw a more striking coincidence . . . Even his terms now stand as Heads of my Chapters." He added despairingly: "So all my originality, whatever it may amount to, will be smashed."

His originality was not smashed—thanks to Wallace's modesty (and absence) and the intervention of Darwin's friends, powerful and wellborn members of the Royal Society who took action to protect Darwin's "priority." Whether or not Wallace was royally screwed is a matter of opinion. His paper, without his permission, was bundled with an old outline and letter of Darwin's—dug up to establish Darwinian primacy—at a presentation at the Linnean Society in London. After which Darwin, his fear of being unknown suddenly greater than his fear of being known, hurled himself into *The Origin of Species*, which came out the following year.

It is important to point out that Wallace didn't mind. He was in the first place used to setbacks of every sort. Before his Malay trip he had spent four years in the Amazon, only to have his ship catch fire on the way home; Wallace was rescued, but his vast South American collection, along with his dreams of a comfortable life, sank into the Sargasso Sea.

He was also a remarkably humble man who went so far as to call his own book-length summation of evolutionary theory "Darwinism." In keeping with his later socialism, Wallace believed that life was a collaboration as much as it was a competition. It was characteristic of him that in his autobiography he included the name and photograph of Ali, his trusted Malay servant, identifying him as "the faithful companion of almost all my journeying among the islands of the far East."

It is also significant that Wallace did not race home to gather his laurels. Solving the origin of species was all well and good, but lacking the private fortune of most naturalists of the day, Wallace still needed to make a living—it wasn't as though he could start doing product endorsements. He spent four more years in the Malay Archipelago, in part because he could not afford to leave, but in part because he did not want to.

This was the age when naturalists, armed only with pins and jars and magnifying glasses, were on the cutting edge of the scientific world. But however much their findings gave rise to materialism in others, there remained a near-mysticism to their love affair with what we would today call biodiversity: the overwhelming plenitude they found in the rain forest and even in their private gardens when they retired to the English countryside. Wallace's friend the botanist Richard Spruce—whom he had gotten to know in the Amazon—had left South America only when shattered health forced him out after fifteen years; Spruce was so heartbroken he hid his face in his hands as his boat pulled away, rather than look at the receding rain forest for the last time.

Unlike Darwin, who returned from his voyage around the world and never left home again, Wallace exemplified the belief that there was something about the natural world that transcended any theory one might devise about it. One simply had to be there. This is the collector's credo, and it is even more the birdwatcher's. Being out in the field isn't a means to an end, it is itself the end. It is bound up with what Wallace Stevens called "mere being," when he described a bird sitting in the palm at the end of the mind, beyond all thought or reason.

Throughout his long life Wallace would return to collecting like Antaeus touching the earth, whether it was in the Rocky Mountains or the Alps or the mountains of Wales; days before his death, at ninety, he was still being wheeled through his garden to look at favorite flowers. Wallace, who was the kind of man who bottle-fed a baby orangutan for three months after he'd saved it from a swamp—unconcernedly noting its resemblance to a human infant—never lost his sense that the natural world contained more than the answers derived from it. He wanted to stay in the tropics as long as he could. The bird of paradise was calling to him.

Wallace embarked on three specific expeditions while in the Malay Archipelago to find birds of paradise—in 1857, when he went to the Aru Islands; in 1858, when he went to mainland New Guinea (considered part of the Malay Archipelago); and in 1860, when he went to the western Molucca Islands. These were some of the most remote places in the world, and Europeans had not yet settled them. He relied almost entirely on the natives of each place, and the native servants he brought with him, for his survival, first of all, and for help locating and collecting the birds, which favored tall trees deep in the forest.

The natives of Aru had a special method for killing birds of paradise. The birds had long been prized by Chinese and Arab traders, and so Aru Islanders had found a way to get them that would not damage their feathers. Before first light, they climbed the tall trees where the male birds displayed in mating season. Hiding behind crude shelters that the hunters constructed as blinds among the branches, they were equipped with bows and arrows, having fitted the tips of the arrows with a conical wooden cap the size of a teacup, which allowed them to bring down the birds without damaging them. When the sun came up, the birds arrived and, according to Wallace, were so involved in their elaborate displays that it was possible for the hunters to bring them down one after the other in rapid succession, with the rest scarcely noticing until they were shot in turn.

Wallace's description of the native method of capturing birds of paradise reminds me of a story I've read about Joseph Hickey, the influential conservationist and ornithologist, who as a boy in the Bronx during the First World War had climbed trees to get a closer look at migrating warblers until someone took pity on him and gave him a pair of opera glasses. Hickey was a member of the Bronx County Bird Club, created by a group of scrappy young urban birders who made up in energy and ingenuity what they lacked in equipment—they shared opera glasses and the pages of a guidebook salvaged from a trashcan. The group helped revolutionize birding in the early 1930s—Roger Tory Peterson, who sometimes birded with the group, later spoke of pulling together the Bronx-born methods in creating his guide.

It is worth reading in full the description Wallace offered of getting his hands on a bird of paradise. The passage comes from his classic work of scientific travel, *The Malay Archipelago: The Land of the Orang-utan and the Bird of Paradise, a Narrative of Travel with Studies of Man and Nature.* (The ecstatic precision of the prose made the book a favorite of Joseph Conrad, who borrowed from it for *Lord Jim* when creating the fanatical collector Stein, who rhapsodizes, as Wallace also did, over butterflies.)

The first two or three days of our stay here were very wet, and I obtained but few insects or birds, but at length, when I was beginning to despair, my boy Baderoon returned one day with a specimen which repaid me for months of delay and expectation. It was a small bird a little less than a thrush. The greater part of its plumage was of an intense cinnabar red, with a gloss as of spun glass. On the head the feathers became short and velvety, and shaded into rich orange. Beneath, from the breast downwards, was pure white, with the softness and gloss of silk, and across the breast a band of deep metallic green separated this colour from the red of the throat. Above each eye was a round spot of the same metallic green; the bill was yellow, and the feet and legs were of a fine cobalt blue, strikingly contrasting with all the other parts of the body.

Wallace is still not done recording and rhapsodizing. All the varied hues, so carefully noted, are just part of the bird's magic. There are emerald green plumes that can be raised and lowered at the "will of the bird"; there are long hanging feathers, in the form of slender wires, that curl and spiral: "These two ornaments, the breast fans and the spiral tipped tail wires, are altogether unique, not occurring on any other species of the eight thousand different birds that are known to exist upon the earth; and, combined with the most exquisite beauty of plumage, render this one of the most perfectly lovely of the many lovely productions of nature."

When Wallace finally got his hands on a new species of the bird—which was named after him, *Paradisea wallacei*, or Wallace's standard wing—he called it "my greatest discovery yet," even though the discovery of the origin of the species was already behind him. Reading his description, I find it hard not to imagine that this is the bird Wallace Stevens had in mind in "Of Mere Being"—a bird whose "fire-fangled feathers dangle down."

A gold-feathered bird
Sings in the palm, without human meaning,
Without human feeling, a foreign song.

In Malay, Wallace heard this inhuman song and understood it. Holding that first bird in his hand, Wallace begins, almost, to prophesy:

I thought of the long ages of the past, during which the successive generations of this little creature had run their course—year by year being born, and living and dying amid these dark and gloomy woods, with no intelligent eye to gaze upon their loveliness; to all appearances such a wanton waste of beauty. Such ideas excite a feeling of melancholy. It seems sad, that on the one hand such exquisite creatures should live out their lives and exhibit their charms only in these wild inhospitable regions, doomed for ages yet to come to hopeless barbarism; while on the other hand, should civilized man ever reach these distant lands, and bring moral, intellectual, and physical light into the recesses of these virgin forests, we may be sure that he will so disturb the nicely-balanced relations of organic and inorganic nature as to cause the disappearance, and finally the extinction, of these very beings whose wonderful structure and beauty he alone is fitted to appreciate and enjoy.

Is there a better description of Western man as a sort of god of creation and destruction? Though he can sound utterly Victorian, with his allusion to the "barbaric" state of Aru, and the absence of an "intelligent eye" to behold the birds (until of course he showed up), he also articulates something his contemporaries spent little time talking about but that our own age is all too familiar with. Wallace is downright modern in his recognition that Europeans en masse would bring death to the birds he has traveled so far to find, even though they, like him, would rhapsodize over their beauty, covet them, describe them, dissect them, study them, and name them. Real barbarism—extinction—would come with the spread of civilization to the region. This was a paradox that Wallace spent a great deal of his life working out, in the end pretty much finding in favor of the "savages" whose world profoundly influenced his own. Or rather, he found in favor of a future that he saw combining elements of the tropical world, with its alien yet ineluctably human inhabitants, and the Western world that produced him, from whose materialism he found himself increasingly alienated.

This helps explain why Wallace is forever yoked to the bird of paradise, a real bird that is also a mythical creature. It is his totemic bird. It represents him the way Darwin is represented by the finches of the Galápagos. Darwin actually spent much more time thinking about pigeons, which he could breed at home—he hadn't even written down which finch came from which island while on the *Beagle* and had to fill it all in later—but his finches are perhaps the most famous birds in the world. They are perfect for teaching the rudiments of natural selection, with their beaks like puzzle pieces evolved to fit into different environmental nooks and crannies. Nothing wrong with a finch; it is in many ways emblematic of Darwin himself. The finch is familiar, even drab (in his autobiography Darwin boasted that he had his whole life avoided controversy), but quietly embodies an explosive truth, and the whole point of evolution is that it is true for the highest as well as the lowest. It may even be that Darwin's totem shouldn't be a bird at all but something more basic, like the barnacle or the earthworm, which was the subject of his last book. Certainly his own capacity to cling to a single subject while chewing through masses of data remains impressive. But birds of paradise are something else again.

Start with the name. And not just the common name. The Latin name that Linnaeus gave the "greater bird of paradise," which Wallace so rhapsodically describes above, was *Paradisea apoda*—*apoda* meaning "without feet"—because the original specimens that reached the West were so mangled that it was actually believed by Europeans that they had no feet at all and simply spent their life on the wing, like angels. Here was a case of Europeans behaving more like the "savages" they often derided, seeing the supernatural in the natural world. (In a sort of inverse error, Linnaeus also believed that swallows hibernated under the mud of lakes.) When Wallace went into raptures over a single species of bird of paradise, the natives laughed: "My transports of admiration and delight quite amused my Aru hosts, who saw nothing more in the 'Burong raja' than we do in the robin or the goldfinch."

But the birds were hardly irrelevant to the natives. In addition to their value in trade, the feathers were used in ceremonial headdresses (just as egret and spoonbill feathers adorned ladies' hats in New York and London) and had been traded locally for centuries both in the Malay Archipelago and New Guinea. Wallace also noted that there were myths among the natives that these birds had their origins in the sky and that they had somehow descended to earth. If they embodied for Europeans drawn to the Far East a vision of paradise regained, they were for the natives emissaries from a magic realm that they to some degree still inhabited. The Aru natives firmly believed that the birds and bugs that Wallace collected and carefully stowed in boxes would come back to life once he was out at sea.

Audubon would have understood this magical supposition well, since it fueled his own artistic dreams. So would Walt Whitman, wondering around this time whether the mockingbird of his childhood was "demon or bird," demon in this case meaning a mediating power between gods and men, not necessarily something malevolent. But Wallace came to understand best of all the native belief that spirits of the dead live on, because in a certain way he came to believe it himself.

14

RIVERS OF DOUBT

The abdication of Belief
Makes the Behavior small—

—EMILY DICKINSON

Wallace came home in 1862, escorting his two live birds of paradise. His reputation as a great collector and as a great thinker had preceded him. He was now a scientist of stature, and he had earned Darwin's marveling gratitude as well as his respect. "Most persons," Darwin wrote him after *The Origin of Species* came out, "would in your position have felt bitter envy and jealousy. How nobly free you seem to be of this common failing of mankind." He added that he had no doubt Wallace would have written his own definitive book on the subject just as well or better "if you had had my leisure."

But Wallace recognized that he could not have written a book like *The Origin of Species*. He was a terrific writer and a fine conceptual thinker who tackled many complex subjects, including the vital field of biogeography, which he virtually created and which combines questions about the distribution of animals and plant life with an understanding of the forces of evolution. But he was not the model of the careful systematic thinker who slowly piled up overwhelming evidence and then derived a theory. Unlike Darwin, endlessly breeding pigeons and poring over barnacles, Wallace had discovered the theory of natural selection in a fit of fevered inspiration. It had descended, like a bird or a poem, out of the blue, a sort of visitation. And Wallace was a sucker for visitations.

Wallace's sister Fanny had become a spiritualist while he was away in the tropics, and partly through her interest Wallace began attending séances in 1865. Though he was skeptical, looking behind doors and under tables in advance of the proceedings, he quickly fell under the spell of these events, enthusiastically recording what he saw—fresh flowers materialized on the table (Wallace duly noted each species); a spirit hand reached down to touch the keys of an accordion; the name of his deceased brother turned up on a piece of paper Wallace had hidden.

Ah, if only my hero didn't look like a crackpot on occasion. But it is worth recalling that Jean Baptiste Lamarck, who erroneously believed that acquired characteristics were passed down to the next generation, was right in his basic intuition that species did in fact change. Though when I was in school Lamarck was taught as the idiot who thought a papa giraffe stretching for leaves at the top of a tree wound up with children that had long necks, he in fact was revolutionary in recognizing, before Darwin, the evolutionary mutability of species. He just had the mechanism wrong. (And even Darwin speculated that certain acquired characteristics might be passed down—unlike Wallace, who embraced what became genetic theory.)

Wallace was part of a group of highly reputable scientists who believed that unseen phenomena might turn out to be quantifiable, even if they were spirits of the dead. Who would have thought that tiny creatures called germs caused disease, that radio waves travel through the air, that we really do spring from unicellular blobs, had it not been for intrepid scientists who believed unseen forces could be tracked to their source?

Why am I writing about this in a book on birdwatching? Certainly not to defend a theory about ghosts. Binoculars are for finding birds; if you aim at the sun you will only lose your vision. But Wallace was much more than the holy fool of nineteenth-century science, and his life is part of the story I am telling. Because the world cracked in Wallace's lifetime and we are still figuring out how to put the fragments together. For me, birding is part of that process.

Peter Raby, a fine biographer of Wallace and other explorer-naturalists, likens the simplicity of the eighteenth-century Linnaean world to a jigsaw puzzle with pieces still missing but whose outline was drawn on the box. It was assumed that subsequent generations of scientist-collectors would complete the picture over time and that, when they had, a picture of God's world would lie before us, like a painting of Eden. Instead, men like Darwin and Wallace went out into the jungle, nets and pins in hand, and came back with more pieces than the puzzle could hold—extinct species and in-between species—and suddenly the old frame was no good. Where to put all that had been gathered? Is there a larger puzzle frame we can build that can hold these pieces in a way that makes sense not simply biologically but theologically, too?

Wallace came to believe that, though the old frame was wrong, perhaps we'd find a new one that also offered a satisfactory explanation of who we are and what our existence signifies. I choose to see Wallace not so much as a credulous softy but as a perennial skeptic. He had been skeptical of the teachings of organized religion, which he blithely overturned, and then he was skeptical of the materialist certitudes that for many displaced those teachings. In this sense, doubt kept open the possibility of faith.

For Wallace, a scientific theory was more like what Yeats

called art, "an accident that happens in the course of one's search for reality." Though he had shed without sorrow the religious convictions of his childhood before the time of his first voyage, Wallace gradually developed an idea of "reality" that extended beyond the observable world, even though he kept trying to provide tangible evidence for that world.

Wallace hovers over what to me are birdwatching's largest impulses: a hunger for life; a need to order it while recognizing that perfect order is an illusion; a desire to live in a scientific world that is also a symbolic world, a world of special human responsibility in which the sudden descent of a creature of great beauty holds out the promise of meaning or purpose, even if that creature turns out not to be a bird but the human being watching the bird.

Wallace's desire to find large connections that bind together disparate worlds can still be seen in the work of naturalists like Edward O. Wilson, who incorporated human nature into his theory of sociobiology (to wide scientific outrage) despite having begun as a cataloger of ants, and who continues to dream of what he calls "consilience," the synthesis of knowledge from multiple disciplines in accordance with a handful of simple principles. Though Wilson is not a theist, 40 percent of American scientists, when polled, acknowledge a belief in some sort of divine power.

Can you look for birds without looking for God? Of course; but I do believe that even if we are not consciously working out certain questions, these questions are working themselves out in us nevertheless, and Wallace makes these questions explicit. So, too, does poetry, especially the poetry born out of that time.

Lévi-Strauss, marching around the Amazon hunting for the most primitive tribes in the world, was disappointed when the strains of a Chopin étude cropped up in his head. I feel a little like that myself—I went looking for birds and here I am talking about poetry. And about God, that old embarrassment. But Emily Dickinson, who burst into poetic life just as the Civil War, Darwin, and Wallace were wrecking the religious order she had been raised in—and who wrote and lived along the knife edge of faith and doubt—has it right:

> *Embarrassment of one another*
> *And God*
> *Is Revelation's limit . . .*

I take these lines to mean that it is not merely doubt but "embarrassment" that plagues us in a modern age—revelation cannot penetrate a culture ashamed about God, the need for God, the possibility of God. Such vulnerabilities and childlike dependencies and ancient hungers are frankly at odds with our modern ideas of ourselves as autonomous and self-sustaining. Dickinson was shockingly modern in this insight—for all her cloistered virginal life she anticipated that it wasn't animal embarrassment or sexual secrecy but religious embarrassment that was going to become a dominant post-Darwinian theme of modern life. And indeed, in our own age, the nakedness of religious questions and declarations, when they are exposed directly and not hidden by metaphor or narrative or some sort of artful indirection, makes us blush.

Dickinson was born in 1830 in Amherst, Massachusetts, where she famously sequestered herself. For the last twenty years of her life, she never left the grounds of her family home. In her seclusion she managed to wrestle with all the embarrassing questions, writing about infinity and eternity and desire and the difficulty of reconciling what we crave with what we experience—and always about death, wondering whether it was or was not the final punctuation mark of our existence. Though shut away from a certain sort of human society, the radical ideas transforming the West came to her through reading, and she was also surrounded by nature. A devoted gardener, she was as likely to enclose a flower in a letter as a poem. And of course there are many birds in her poetry—the only wild animals that make house calls with any regularity, especially in semi-rural nineteenth-century New England.

Her birds often exhibit a quaint residual anthropomorphism mingled with the harsh realities of a biological world:

> *A Bird came down the Walk—*
> *He did not know I saw—*
> *He bit an Angleworm in halves*
> *And ate the fellow, raw . . .*

Written in 1862, the poem's not exactly a brutal Darwinian landscape, but Dickinson's poems register, in infinitely subtle ways, the consequences of evolutionary thought, as when she writes:

> *Some keep the Sabbath going to Church—*
> *I keep it, staying at Home—*
> *With a Bobolink for a Chorister—*
> *And an Orchard, for a Dome—*

So far this is an innocent enough poem in defense of staying home, which Dickinson did even more zealously than Thoreau, who imprisoned himself to be near birds. She has her birds and her orchard, she is in Eden. It seems sweetly innocuous to say that birdsong has taken the place of church music in this poem. But is Dickinson saying that she finds God everywhere so has no need of church because the singing of birds is prayer enough? Or is she saying that there isn't a traditional God anymore, so going to church is somehow irrelevant? Is she herself an angel or a bird or merely in costume when she writes, in the middle stanza of the same poem:

> *Some keep the Sabbath in Surplice—*
> *I just wear my Wings—*
> *And instead of tolling the Bell, for Church,*
> *Our little Sexton—sings.*

The end of the poem is even more ambiguous:

> *God preaches, a noted Clergyman—*
> *And the sermon is never long,*
> *So instead of getting to Heaven, at last—*
> *I'm going, all along.*

Is the sermon she hears from God also birdsong? Is God speaking through the bird, or is a bird as much of God as we have now? Is the poet going to heaven all along because the road to heaven now leads through spontaneous communion with the natural world God made, or is the poet going to heaven all along because earth is all we have of heaven and while you're alive you're already there? In which case birds are not a glimpse of angels to come, they are all we'll ever have of angels.

That poem, which was written in 1860, has a gentleness you might almost mistake for the semi-paganism of Thoreau, who transferred his religious life to the natural world in anticipation of the environmental movement. But Dickinson had been raised with more attachment to a traditional God and therefore could not let go as easily as Thoreau:

Of Course—I prayed—
And did God Care?
He cared as much as on the Air
A Bird—had stamped her foot—
And cried "Give Me"—

Dickinson wrote this poem in 1862, the year the brutal carnage of the Civil War brought home the savage nature of the human struggle. That year she wrote in a letter describing her family: "They are religious—except me—and address an Eclipse, every morning—whom they call their 'Father.'"

Dickinson spent a great deal of her life working out her relationship to the "Eclipse." Her poetry captures the ambiguity of that time, and our own, better than anything I know. Despite the fact that her tombstone confidently declares that she was "gathered back" in 1886, she herself knew there was no going back to a simple religious world; that an element of darkness now was built

into daily life. "The Missionary to the Mole / Must prove there is a Sky," she wrote, in a poem that begins "So much of Heaven has gone from Earth." Birdwatching had missionary force for me because I felt like a mole before I found it. Having shown me the sky, it could not, of course, explain the meaning of what I saw; but it did, like poetry, force me to look up.

Whether or not we are poets, it is very hard to dispense with metaphors. Nature with a capital *N* was too thickly intertwined with divine associations for any nineteenth-century naturalist— even the hardheaded Darwin—to distinguish metaphor from reality completely. It was Wallace who in 1866 chided Darwin that "natural selection" was a misleading, overly metaphorical term, allowing readers to imagine a controlling intelligence rather than the blind workings of chance. Wallace preferred Herbert Spencer's "survival of the fittest." But on the whole, it was Wallace who could not dispense with metaphor.

Literary questions lurk at the heart of the debate over evolution. Does the universe have an author? Is natural history a story with a plot, or is it merely a random accumulation of anecdotes? Do things reverberate with secondary, higher meaning, or are they merely what they are? Science and religion were coming apart at the seams and so were the metaphors that had held them together.

In 1882, the year of Darwin's death, Dickinson wrote about those who had come before her:

Those—dying then,
Knew where they went—
They went to God's Right Hand—
That Hand is amputated now
And God cannot be found—

Those five lines of poetry say as much about the post-Darwinian world as anything ever written. And they contain enough complex ambiguity to fill a book. Did the dead who knew where they were going really go there, or did they only think they knew where they were going? Is God now missing because we've killed the old metaphors—God's right hand—and need now to find new ones in order to recapture a sense of the divine? Or is God missing because we've killed God literally? Or does the amputation of God's hand mean God is gone altogether and we've discovered an absence for which there is no substitute?

The poet offers no answers, of course—merely the observation that "The abdication of Belief / Makes the Behavior small." There is no answer—this is, after all, a poem—just the question, like the one framed by Frost's ovenbird: "what to make of a diminished thing."

Darwin noted in his autobiography that as he grew older, he completely lost the ability to read poetry. He wondered if this was not, along with his waning interest in music, a symptom of mental decline, but it seems symbolic of a change in the fabric of intellectual life. The age of metaphor—when science, religion, and poetic imagination were braided together—was passing away. Wallace, meanwhile, read poetry more and more, sprinkling poetic epigraphs through his books. In *his* autobiography, Wallace, thinking of all the ways his setbacks, his poverty, and the loss of his early collections had ultimately led him to his present life, quotes Hamlet: "There's a divinity that shapes our ends, / Rough-hew them how we will."

Though most if not all of Wallace's arguments for the uniqueness of human beings—hairlessness and upright posture, facial beauty and moral capacity, the complexity of the human hand—can be refuted today by scientists, and certainly his arguments for spiritual manifestations do not survive the most basic scrutiny, the essence of his argument was never really dependent on individual biological proofs. He intuited larger meaning in life, just as he intuited the theory of evolution by means of natural selection. His proofs for evolution turned out to be science and his proofs for higher meaning turned out to live in an extra-scientific realm. But the impulses behind both discoveries are still with us, even if

Wallace—too Darwinian for the champions of intelligent design and too theistic for the Darwinians—has fallen into eclipse. But Wallace was able to "dwell in possibility," in Emily Dickinson's great phrase, which is why we still need him.

Theodore Roosevelt, who had swerved from his original intention to become a naturalist but retained a keen interest in the field, reviewed Wallace's *The World of Life* in 1911 for *Outlook*. Roosevelt, considering Wallace alongside William James and Henri Bergson, was persuaded by both aspects of Wallace's thought, writing that there surely was "an overwhelming argument for 'creative power, directional mind, and ultimate purpose' in the process of evolution."

An argument, but, alas, not proof. There remains no proof for the existence of God, just as there remains none for God's absence. For me, birdwatching—vacillating as it does between the practical and the emblematic, the literal and the lofty—allows us to "dwell in possibility." The Dickinson poem that begins with that phrase, which was written the year Wallace came home with his birds, ends with a description of the life of the poet that can equally describe the environmentalist and the religious seeker:

For Occupation—This—
The spreading wide my narrow Hands
To gather Paradise—

Two years after Roosevelt's review appeared in *Outlook* endorsing Wallace's grand view of life, Wallace died at the age of ninety. That same year, Roosevelt sailed for Brazil, where Wallace's work had begun, to explore a tributary of the Amazon fittingly called the River of Doubt. The journey nearly killed him, but Roosevelt being Roosevelt, he managed to survive and the river was duly renamed Rio Teodoro.

Roosevelt came home physically broken, and the world he came back to was fundamentally changed by the First World War, which claimed the life of his beloved youngest son and unleashed the kind of carnage that beggared even the horrors of the Civil War and seemed to extend more fully than ever the dominion of brute, blind forces over human destiny. The Armenian genocide of 1915 made extinction not simply a by-product but an actual goal of human behavior.

The altered world of the twentieth century was perhaps another reason why Wallace, Victorian optimist that he was, seemed unsuitable as an emblematic scientist to a later generation. But we cannot rid ourselves of the old questions that still lurk at the heart of his work, and that our relationship to the natural world is particularly charged with.

It may be that, as Edward O. Wilson maintains, saving the environment is a matter of pure self-interest, because there are so many healing drugs as yet undiscovered in the plants of the rain forest, because the threat of global warming endangers us all, because so much of the food we eat—essentially four domesticated grains—puts all our nutritional needs in just a few baskets. But for me, Wilson's religious childhood, though abandoned, still runs like a stream under his environmentalism, keeping his thoughts green. Why not kill Armenians if it suits the struggle of one group of humans for survival? Why not let a single bird species die out, since species through history die out all the time? Surely there are reasons beyond the scientific that dictate our fundamental understanding that these things are wrong and disturb a larger balance.

Roosevelt made his triumphal journey down the River of Doubt in a more heroic age, perhaps. But it is still a journey that, metaphorically at least, each of us must make.

A PASSAGE TO PALESTINE

"There goes a Sainte-Terrer,*"*
a Saunterer, a Holy-Lander.

—HENRY DAVID THOREAU,
"Walking"

I n early spring of 2000, the year I'd first gone looking for the ivory-billed woodpecker, I went birdwatching in Israel. I had been to Israel before—to study biblical Hebrew, to visit relatives, to work on a kibbutz. Once, in college, I'd even won a fellowship to follow in the footsteps of Herman Melville, who visited the Holy Land in 1857. But I had never gone to look for birds.

Jeremiah may have said, "Yea, the stork in the heavens knoweth her appointed times," and Jesus may have said, "Behold the fowls of the air, for they sow not, neither do they reap," but I never thought twice about the avifauna of the place. I have so many personal, political, and religious associations and expectations connected to the region that they eclipsed the natural world there for me even after I started birding.

I was missing a lot. In spring and fall half a billion birds funnel over the tiny country, riding the thermals of the Great Rift Valley from Kenya all the way to Turkey. Whether you see them as having arrived on the fifth day of creation, or after millions of years of slow divergence from reptilian ancestors, they are an inspiring sight. Israel is second only to Panama in the density and variety of its spring migration.

Since Israel is where the allegorical meets the actual—sometimes violently—it is also an ideal place not merely to see birds but to think about them. East and West literally collide in this tiny place that forms a land bridge connecting Africa, Europe, and Asia, making it a magnet for migrating birds from all three continents, just as it has been, throughout history, a magnet for invading armies. It was a place that threw people and wilderness together in theologically formative ways that reverberate in the great spaces of America but that have their origins there.

Israel is six thousand miles from my home, but the trip turned out to be a natural extension of what I had been doing in Central Park. It made the impulses behind my backyard birding—and my foray into a Louisiana swamp to find the Lord God bird—explicit. And although neither Darwin nor Wallace traveled there, they haunt the place nevertheless, as do the ruptures of the nineteenth century.

I'm a little wary of talking about making the impulses behind birdwatching "explicit." It is an activity that lives in the doing, as its humble name implies. But just as it is possible to hold the named, identified bird in your sight while recognizing the wild animal that eludes all classification, so I think it is possible, even necessary, to pair the humble act of looking with the hidden desire to see in all birds a bird of paradise. Wandering off the beaten path and looking for rarities—only to realize that your rarities are another person's backyard birds—is a noble part of birding.

I remember traveling to Orkney, a group of islands off the northern coast of Scotland, where I saw thousands of seabirds—fulmars and kittiwakes—nesting in the high, sea-battered cliffs. It would have been enough just to look at these birds, and at the fierce skua, who dive-bombed me and my wife as we ran haplessly through their nesting ground on the island of Hoy—but then I visited the Tomb of the Eagles, a Neolithic burial mound constructed some five thousand years ago, and was forced to think of birds in another way. It was there that the bones of men and women  and children mingled with the skulls and claws of sea eagles. Archaeologists speculate that these birds may have been used to pick the corpses clean—the way the American Museum of Natural History uses beetles today to strip its specimens—and speculate further that these birds played some sacred role in the lives of those mysterious human beings who may have seen in the eagles a sort of bird of paradise, something fierce and transcendent that we ourselves still crave.

But Israel is even closer to the heart of the matter than Orkney. Nature and monotheism fit together easily in the Western mind until the nineteenth century, and it is in Israel that the overlap was born, where Eden was imagined and the Bible, that pre-Darwinian blueprint for life on earth, was written. If one is going to make a journey down one's own personal River of Doubt, it might as well be in Israel.

Certainly it functioned that way for Melville, who felt the blasted landscape he saw was a geographical analog to a world God had abandoned. Though he visited two years before *The Origin of Species* was published, he already wrote like somebody touched by Darwinian insights—he saw human history as a valley of dry bones without any divine wind promising to breathe life or meaning back into the dead. In his Palestine diary, Melville notes:

> Whitish mildew pervading whole tracts of landscape—bleached—leprosy—encrustation of curses—old cheese—bones of rocks,—crunched, gnawed, & mumbled— . . . You see the anatomy—compares with ordinary regions as skeleton with living & rosy man.

If only he had looked up! Of course, he had non-Darwinian sorrows, too: *Moby-Dick* had sunk without a ripple, his country was inching toward disunion, and his family thought he was losing his mind, which is why they had encouraged him to make the trip to the Levant in the first place. But his description of the land is charged with modern theological anguish. In his journal entry he sounds like Leopold Bloom, the Jewish hero of Joyce's *Ulysses*, thinking with horror of Zion in 1922: "A dead sea in a dead land, grey and old . . . Now it could bear no more. Dead: an old woman's: the grey sunken cunt of the world."

Melville turned his journal into a verse epic set in Palestine, *Clarel*, which he published in 1876; a character in that book is an American Christian who has gone native and become a Jew. This figure was based on an actual convert Melville met on his journey, but there is a kind of logic to his appearance in Melville's poem, just as there is logic to the Catholic-born Joyce making Leopold Bloom a Jew in his great epic of twentieth-century modern life. After Darwin, Christians themselves were cast in the role of Jews—people displaced by a new dispensation, clinging superstitiously to an outworn creed with no hope of redemption. Christians had been out-New-Testamented by *The*

Origin of Species and so they often saw their fate, indirectly and unconsciously, through Jews.

There is another nineteenth-century figure whose footsteps through Palestine I wish I had traced while in college, who did spend a great deal of time looking up, though if someone had talked to me about an Anglican minister and ornithologist in those days, I don't think I'd have much cared. I learned about Henry Baker Tristram, appropriately enough, from a bird. There is a black bird I wanted to see, found in the region of the Dead Sea, that bears his name: Tristram's grackle. The bird is known for landing on Nubian ibex and picking them clean of parasites while the beasts stand obligingly still. I'm always curious about who gives his name to what, and before I knew it, I was reading about Tristram and Darwin and Wallace in the middle of the nineteenth century, where it is worth returning before I describe any more about birding in modern-day Israel.

IN LATE JUNE OF 1860, a legendary battle took place in England that was like one of those early Civil War battles where well-dressed audiences arrived in carriages to see the bloodshed. The British Association for the Advancement of Science was holding its annual meeting at Oxford, and though these weeklong events were formal and informative but seldom controversial, Darwin had published *The Origin of Species* in November of 1859 and everything had changed. Darwin did not speak of men and monkeys in his book, and had in fact fearfully refrained from spelling out any theological implications in it beyond his famous conclusion, which continues to give hope to close readers craving Darwinian science and divine possibility: "There is grandeur in this view of life, with its several powers, having been originally breathed into a few forms or into one." But though our own age may draw hope from that conclusion, the established Church of England was hardly satisfied with it.

Bishop Samuel Wilberforce, a prominent Anglican who had scathingly reviewed *The Origin of Species*, was looking forward to having an opportunity to denounce the theory of natural selection at one of the society's sessions. Though he considered attending, Darwin, as usual, took fright, got ill, and went off to a water cure, while the fearless Wallace was still shivering his way through the Malay Archipelago looking for birds of paradise. But Darwin's loyal defenders, Joseph Hooker and T. H. Huxley (who would earn the name "Darwin's Bulldog"), were there to do battle. At a session held on June 30 in the new Natural History Museum at Oxford, as many as a thousand people, by Hooker's estimate, packed into an auditorium to see religion face off against science.

The weather was hot, the mood was expectant, ladies fainted. Robert FitzRoy, captain of the *Beagle*, was in the audience—he stood up and denounced Darwin's book, declaring that he had often spoken of Genesis with Darwin on board the *Beagle* and was now horrified by his former passenger's blasphemy. FitzRoy, who waved a Bible in the air, was not doing well mentally or financially and would later commit suicide.

Apparently nobody could hear anything very well, but the story, which has become legend, goes that at some point during the proceedings Bishop Wilberforce, who had offered a long critique of Darwin's *Origin*, turned to Huxley and asked if he was related to an ape on his grandmother's or his grandfather's side. At which point Huxley is reported to have murmured, "The Lord has delivered him into my hand." He then offered a defense of Darwin and an attack on Wilberforce that concluded with words to the effect that he would rather be related to an ape than a clergyman. Hooker, who had stage fright and wasn't going to attend but was talked into it by Robert Chambers, the author of *Vestiges*, also spoke in defense of Darwin—some, including Hooker himself, say more effectively, as well as more audibly—but it was Huxley's remark about clergymen and apes that has gone down in history as the coup de grâce in the death match where science did in religion. Wilberforce's question and Huxley's riposte helped set the terms and tone of the battle still found in the Scopes "monkey trial" of 1925 and sadly alive in much of the United States even today.

Sitting in the audience that day in 1860 was a young clergyman named Henry Baker Tristram. Though Tristram was a man of the cloth, it is unlikely he went in support of Bishop Wilberforce. Born in 1822, Tristram was ordained an Anglican priest in 1847. The following year ill health sent him to Bermuda, where he spent two years, working in part as a military chaplain. There he took up the study of birds and shells. Other travels—and more bird study—followed. In 1859 he helped found the British Ornithologists' Union; that same year another founder of the BOU, Alfred Newton, gave him a copy of the Wallace-Darwin papers delivered at the Linnean Society. Tristram was impressed and made his own small, historic contribution by applying the Wallace-Darwin theory of natural selection to account for differences in bill size and color in desert larks he had collected in the Sahara. Tristram published his results in *Ibis*, the journal of the BOU, one month before the *Origin* had even appeared, and he thus has the distinction of being the first naturalist to publicly apply the Wallace-Darwin theory.

Tristram was sitting next to his friend Newton at the Huxley-Wilberforce debate when Huxley made his famous comment about apes and clergymen, at which point Tristram turned to his friend and observed that he was no longer a Darwinian. As he later wrote to Newton, he couldn't bear the "argument of noise and sneers" that greeted anyone who "did not subscribe to the God Darwin and his prophet Huxley."

Scholars debate whether Tristram had ever truly been converted to natural selection and could therefore become unconverted, but that matters less to me than the place he occupies as one of those emblematic people, like Wallace, who shuttled, birdlike, between worlds. Alongside his church duties, Tristram pursued an increasingly active life as a naturalist, and the place he returned to most often, and wrote about most frequently, was Palestine.

There were certainly good zoological reasons for this—when he'd gone first to Palestine in the winter of 1858–59, he had noted how little was known about the flora and fauna of the region. But after the great Darwin division, Palestine became a perfect refuge for him. He wasn't just running back into the bosom of old-time religion; he was also running into the natural world, and so into the scientific future, going into the wilderness and looking with a naturalist's eye. Palestine gave him an opportunity to combine the two halves of himself. There he could expend his energies determining whether it was really *Coturnix vulgaris*, the common quail, that blew in abundance toward the Israelites in the desert, as the Book of Numbers says, or perhaps the black stork or the sandgrouse, as later commentators argued. Consulting migratory routes, flock size, the behavior of the birds, Hebrew and Arabic grammar, various natural histories, and his own experience—he caught by hand several exhausted quail in the Jordan Valley and his horse even crushed one—he concludes that "the miracle consisted in the supply being brought to the tents of Israel by the special guidance of the Lord, in exact harmony with the known habits of the bird." This conclusion is not really so different from Wallace's—not about organized religion or the Bible, which he never regained an interest in, but the general belief that God works in mysterious ways that look an awful lot like the ways of nature.

Tristram went back to Palestine in 1863 and many times after that, and his popular books—with titles like *The Fauna and Flora of Palestine* and *The Natural History of the Bible*—made him a religious, and simultaneously a biological, authority. He is still indispensable to the study of the region. But his trips, and his books, were a kind of therapy he offered himself to heal the Darwinian trauma.

The Western world needed therapy at that moment (without Darwin, no Freud) and got it where it could. Thanksgiving, for example, which Abraham Lincoln officially proclaimed in 1863. Lincoln was trying to create a national holiday that would bring together the citizens of a divided country, but he was also doing something, no doubt unintentionally, connected to that other civil war that broke out in 1859 in England. The fantasy of Pilgrims and Indians feasting together has a Darwinian resonance— that the civilized and the "savage" in us, the wild and the tame, the known and the unknown, can sit down at the same table.

The holiday was less about actual Indians, of course, who were by then more a metaphor than a reality in American culture—despite the Indian Wars still ahead of the country in the aftermath of the Civil War—or about actual Pilgrims, those religious fundamentalists then in eclipse, than about the divided state of humankind at that broken moment. Fittingly, there is a bird at the center. No turkeys were mentioned by William Bradford, governor of Plymouth Colony, in his account of the 1621 celebration, but the turkey was a perfect bird to build the feast around—the feisty bird that Benjamin Franklin wanted to serve as the national symbol, rather than the eagle, which he derided as a cowardly scavenger. The turkey had been domesticated in Europe but had its own wild autonomy as a bird of the American wilderness. It was a bird that could bring Indians and Englishmen together, just as quail could bring Englishmen and Israelites together.

In this regard, the turkey was the opposite of a little bird dividing America around the same time—the English sparrow, also known as the house sparrow. Introduced first in Brooklyn shortly after 1850 and zealously imported during the following decade in the hope that it would eat farming pests, and for reasons of immigrant nostalgia as well, the sparrow quickly spread throughout the United States. The bird failed to fulfill its promise as a consumer of canker worms, settling most often for the undigested seeds in horse droppings. Resentment of the bird erupted in the "Sparrow War," which raged in the 1870s. The great American ornithologist Elliott Coues (who had met Wallace in Washington and who, like him, was a spiritualist) led the charge against *Passer domesticus*. "I despise the sight of that bird in this country," he wrote to one correspondent. Coues was denounced for "treason" by Henry Ward Beecher; he was called a murderer by the founder of the American Society for the Prevention of Cruelty to Animals. Young Teddy Roosevelt, a sophomore at Harvard, piped in with his own anecdotes of sparrows harassing native birds in New York, and recalled that in Egypt he had seen farmers shooting the birds. The house sparrow, in fact, probably first attached itself to human beings in the Middle East, with the development of agriculture thousands of years ago.

Nearly all ornithologists came out against the sparrow in America, and I sometimes think that in some unconscious way they were acknowledging, through their hatred of this bird, a certain dark awareness of what European settlers had done to the native human population of America. This was especially true for someone like Coues, who was a frontier historian, the editor of the journals of Lewis and Clark, and who, as an army surgeon (and ornithologist) in Arizona among the Apache, had seen the Indian wars up close. In indicting the sparrow, men like Coues were in some sense indicting themselves. The turkey, on the other hand, was native and foreign both, and so a balm to the American conscience.

Tristram was in some sense looking for turkeys, or for something that could bring clashing cultures together. But the place he went looking wasn't the new promised land, it was the old one, the actual original land described in the Bible—the document whose autonomy and historical and theological value was most shaken by evolutionary theory.

His books are filled with fine scientific observation, but simultaneously strive to combine an accurate representation of the zoology and geology and meteorology of the region with the sense that it is a theological landscape—not an easy undertaking for a field biologist working in the wake of natural selection. In youth he was lean and dashing, posing with a long gun and belted safari suit, but there is a photograph of him from later life,

a stout man with a great white beard, wearing a black frock coat and black broad-brimmed hat, sitting on a donkey. He looks like a hybrid of Don Quixote and Sancho Panza.

Tristram went to Palestine because certain of his beliefs emanated from that tiny place and because biblical figures that mattered to him had lived there. The birds and animals that had been there three thousand years before had, with certain variations, remained and became for him a sort of zoological link to a spiritual reality he craved contact with.

I, too, emanate in some sense from that specific place as much as, biologically, I derive from unseen primate ancestors. Discovering birds in Israel linked me to my double heritage, human and wild, just as discovering the birdlife in Central Park transformed my sense of New York City, of America, and ultimately of myself. I was looking at the same landscape, but it had been completely transformed. The physical world was no longer a mere backdrop for human interaction. It stirred with its own wildlife, without which there would be no human life. I had known Israel as a modern country, and as an ancient biblical place, and I knew it as an idea, but somehow seeing the birds—really seeing them—made everything older and simultaneously more alive than ever before. They knit my multiple realities together.

THE HIDDEN SWAMP

Beneath the checkered carpet of plowed field, stubble,
and orchard, waiting for the first signs of Doubt,
growled the most legendary beast of all, the great
swamp imprisoned by the founders.

—MEIR SHALEV,
The Blue Mountain

M y guide for my first day of birding in Israel was an ornithologist from Tel Aviv University, Yossi Leshem. A tall, stooped, open-faced man of about fifty, Leshem is the king of Israeli birding, an international ambassador of the pursuit, with an easy smile that is half a squint, as if he's looked up so long he expects to see the sun. When we first met, at the Jerusalem Bird Observatory in the early morning, I was surprised to discover, on top of his wild but wispy hair, a small knitted *kippa.* He is an observant Jew and covers his head, contradicting my preconceived prejudice that the Orthodox don't birdwatch. (Leshem was raised in a secular family of Holocaust survivors and didn't become observant until the age of eleven, so he doesn't completely challenge the theory.) I felt the strange excitement I always do around religious scientists, a promise of harmony that birding itself holds out. Though thoroughly modern, there is a whisper of Tristram about him. He likes to quote biblical or rabbinic passages associated with the bird he is discussing, and prefaced a chapter about migration in one of his books with a verse from Proverbs:

There be three things which are too wonderful for me,
Indeed, four which I know not:
The way of a vulture in the sky;
The way of a serpent upon a rock;
The way of a ship in the midst of the sea;
And the way of a man with a young woman.

Leshem and I quickly left Jerusalem and were soon driving through the Judean desert and up the "Rift Road," which mirrors the migratory route of the birds. The mountains of Moab, which are in Jordan, were off to our right; to our left were the Judean Mountains. The heat that rises from the earth and bounces off these mountain walls creates the thermal highway that soaring birds ride, expending a minimum of their own energy.

The West Bank, which we drove through, had become intensely dangerous in the winter of 2001 when I was there—there had been a number of shootings on the road, though I found Leshem's driving as frightening as the specter of an attack. He is a frenetic talker and was whirling with bird-related plans: he helped create a festival of the cranes at a holistic spa near the Huleh Valley. He got a local winery to bottle Lesser Kestrel wine, with a picture of the endangered raptor on the label. Lufthansa, which has a crane as its motto, was supporting his website for tracking migrating birds. He'd been trying to interest the Palestinian Authority in a joint ecotourism venture (which, given the political collapse of winter 2000 had stalled indefinitely). Meanwhile, he was raising money for his international birding center at Latrun—the auditorium was not yet completed, did I know any donors?

All the while, Leshem kept interrupting himself to answer his constantly ringing cell phone, placing calls of his own to arrange a birding trip for me to Eilat and scrunching down behind the steering wheel whenever we passed a police car, since it is illegal to talk on the phone while driving in Israel. Leshem not only managed to do both, he was able to turn away from the road so that he could rummage in the backseat for a picture of himself and the Palestinian Minister of the Environment releasing a banded bird together in 1998, find a video about bird strikes and the air force (an area Leshem has pioneered), or snag me a loose bottle of Lesser Kestrel wine that was rolling free. Occasionally, he slammed on the brakes so we could get out to see a Barbary falcon or honey buzzard migrating overhead.

Our first stop was a kibbutz in the Jordan Valley, Kfar Rupin, that, because of its fishponds, attracts splendid waterfowl. A few years earlier, the kibbutz had decided to put some money into guided bird tours, though, because of the violence, I was the only tourist. It happens that I had been a volunteer for a summer at Kfar Rupin eighteen years earlier, when I was a sophomore in college. The kibbutz was then selling sod and I would wake up at 4:00 A.M. to work in the grass fields. I still remember being in the field at dawn—the date palms along the horizon like feather dusters in the pink light; the squares of sod rolled up into my hands along the conveyor-belt ramp built into the tractor. The grass was cool, but when you dug your fingers in, the clinging dirt was warm, like the pelt of an animal, as if the earth had been skinned.

I had no idea at the time how irrelevant kibbutz life had become to Israeli society, but I might have guessed, since most of the other volunteers were drifting European kids, stopping off in Israel to catch up on their sleep and nutrition on their way back from Thailand. The pastoral dream still matters to the country—just as the Jeffersonian ideal of yeoman farmers still lingers in America—but it is a high-tech, urban country. I used to rumble out to the fields each morning in the back of a truck with a tattooed skinhead and a punk rocker who looked like a skinhead because the kibbutz had forced him to shave his green Mohawk. The only other Jewish volunteer was a dark-haired young woman from France who filled me with bashful longing. She wore her name in Hebrew around her neck and was rumored by the end of the summer to have given a volunteer from Ireland syphilis.

That summer I had no interest in birds. I spent a lot of time staring at the Gilboa Mountains, where my biblical namesake fell in battle fighting the Philistines alongside his father, the deposed King Saul. This time, however, I was delighted to see rare pygmy cormorants, all three of Israel's beautiful kingfishers, and a flock of black storks—only 30,000 pass through the country each year, compared to some 500,000 white storks. The white storks were there in abundance, too, gliding endlessly overhead. There was something deeply soothing in the ancient patterns whirling above so much chaos. The stork still knows his appointed time.

From the Jordan Valley we drove to the Golan Heights, where I saw griffon vultures flying over the ruins of Gamla, a Jewish city in the time of Joshua and, in 66 C.E., the site of an ill-fated revolt against the Romans. I very much wanted to see a lammergeier, or bearded vulture, an enormous bird nearly four feet in length with a wingspan of eight or nine feet, which Tristram describes soaring back and forth in front of his camp, dropping turtles and snakes from a great height onto the rocks below. The practice earned it the Latin name *ossifrage*, which means "bone breaker." (Tristram speculates that it was a lammergeier that must have killed Aeschylus by dropping a tortoise on him, mistaking the playwright's bald

head for a rock and caus-
ing the only instance of
death by tortoise in literary
history—though perhaps it
is the bird who should be
held accountable.)

But there aren't any
lammergeiers in Israel anymore, though there were in
the early years of the state.
Yossi Leshem informed
me that Shimon Peres was
out walking with Heinrich
Mendelssohn, the father of Israeli ornithology—Mendelssohn often led "nature walks" that doubled as reconnaissance missions—
when he looked up and saw a great bird with huge wings soaring
above him and decided on the spot to take the Hebrew name for
the bird, *peres*, substituting it for Perske in the manner of many
Israelis who forsook their European names as if they were slave
names and gave themselves new heroic, nature-born Hebrew
ones. *Peres*, like *ossifrage*, means "the breaker."

Here is the paradox of the modern relationship to nature in a
nutshell—the natural world gave the founders of Israel their inspiration and allowed them to create a modern country that at
once, in the manner of modern countries, imperiled the natural
world that had originally inspired them. Leshem told me that he
tried to get Peres to pose for a photograph with his avian doppel-
gänger—Leshem would like to raise awareness of the bird,
which is still an occasional visitor—but it was an election year
and Peres's aides dissuaded him when they realized it was in fact
a vulture that scavenged dead creatures.

From the Golan, Leshem drove me to the Huleh Valley, near

the shrunken remains of the once great Huleh Lake and the swamp that surrounded it. If there is an environmental symbol of the way the founding myths of early Zionism have been turned on their head, it is the Huleh Lake, which was drained in 1953. This body of water and the swamp connected to it were identified in the Bible as the "waters of Merom." Tristram visited the area and describes it as "an impenetrable swamp of unknown depth, whence the seething vapour, under the rays of an almost tropcial sun, is constantly ascending into the upper atmosphere during the day." He puts the dimensions of the "morass" at four miles by eight miles, "one mass of floating papyrus and reeds, on which it is impossible to find a footing, and through and under which the Jordan works its way to the open water."

As in Louisiana, where, just a few months earlier, I had been looking for the ivory-billed woodpecker, the needs of the swamp and the needs of the modern world alongside the swamp did not overlap—at least not at that moment in Israel's precarious founding, when every inch of land was contested and needed. Draining the Huleh was one of the most ambitious public-works projects to date in Israel and in accord with the ethos of making the desert bloom and the swamps dry; it was also an astonishing act of habitat destruction that eliminated a stopover for thousands of migratory birds and led to the extinction of plant and animal species found only there. As the Israeli poet Yehuda Amichai wrote:

> When I was young I believed with all my heart
> the Huleh swamp had to be drained.
> Then all the bright-colored birds fled for their lives.
> Now half a century later they are filling it with water again
> because it was all a mistake. Perhaps my entire life
> I've been living a mistake.

The draining of the Huleh swamp galvanized a nascent environmental movement that morphed into the Society for the Protection of Nature; in recent years, the society has led efforts to reflood a few areas around the lake in the hope of drawing back the millions of migrating birds that spent the winter in the area. Edward O. Wilson wrote in his recent book *The Creation*: "Civilization was purchased by the betrayal of nature." This does not make civilization bad, of course; it just makes it founded on a paradox that—paradoxically—civilization alone is capable of acknowledging.

Contemporary Israel was a five-year-old country when it drained the Huleh swamp and imposed a modern vision on a land that was always threatening to undo what was done to it. The accelerated pace of a country formed in a post-industrial age gives it an almost allegorical quality—it took America in its expanding vastness longer to achieve what is made so emblematic in the story of the Huleh swamp. In the Israeli novel *The Blue Mountain*, an ironic but affectionate portrait of Israel's land-loving, land-subduing founders, Meir Shalev writes that "beneath the checkered carpet of plowed field, stubble, and orchard, waiting for the first signs of Doubt, growled the most legendary beast of all, the great swamp imprisoned by the founders."

Today, preservation of the remnant scrap of swamp, and a more recent program to plant peanuts and corn in neighboring fields, have coaxed back five thousand cranes who now winter in what's left of the Huleh Lake. It was to see these birds, along with the flocks of black kites that gather at dusk, that Leshem and I traveled to the Huleh. It is not the great swarm of birds the swamp once drew, just as it is not the swamp that Tristram knew, but then birders in every place must get used to asking "what to make of a diminished thing." England, as Tristram notes in his

Natural History of the Bible, once had cranes—and black kites—but they were long gone by the time he was writing.

The cranes were not where they were supposed to be, and as Leshem and I chased them by car from field to field, I thought about my aunt, long dead, who helped found a kibbutz just a few miles away on the banks of the Jordan River, which had fed the swamp. I thought of the beautiful eucalyptus tree my aunt planted, a great thirsty anchor on the bank of the narrow Jordan, and felt a pang. It was hard to suppress a melancholy qualm that the country had turned out so different from the dreams of those early Zionists, and that kibbutz life itself, so utopian in its origins, was passing away. Death is always the flip side of evolution—if someday we evolve as a species, it will entail mourning the selves we now are. How much easier it must have been to live in a world of static species and fixed beliefs.

At last we found our cranes, not on the ground, but in the air, where they were reeling off into the darkening sky, long necks stretched out in flight, black-fingered wings gripping the air, legs hanging straight out behind, suggesting crucified bodies. There were hundreds of giant birds, a magnificent sight, though Tristram offers a description of the birds crossing the Red Sea from Africa and filling the whole breadth of the sea that beggars the present vision.

It would be wonderful to see the land as Tristram saw it. And it would be wonderful to show it to him now. Tristram could hardly have imagined that Jews would return in great numbers, like migrating birds who lost their way for a couple of thousand years, to join the little flock that had stayed behind. Would he have been heartbroken to discover that reclaiming the biblical land also transformed it into a place where biblical biodiversity has retreated beneath human habitation? We'd have to tell him the swamp was gone and the ostrich was gone and the lammergeier and a number of other animals and birds he knew intimately were gone. (On the other hand, an Israeli naturalist once told me that Tristram was hell-bent on shooting the last known wild bear in Palestine.) Of course, we'd also have to tell him about World War I with its 15 million dead (a number that more than doubles if you add in the deaths from the related influenza epidemic of 1918), and about World War II—62 million dead—and inside that number, one-third of the world's Jews, to whom, as a Protestant minister and Hebraist, he might have felt some attachment.

The extremes of the modern world would no doubt terrify and depress him, but would offer up some context for the destruction of the physical world he loved so deeply. Certain dilemmas Tristram would no doubt recognize from his own age. There is far more irrefutable evidence for Darwin's theory today than there was in Darwin's encyclopedic but hastily written *The Origin of Species*. But Tristram would notice that religious beliefs have not gone away. For millions, science and reason and evolutionary findings are enemies that have heightened a terrifying religious fundamentalism; for others, science is a new religion that leaves no room for transcendent beliefs at all. But he would discover that there are educated people who dwell in possibility and try to inhabit a middle ground between scientific and religious extremes. He and Yossi Leshem would have much to talk about.

Even in Tristram's own day there was a middle terrain far more complex and interesting than the black-and-white regions staked out by Huxley and Bishop Wilberforce in 1860. Tristram himself came to inhabit it. He was, in addition to being a minister, an active freemason, with its acceptance of an unspecified, almost Wallacian "Supreme Being" rather than any specific deity. In 1868 Tristram appeared alongside Wallace on a panel responding to the Reverend Francis Orpen Morris, who was, like Tristram, a naturalist and a minister. Morris denounced natural selection in his paper "On the Difficulties of Darwinism," and after Wallace's response, Tristram said he "thought it best to make a compromise between the extremes of the Darwinians and the religious party." In this regard he was a Wallacist, and indeed credited Wallace, in an 1879 review, with allowing naturalists to combine a belief in God with "a frank and cordial acceptance of the theory of natural selection." That year, Disraeli offered Tristram the Anglican bishopric of Jerusalem, but Tristram respectfully declined.

In 1893, thirty-three years after Tristram had been traumatized by the Huxley-Wilberforce debate, Tristram was chairman of the biological section of the British Association for the Advancement of Science. This was the organization that had sponsored the event that led Tristram to denounce "the God Darwin and his prophet Huxley." At the association's meetings in that year, Tristram referred proudly to his own early application of natural selection, in his study of desert larks, and referred to Darwin as "our great master."

Tristram, who died a hundred years ago, found a middle ground that made room for science and religion, the Bible and *The Origin of Species*. He followed birds backward to a biblical landscape, and he also followed birds into the Darwinian future. And somehow he managed to find a home in both. I associate him with the bird that bears his name, Tristram's grackle, which is found in Israel primarily near the Dead Sea. It is a somber black bird living in a lonely spot, but when it flies, it reveals an unexpected patch of orange on the wing.

BIRDING IN THE DARK

Downward to darkness, on extended wings.

—WALLACE STEVENS,
"Sunday Morning"

On my last night in Israel I found myself at midnight in a pitch-black *wadi* in the desert near Eilat. The stars were everywhere above me, glowing in their dark sockets, but I was not watching the stars. My eyes were fixed on a single spot high up on the cliff wall, a tiny ledge that my guide illuminated with a searchlight plugged into the cigarette lighter of his four-wheel-drive Audi. This is where the bird that we were hoping to summon with a tape recording, the rare Hume's tawny owl, was likely to perch.

Hume's tawny owl was named for Allan Octavian Hume, a contemporary of Wallace and Tristram who, like them, sought to escape the materialism of the age on eagle's wings. Hume moved to India as a civil servant; there, in his spare time, he became the father of Indian ornithology, amassing the largest collection of Asiatic bird skins in the world. In a typically Wallacian episode, however, Hume's masterwork, *The Birds of India*, vanished after a servant sold the manuscript as scrap paper. In a further stroke of bad luck, he lost twenty thousand bird skins when the ground shifted under his grand house in Shimla, India. Heartbroken, he turned his attention to other matters. A political radical, Hume helped create the Indian National Congress; a theosophist, he briefly fell under the sway of Madame Blavatsky, and was deeply drawn to Tibetan mysticism.

I liked it that the owl I was waiting for had an interesting person attached. Human associations with birds are not always pleasant. I'd read in a twelfth-century bestiary, translated by T. H. White: "Owls are symbolical of the Jews, who repulse Our Saviour when he comes to redeem them, saying: 'We have no King but Caesar.' They value darkness more than light." Perhaps this is why I took special pleasure looking for owls in Israel. There I was in darkness, where the Crusaders would have expected to find me—but I was, after all, in the Jewish state.

And I was determining for myself the meaning of the birds. King Solomon, according to legend, spoke the language of the birds—and all the animals. This seems to me a universal human desire, though it wasn't until I started birdwatching that I left behind a generic Dr. Dolittle fantasy and encountered it in a personal way. The impulse is well expressed by the Austrian zoologist Konrad Lorenz, in his classic 1955 book on animal behavior, *King Solomon's Ring*. Lorenz points out that what the Bible actually says is that Solomon "spake also of beasts, and of fowl, and of creeping things, and of fishes," not that he spoke *with* them, but Lorenz then endorses the myth that Solomon spoke not only of but with animals: "I am quite ready to believe that Solomon really could do so, even without the help of the magic ring which is attributed to him by the legend in question, and I have very good reason for crediting it; I can do it myself."

With less boasting, this is a belief shared by most naturalists. In *Biophilia: The Human Bond with Other Species*, Edward O. Wilson recalls a tour he took of the Old City of Jerusalem. Not far from the spot where the throne of King Solomon is believed to have stood, the eminent entomologist gets down on his hands and knees to watch carpenter ants disappear through cracks in the cobblestones. As he walks past the Temple Mount, Wilson makes "inner calculations of the number of ant species found within the city walls." For Wilson, the natural history of the place means as much as its human history: "The million year history of Jerusalem is at least as compelling as its past three thousand years."

Looking for ants under the throne, Wilson isn't refuting King Solomon, he is joining him. After all, it was Solomon—reputed to have written the book of Proverbs—who declared, "Go to the ant, thou sluggard. Consider her ways and be wise."

For me, birding offers what Wilson—who initially planned to pursue birds but abandoned them after an eye injury in childhood—found in ants. It is a way of bridging disparate worlds—continents, the air and the earth, the symbolic and the actual, the scientific and the religious. It is a way of joining the million-year history of Jerusalem with the Jerusalem of the past three thousand years. Birdwatching has given me a way to reconcile Solomon's throne and the ants underneath it.

But the Jews were not a nation of Solomons, or zoologists, and the natural world held its primal terrors for them as much as for Christians. They associated owls with Lilith, Adam's first wife, a demon who causes nocturnal emissions and carries off children. (A name for owl in Hebrew is *lilit*; the tawny owl is called *lilit midbar*, or desert owl.) Lilith in folklore often takes the form of a beautiful woman. As a birdwatcher I easily understand the link to Lilith—birdwatching is a sport of seduction and pursuit. Birdwatchers are, in token, transmuted form, a tamed remnant of the conquistadors in Elizabeth Bishop's poem who go tearing into the jungle:

they ripped away into the hanging fabric,
each out to catch an Indian for himself—
those maddening little women who kept calling,
calling to each other (or had the birds waked up?)
and retreating, always retreating, behind it.

Or at least it is a pursuit for peeping Toms. I was forced to acknowledge this in the chilly darkness of the desert as I waited, heart pounding, searchlight at the ready, preparing to peel back a corner of the night and spotlight my prize. The day before my owl excursion I had watched through binoculars as two Egyptian vultures—just arrived from Africa—copulated in the Golan Heights. These are fantastic, grotesque birds with a ruff of white feathers that rise to form a hood around their yellow, featherless faces. They look like sinister Elizabethan courtiers. My birds were sitting side by side on a rock, touching bills. Suddenly the male jumped awkwardly on the female's back in that hunching, vulturish way, as if she were a piece of carrion, flapping once or twice to keep his balance. A moment later he was off again, staring indifferently into space.

Yeats knew what he was writing about when he imagined Zeus, in the form of a swan, raping Leda: "A sudden blow, the great wings beating still / Above the staggering girl." Yeats's fantasy of bird-human intercourse is ancient and strange, older than the Greek myth he was evoking, a mixture of horror and envy, and it goes beyond voyeurism. Yeats dares his reader to actually visualize the coupling:

How can those terrified vague fingers push
The feathered glory from her loosening thighs?
And how can body, laid in that white rush,
But feel the strange heart beating where it lies?

As a child wandering the American Museum of Natural History, I found the great beaked bird masks and shaggy costumes in the hall of native peoples far more terrifying than mere animals posed in their wildest state. How do the divine, the animal, and the human fit together—is it a violent joining? For Yeats it is; in the moment of their coupling, the destruction of Troy is sown (Leda will give birth to Helen of Troy):

A shudder in the loins engenders there
The broken wall, the burning roof and tower . . .

But all this violence doesn't diminish the human desire to feel the "strange heart beating where it lies," for all that it terrifies us.

Jews feared more than the seductions of Lilith. In the Bible, owls, which roosted in the ruins of the Temple in Jerusalem, are associated with ghosts haunting the abandoned house of God.

They embody pagan terrors, *the broken wall, the burning roof and tower,* and they are omens of loss and sorrow. With their pale bellies, white faces, and strange cries, barn owls—sometimes called ghost owls in the United States—may well have been the origin of many spectral encounters. Tristram, in *The Natural History of the Bible,* notes that the word *lilit* appears only once in the

Bible, in Isaiah, who, envisioning the destruction of Idumea, uses it to designate the screech owl, which will "find for herself a place of rest" in the vanquished land.

Nowadays people haunt the ruined wild places as much as wild animals haunt us. But in my pitch-black *wadi* I can feel a little echo of primal natural terrors. There might be scorpions or snakes; there is no water; the darkness is profound. But I have sought out this spot like a tourist, and it is a place conservationists will have to fight to conserve. I crave this experience, staged though it may be.

And it is easier to absorb than the other terrors of the land, which are human terrors and form the backdrop against which I looked at birds. The ghosts of the ruined Temple were everywhere around me on my birdwatching trip, no matter where in Israel I went. I was there in early March, six months into the violence that began the day Ariel Sharon, in October 2000, visited the Temple Mount with an armed entourage. Solomon's Temple, Edward O. Wilson's ants, and a modern political state are hard things to balance. In the course of my trip, the fallen Temple felt less like an ancient calamity redeemed by modern statecraft and more like a grim reflection of contemporary reality—a reminder of the friable state of human aspirations, of broken alliances between both people and God, and of the unpredictable and often tragic nature of human history.

How nice it would be to keep history and politics and superstition and religious desire out of birdwatching altogether, but these things crowd around me, I cannot keep them at bay, and this is the place to let them in. I cannot belong to that school of nature writing where you set off with a knapsack and nothing else—seemingly without parents or children or religion or tradition or friends or country. Emerson, in his essay "Nature," wishes to be a "transparent eyeball," but is there anything more grotesque? Emerson certainly failed in that attempt, and knew he was failing, which is why he is such a great essayist.

Context endlessly matters. I feel different about Konrad Lorenz, who won a Nobel Prize in 1973, knowing that he joined the Nazi Party in 1938 and that he referred to the "ugly Jewish nose" of the shoveler duck and that his theories of animal behavior, of the ideal forms of wild animals and the corrupted forms of the domesticated ones, informed and were informed by Nazi thinking. The famous image of Lorenz followed by geese who had imprinted on him because he took the place of their mother looks different to me now. Goose-stepping takes on a whole new meaning, and so does admiration for the rigid laws of nature. Different, too, is the meaning of Lorenz's most famous chapter of *King Solomon's Ring*, in which he describes how, when two wolves fight, the vanquished wolf presents his throat and the victor, bound by nature, is unable to bite it, snap his jaws as he might, because he is governed by an inner law. This was an idea I loved until I recently discovered that this is dubious science and disturbingly bound up with the Nazi obsession with the "Order of the Wolf," the urge not merely to feel the strange heart of wildness beating but to have it beat in your own breast. The "Order of the Wolf" was part of the Nazis' cult of animal instinct as opposed to the messy disorder of complex human relationships that Jews embodied for them, a gray urban world where instinct is vitiated by reason and reflection. In other words, civilization.

We are always inventing an imaginary Eden of one sort or another for ourselves, to relieve us of the complex burdens of our humanity. The despoiling of America by European settlers was terrible, but America was never paradise so long as humans inhabited it—Neolithic hunters, using primitive tools but driven by recognizably human impulses, are probably responsible for the extinction of the woolly mammoth in North America thousands of years before there even was European civilization.

I can't give in to the facile modern metaphor that might make Israel's founders modern-day Pilgrims who came and despoiled a primitive place in disregard of a native population. The Pilgrims may have seen themselves as Israelites, but Israel's founders did not need to see themselves as Pilgrims. Some, it is true, arrived from Western lands. Some arrived—or were expelled—from Eastern, Arab lands. And some had never left the land and had been living there all along. The Palestinian Arabs were certainly there, too, and they have their own complex narrative and played their own role in the shaping of the land and the country. Their imprint is on the land and is old, if not as ancient as the imprint of the Jews. They, too, have ancient tribal ties and modern national and political ones, a memory of a victorious Muslim conquest and of the defeat by Christians, who were present in the land before Muslims and tried to return during the Crusades, and of defeat of the Christians, who were eventually driven out, and of colonial oppression under the Turks and the British, and of the complex paradigm-shaking return of Jews, who are viewed as modern interlopers, though they gave birth to Christianity and Islam in that very place.

And in some sense Israelis are modern interlopers as well as ancient originals, which is much like our general human relationship to the natural world. Today the majority of Americans are neither Pilgrims nor Indians. We are, if anything, like the turkey at the Thanksgiving feast—a native American bird that had been taken to Europe and domesticated and then brought back—much as the potato had been brought back from the Americas by Columbus and then reintroduced in America as an old-new thing. Israel is a complex modern hybrid—an old-new land, as

Theodor Herzl called it—*Altneuland*, in German—which is what makes it so hard for people to grasp the place and so essential that they do, because it is in so many ways emblematic of modern civilization.

"Old-new land" has environmental as well as political-religious meaning. We all live, no matter where, in an old-new land today. We are part of the natural world and we are separate from the natural world; we are simultaneously the conquerors and the conquered. Birdwatching, which throws people and animals together in complex ways, employing technology to summon our primitive longings, enacts this drama well.

Yossi Leshem understood this when he gave his birdwatching center in Latrun the hopeful motto "Migrating birds know no boundaries." People of course are obsessed with borders, and the center acknowledges that, too. Leshem, with support from Tel Aviv University and the Society for the Preservation of Nature, created his bird center smack in the middle of the Western migration route running between the Judean and Samarian Mountains, halfway between Jerusalem and Tel Aviv. The spot was a human crossroads for millennia, linking the road from Jaffa to Jerusalem and from Gaza to Damascus. Nearby lie the ruins of one of the largest Crusader castles in the Middle East.

Leshem's birding center overlooks the Ayalon Valley, where Joshua commanded the sun to stand still while he defeated the Amorites. Centuries later, not far from the valley, Judah Maccabee routed Syrian forces in the battle of Emmaus. Latrun is also the sight of the first armored battle in Israeli history: in the 1948 War of Independence, David Ben-Gurion ordered an attack on Arab forces occupying a British police fort at Latrun. Victory would have given Israel control over the road to Jerusalem and a way to break the Arab blockade that cut Jerusalem off from the rest of the country. (This was the first of three bloody, unsuccessful battles—in the end it was the construction of the "Burma Road," which performed a sort of end run around Latrun, that broke the siege.)

By design the International Center of Bird Migration is half war memorial, half ornithological observatory. Leshem hopes to bring together the battle-scarred past of the country with a utopian vision of the future. One hundred and fifty tanks serve as a memorial to the Armored Corps soldiers who fell in Israel's wars; the migrating raptors overhead and the radar devices that track them from the ground emblematize a future without borders, as free as the birds.

But that future felt far off when I was in Israel in 2001 and suicide bombings of buses and shopping malls punctuated my visit, the death throes of the Oslo peace accord and the birth pangs of something worse.

Leshem's utopian future feels even further off as I write this

in 2006, after another war—with Iran and Syria by proxy, Hezbollah and Hamas directly—has temporarily ended with no sign of larger resolution. During the fighting I received an e-mail from Leshem—he regularly sends out dispatches to a long list of correspondents—containing a picture of a migrating stork that had been speared in Africa but somehow made the migratory journey, the spear still in its body. The photo somehow said it all.

You don't go birdwatching in a vacuum; the world, natural and man-made, intrudes, just as it did for Abraham Cahan back in 1903, when the Yiddish journalist raced back from a birdwatching trip because he had learned about the Kishinev pogrom. I will never forget the birdwatching I did on September 10, 2001. I was in Guilford, Connecticut, for a "bioblitz," a twenty-four-hour natural history marathon inspired by Edward O. Wilson, who participated in the first bioblitz at Walden Pond in 1999, in which a tally of all detectable life within a designated area is produced at the end of a day and night of intensive searching.

The bioblitz in Guilford boasted many amateurs and experts, people who studied bats and mushrooms and insects and birds. I spent the day with Noble Proctor, a world-class birder and protégé of Roger Tory Peterson who is also an old-fashioned naturalist with the sort of encyclopedic knowledge that can be acquired only by long days in the field. Naming every lichen below and bird overhead, slipping on hip waders to go after rails in a marsh, he blithely described what it feels like to have West Nile virus, which he had contracted on his rovings and had at first mistaken for a stiff neck. When the sun went down, Proctor went to look at pond water under a microscope to count those minuscule creatures for the final tally, so I transferred my allegiance to the bug people, who came out at night, hung a sheet between two trees, put a generator-powered ultraviolet light above it, and sat down in deck chairs to drink beer and watch, jumping up from time to time to examine the bugs projected like moving images on the screen, rattling off the Latin names and writing them down.

The next day, September 11, I was home in Manhattan, organizing my notebook, writing about what I'd seen and the devoted, eccentric people I'd met, when terrorists flew two planes into the World Trade Center towers. Later, I could not help thinking that while those terrorists were plotting death, I had been with a group of people so focused on life that no pondwater organism was too small to be recorded. I remembered seeing a film strip in a college biology course featuring Roman Vishniac, the Russian-born photographer famous for documenting Eastern European Jewish life on the eve of its destruction. Vishniac was also a pioneering photomicroscopist who even as a boy had hooked his camera up to a microscope. In the film, he took pond water from Central Park in Manhattan and examined the microorganisms it contained back in his apartment on Central Park West. When he was done filming and discussing the universe of tiny organisms that lived in the water, he trudged back to Central Park with his pail of pond water and poured it into the same spot he had ladled it out of.

I also thought about what Arthur Allen had written in his preface to "The Ivory-billed Woodpecker" in 1942:

> Today we are measuring our love of freedom in billions of dollars and thousands of lives. The American way of living is worth anything we have to pay to preserve it, and the Ivory-billed Woodpecker is one little guide post on our way of life, a reminder of that pioneering spirit that has made us what we are, a people rich in resourcefulness and powerful to accomplish what is right.

His observation still makes sense today; what kind of society do you want to live in and are you willing to die for? Surely we want a world of people like Roman Vishniac, returning even pond water to its source, though to defend that world we will automatically change our behavior and may cease to take such care with microorganisms, to say nothing of larger animals.

I had often derided the twin towers before their destruction—they were false beacons leading migratory birds astray, and they were hubristic assertions of material power, and I remembered being a child when they were built and the protests they spawned. But after their destruction I would have done anything to bring them back. This was of course because of all the lives lost inside them, but it was also because the towers themselves suddenly seemed a tangible expression of the culture I valued. In fact, in the immediate days afterward, my twenty-four-hour treasure hunt seemed almost frivolous, an activity that belonged to a more innocent world that I almost required binoculars to see clearly. War is not a good time to make environmental decisions. One feels this particularly keenly in Israel, which has never been at peace since its founding; this gives its relationship to nature a strangely prophetic quality.

There is so much to worry about in Israel—the irreconcilable nature of competing national narratives, the terrifying specter of war without end, the threat of genocide voiced daily by its neighbors recalling the medieval hatred that once turned Jews into owls but amplified by technology that gives people godlike powers of destruction—that it becomes harder and harder to see the natural world as neutral or free. It becomes harder to see the natural world at all, like poor Shimon Peres robbed of the noble bird he took his name from because it suddenly had grim symbolic overtones.

And yet the urge to bring birds into focus, Yossi Leshem's

heroic work embracing the natural world in a political landscape, takes on a transcendent nobility and gives birdwatching a
sort of moral imperative wherever it is practiced. The latest dis-
patch from Leshem arrived as I was completing this chapter, on
September 12, 2006. With his characteristic optimism, Leshem
included a photograph of a Jordanian, General Monsour Abu
Rashed, chairman of the Amman Center for Peace and Development, holding a barn owl "as a token of the Israeli-Jordanian co-
operation, while shattering an ancient Middle East myth which
holds that this bird is the bringer of bad luck."

The rare owl that I waited for in darkness on my last birding
day in Israel had its burden of lore and human association. It was
a ghost bird and a seductive spirit. It was a disbelieving Jew and
an incarnation of wisdom. It was a million things in myth and
legend and in science. But when it finally arrived, it was just an
owl. A bird feathered even on its toes so that it made no sound
at all as it flew. And when it suddenly began hooting into the
night, the sound was inhuman, chilling, like a stylus torn across
the surface of a record. It sang straight into my bones.

We snapped on our searchlight, and the bird was just where
we'd hoped it would land. I expected it to look enormous, but it
was tiny on its high perch, nearly indistinguishable from the pale
rock. In the scope I found its orange eyes and white belly feathers catching the glare. We had tricked it into coming with a
recording of its own voice, but its arrival still felt like an unexpected blessing. It was a real owl, even if it had come to drive
away an imaginary rival. We took turns watching it through our
scope. Then, out of respect for the animal, we turned off our
light and listened in darkness.

THE DOCTOR BIRD

Another bird said: "Hoopoe, you can find
The way from here, but we are almost blind—
The path seems full of terrors and despair.
Dear hoopoe, how much further till we're there?"

—FARID UD-DIN ATTAR,
The Conference of Birds
(translated from the Persian by Afkham Darbandi and Dick Davis)

Before we leave Israel, there is one more bird to consider. This bird, the hoopoe, has a striking appearance—a punky crest tipped in black, a pinkish-cinnamon face and shoulders, long decurved bill blackened as if it had been dipped in ink. But the bird is also a mythical creature. Tristram notes in his *Natural History of the Bible* that while the Bible mentions it only once—in the catalog of unclean birds in Deuteronomy—"Few birds have had more absurd fables attached to them than this. The Arabs have a superstitious reverence for it, and, believing it to possess marvelous medicinal qualities, they call it 'the Doctor Bird.'"

Tristram does not say why this is so, but my twelfth-century bestiary describes the hoopoe (which is European as well as Mediterranean) as a bird that cares for its parents in their old age—it "preens their feathers for them, keeps them warm and licks their eyes. Thus the parents feel restored."

I knew of the bird from a childhood collection, *The Legends of King Solomon*, where it plays a dramatic role in the story of how King Solomon built the Temple. Solomon was forbidden to use iron, since iron is used to fashion weapons, and so Solomon needs to get his hands on a magic worm, called the shamir, that eats

U. Epops.   *Hoopoe*.

through rock and that will help him cut the giant stones the Temple requires. In order to find the location of the worm, he must capture Asmodeus, the king of the demons, who knows many secrets of the universe, including the whereabouts of the shamir. After capturing Asmodeus and binding him in chains secured with Solomon's magic ring—the one bearing God's name—Solomon learns that the worm is guarded by the hoopoe.

Asmodeus explains to Solomon that the hoopoe brings the worm to desolate mountain places, the worm splits the stone, and then the bird drops in seeds. The seeds grow, and in this way the desolate parts of the earth are made to bloom. The worm is hidden, but Asmodeus tells Solomon where to find the bird. Solomon dispatches his servant, who finds the hoopoe's nest and covers it with glass while the bird is away. The bird, when it returns to its nest, cannot get past the glass, its children are hungry and crying, and so, in desperation, the hoopoe fetches the worm and drops it on the glass, hoping it will split it. At that moment, Solomon's servant jumps forward and snatches the glass with the worm still on it and brings it to the king, who is at last able to build the Temple.

I was very keen to see a hoopoe in Israel. The bird that occasioned an ancient quest would, I felt, play a role in my own birding quest—I imagined myself pursuing the bird all over the country. The bird that made the wasteland bloom. The bird that held the key to the house of God but that somehow necessitated demonic intervention.

But my own encounter with a hoopoe took me by surprise. It came while I was waiting for Yossi Leshem to meet me in the Jerusalem Bird Observatory on my first day birdwatching in Israel. The observatory is on a one-acre plot of ground tucked between the Knesset and the Supreme Court. There is an old cemetery on the site, which may explain why it was left undeveloped. While waiting for Leshem, I watched a young soldier named Eran, who manned the observatory, band birds that he plucked out of mist nets.

In addition to the binoculars around his neck and the rifle over his shoulder, Eran had a small canvas pouch in his hands, tied with a drawstring. He sat down at a table, weighed the pouch on an ounce scale, and then extracted from it a small gray bird, a chiffchaff, which he held, wings together, in one large hand. The bird was tremulously still as Eran measured the wing with a finely calibrated ruler. He blew on the soft tufted breast feathers to gauge the amount of fat on the bird and, having recorded his findings in a book, clipped a band around the bird's ankle with a small pair of pliers and tossed the bird casually behind him into the air.

The trees were full of tiny gray birds with beautiful names— Orphean warbler, graceful warbler, willow warbler. Many were calling. (The Latin species name of the chiffchaff, *collybita*, means moneylender, because its two-note call is said to sound

like jingling coins.) A
blackbird was singing in a
pomegranate tree still
hung with last year's
pomegranates, which had
the dull maroon coloring
of clotted blood—dry and
light, they stirred in the air
like Christmas ornaments.
Palestine sunbirds, tiny iri-
descent blue-green birds
with sickle-shaped bills,

whizzed by with the sugar-high energy of hummingbirds. Sud-
denly I was distracted by a low, mellow, slightly insane chant.

"There goes a hoopoe," said Eran, as a bird the size of a crow,
with big rounded wings like a black-and-white moth, swooped
down and vanished into a hole in a concrete wall. "Filthy bird,"
he added with disgust. "They smell like shit."

So much for my quest for the magical bird. And so much for
the hoopoe's mystical aura. Indeed, the medieval bestiary has a
second entry for the hoopoe—this, T. H. White explains, often
happens in medieval bestiaries—in which we are told that "the
bird lines its nest with human dung. The filthy creature feeds on
stinking excrement. He lives on this in graves."

Another lesson from the birds—however much we wish to reduce them to symbols, they continually resist us. Their nests really
do stink, though when I took a whiff outside the hole in Jerusalem
I didn't in fact smell anything—it was early yet in the nesting season. The very anticlimax of discovering that the hoopoe is a sort of
yard bird, a Middle Eastern blue jay, was a lesson worth learning.
And every birder knows that some of the best birds on a birding
trip show up in the parking lot before you quite set out.

And still, of course, it is a special bird, and a symbolic bird, and now it has private symbolism for me as well mythological symbolism. For one thing, it is both rare and common, which is what all birds are, or ought to be. And the two-sided nature of the bird has made me value it even more. Indeed, Yossi Leshem told me that the rabbis of the Talmud noticed that the hoopoe flattens its crest out in flight, which gives it the appearance of facing forward and backward, since the flattened crest looks like a beak pointing in the opposite direction. This makes the bird a sort of avian Janus, the two-faced god of liminal states. This dual nature—the creature that helps build Solomon's Temple and cares for its parents; the bird that reeks of humanity—makes it even more an emblem for birdwatching, one whose relevance transcends any particular place. Doesn't "hoopoe" (or at least the Latin name *Upupa epops*) sound like utopia? Doesn't "hoopoe" look like a strange spelling of "hope"?

The hoopoe is at the center of *The Conference of Birds*, the great Persian poem by the Sufi mystic Farid ud-Din Attar, written, like the medieval bestiary, in the twelfth century, when the Muslim world was a far more civilized place than the Europe that created the bestiary. The poem is an avian epic in which we learn that the hoopoe was King Solomon's messenger when he was courting the Queen of Sheba, and that the markings on the hoopoe's beak are actually Arabic script, proclaiming *bismillah*, or "In the name of God," the opening words of the Koran.

The Conference of Birds is the story of a quest made by birds that are also looking for a bird. It was composed by Attar (his name describes his profession, druggist; according to his translators, it is the same word as "attar of roses"), who, like other great Persian poets, was revered simultaneously as a poet and as a Sufi master. Though he spent many years, like Henry Baker Tristram, traveling—to Egypt, Damascus, Mecca, Turkestan, and India—

he returned home to Nishapur, birthplace of Omar Khayyam, in northeast Iran, where his grave is now a shrine.

Attar's *The Conference of Birds* had an influence on Chaucer's "The Parliament of Fowls," though it has more in common with *The Canterbury Tales*, since it is about a group of pilgrims who set off on a religious pilgrimage. In the Attar story, a group of birds decide at their conference that they should have a king; they are informed by the hoopoe, who is the wisest among them, that they already have a king called the Simorgh and that they must seek him out. (The Simorgh is itself a mythical bird of Persian folklore that is close to God and sometimes is God.) Despite their enthusiasm, the birds lose their nerve, and each in turn gives reasons why it can't go—the nightingale is in love, the duck must remain near water, the finch is afraid—but each in turn is argued down by the hoopoe, who tells stories and parables and instructs like a Sufi master. The quest, in fact, has already begun, since it is as much an inner journey as an outer one.

In the end, bullied, shamed, and enlightened by the hoopoe, they set out, a group of birds who are in some sense also birdwatchers. The way is as dangerous and desolate as they feared—only thirty birds of a great multitude are left when they finally arrive at the Simorgh's palace. The Simorgh's counselors turn them away, but they persist and are finally admitted, only to discover, in a strange mystical moment, that they are themselves the Simorgh. Looking at the dazzling divine king, they literally see themselves reflected back.

Here's the Simorgh speaking at the end of the poem, as rendered in the fine and lucid modern translation by the husband-and-wife team Afkham Darbandi and Dick Davis, who point out that the mystical union at the end is enforced by the fact that the word "Simorgh" literally means "thirty birds" in Perisan; a pun enacts the fact that the thirty survivors see themselves in the divine bird. They do more than see themselves in the bird; they are in some sense destroyed by and absorbed into the divine bird:

> "... and since you came as thirty birds, you see
> These thirty birds when you discover Me,
> The Simorgh, Truth's last flawless jewel, the light
> In which you will be lost to mortal sight,
> Dispersed to nothingness until once more
> You find in Me the selves you were before."
> Then, as they listened to the Simorgh's words,
> A trembling dissolution filled the birds—
> The substance of their being was undone,
> And they were lost like shade before the sun;
> Neither the pilgrims nor their guide remained.
> The Simorgh ceased to speak, and silence reigned.

The Conference of Birds is a Sufi poem, and it is a poem about Sufism, which, at least as Attar practiced it, holds that all religions lead to ultimate divine truth, a truth that stands apart from and in some sense beyond religion (though religions, especially Islam, are useful on the journey). Sufism has often been heretical within Islam because it seems to challenge the ultimate autonomy of Islam, however steeped it is in it, which is why there is so much parable and recondite indirection in Sufism, of which *The Conference of Birds* is considered a perfect example. The birds' pilgrimage is a religious quest in which, as in Sufism, the self must be annihilated and merge with God, who is found through a descent into one's own divine nature.

Emerson, who began his career by scandalizing the Unitarian Church when he announced that Jesus lives within each person (and possibly no place else), was powerfully drawn to Sufism, and he began studying it starting in the early 1840s. His 1876 essay "Persian Poetry" ends by quoting the passage from the conclusion of *The Conference of Birds*—which he calls "The Bird Conversations"—that I quoted above, in which the birds discover that in some sense they are God.

Emerson read Persian poetry in German translation—he was particularly fond of the poet Hafiz, though he purged a lot of the sensual and homoerotic imagery in his own renderings of that poet. His translation of Attar seems vaguely Germanic, lacking the bright clarity of Darbandi and Davis. It also contains a mistranslation, since he refers to "three birds" not thirty, but here it is, medieval Sufism creeping into nineteenth-century American literature:

> *"You as three birds are amazed,*
> *Impatient, heartless, confused:*
> *Far over you I am raised,*
> *Since I am in act Simorg.*
> *Ye blot out my highest being,*
> *That ye may find yourselves on my throne;*
> *Forever ye blot out yourselves,*
> *As shadows in the sun. Farewell!"*

Better to read Emerson speaking in his own voice and striving toward something that might be called American Sufism, though Emerson called it Transcendentalism—the passage from his essay "Nature" in which he speaks of the transparent eyeball:

> Standing on the bare ground—my head bathed by the blithe air, and uplifted into infinite space—all mean egotism vanishes. I become a transparent eye-ball—I am nothing; I see all; the currents of the Universal Being circulate through me; I am part or particle of God. The

name of the nearest friend sounds then foreign and acci-
dental: to be brothers, to be acquaintances,—master or
servant, is then a trifle and a disturbance. I am the lover
of uncontained and immortal beauty. In the wilderness, I
have something more dear and connate than in streets or
villages. In the tranquil landscape, and especially in the
distant line of the horizon, man beholds somewhat as
beautiful as his own nature.

This is all very stirring, though, perversely, it makes me long
for the bird that smells like shit as well as the bird that whispers in
Solomon's ear, because, after all, we live between earth and sky
ourselves. Why die before we have to, and why should "acquaintances," not to mention "brothers," become "a trifle"? I like birdwatching in part, I suppose, because I am part of the equation, not
an impediment to but an acknowledged part of the natural order.

It was an old ornithologist who put this in perspective for
me, a man I met in Israel who had explored in detail the Huleh
swamp before it was drained, knowing that its days were num-
bered. "If I could have eliminated the Arabs and the Zionists, I
could have created a paradise for birds," Amotz Zahavi told me.
Now a retired professor of zoology, Zahavi was one of the men
who, back in the fifties, created the Society for the Preservation
of Nature. At the time, he was a young biology teacher, and
realizing that the Huleh swamp was going to be "reclaimed," he
spent most of 1950 exploring the place by canoe. Despite official
declarations, malaria was no longer a fear—a few years earlier,
someone had hit on the idea of smearing the walls of houses with
DDT to kill the mosquitoes when they moved inside for the
winter. In those days, Zahavi told me, nobody knew its ill effects
and people often shampooed with DDT to kill lice.

I was surprised that Zahavi would still use the Zionist word "reclaim" for a project that destroyed so much irreplaceable habitat. Almost as soon as the country was born, conservationists understood that developing the land and filling it with people, draining the swamps, watering the desert—in short, several key Zionist principles—bore unintended seeds of environmental destruction. Didn't he, as a naturalist and an environmentalist, feel, with Emerson, that "in the wilderness, I find something more dear and connate than in streets or villages"? Didn't he mourn the destruction of habitat?

Zahavi shrugged when I asked about this. He had the weary tone of someone familiar with the ironies of history. "Since I believe the Jewish state is necessary for the survival of the Jews, the compromise was necessary." He is the kind of man who would not be surprised to learn that the World Health Organization recently declared that DDT, infamous scourge of plants and animals, should once again be used in Africa to fight malaria, which is, after all, the number one cause of death among humans.

The pragmatism of someone like Zahavi gives me hope, though it runs counter to a certain desire for environmental purity I am myself susceptible to—a purity that writers like Emerson and Thoreau helped enshrine. Robert Richardson, in his biography of Thoreau, writes about the ways in which Thoreau's own celibate existence, his sexual chastity, which he often referred to as "purity," was transferred to the environment. Richardson shrewdly sees this as connected to the creation of a new environmental religion that began to take shape in the aftermath of the Darwinian damage to traditional faith. Quoting Mary Douglas, whose anthropological investigations often center on questions of purity and impurity, Richardson writes:

> Mary Douglas, the brilliant modern anthropologist, has argued that even after nature has replaced God in a secu-

lar society, certain old ritual concerns persist, often taking new forms. "The violent emotions that used to be centered on purity of doctrine, purity of cult, purity of sex," says Douglas, "seem now to be focussed on purity of the environment."

Richardson goes on to say that "in Thoreau's awkward and primitive efforts to relate that view of nature to human sexuality, we see a crucial moment in the shift from the old religion of God to the new religion of nature, and the beginnings of the modern views of nature as sacred, and her pollution as profane."

Saving the environment is urgent and necessary, but the "environment" is bound up with the humans who live in it and subject it to all the contradictory impulses of human desire—to save and destroy and settle and preserve. "Nature" is a very broad term. When it was suggested to Jackson Pollock, in response to his great abstract splatterings, that he try painting nature, he responded, "I am nature." And there is truth in that—though human nature isn't all in all and needs that other nature, that was here first, that it is part of and different from.

I like birdwatching because a person with binoculars isn't a transparent eyeball but a human being connected in a particular way to nature. Thoreau could delight in observing that the word "saunter" came from "'à la Sainte Terre,' to the Holy Land," implying that a local stroll in America is a pilgrimage that can take you to holy ground, wherever you go, and so it is. But Thoreau's sense of place, rooted in a vast and growing America, and in circumscribed Concord, was so strong and so secure that he could dream of a certain homelessness without challenging the possibility of an actual homeland. The "Holy Land" of the Middle Ages seemed sufficiently remote for him to make a metaphor out of it and graft it onto his own backyard, just as the wilderness of the

Indians for America at large became the stuff not of their actual homes but a kind of generalized notion of "wilderness." Since Amotz Zahavi lives in an actual land that, because it was considered the Holy Land by the Jews who inhabited it three thousand years ago, was resettled by Jews in the modern era, he cannot afford the purely metaphorical—any more than Penobscot Indians, for whom Mt. Katahdin was sacred, wished to be settled in the Black Hills of Dakota. Zahavi did not wish, any more than the Indians, to become like the Simorgh's obliterated pilgrims in Emerson's translation: "Forever ye blot out yourselves." This sense of the human relationship to the land didn't prevent Zahavi from becoming an environmentalist, but it tempered his vision. It made him simultaneously an environmentalist and a humanist. The great question facing us today is, Can we be both?

There is a darker current to the legend of Solomon building the Temple that haunts me. When Solomon has finished building the Temple, he visits the king of the demons, still his captive, and says to him, "How is it possible that you are king of the demons, and it is written that you are more powerful than man, and yet I have been able to capture you?" Whereupon Asmodeus says to Solomon, "Unbind me and give me your ring and I will show you."

Solomon unbinds Asmodeus, and suddenly the demon king becomes enormous—one wing touches the earth and the other touches the sky. He swallows Solomon and his ring and then spits them out so violently that the ring flies into the sea and is lost and Solomon himself is hurled many hundreds of miles away from his kingdom. Asmodeus meanwhile transforms himself into Solomon, concealing his clawed, demon feet with white stockings. He sits on Solomon's throne and rules in his place.

Solomon spends three years wandering, a lost beggar with no way to prove his kingship. This, the rabbis felt, was punishment for his various sins—too many wives, flirtation with paganism. In the version I read as a child, Solomon, after much hardship and humiliation, becomes a cook for another king, preparing dishes he recalled from his own royal life. The king's daughter falls in love with him; they are discovered and banished, and together flee to a seaside town where, with the last of their money, they buy a fish to eat. Inside the fish is Solomon's lost ring. He returns to Jerusalem and ousts Asmodeus.

The rabbis actually debated whether Solomon was banished for a limited time or in fact forever. This implies that there is another version of the story in which Solomon, the wisest of all men, wanders forever, a lost man.

The idea that you might lose yourself in the act of doing something holy, the fact that in order to make God's Temple it is necessary to descend to hell and consort with demons, is a dark lesson. Solomon, whose ring was a symbol of divine order, an ability to balance the human world and the animal world, the pagan world and the monotheistic world, the upper world and the lower world—even Solomon the wise—loses his true self. A pretender sits on his throne. The story captures the terror of being trapped in a false life, the fear that we are deceiving ourselves and that we are not, in our beliefs and behaviors, "real."

There is also an environmental terror, connected to a psychological one, that an artificial world will replace the real world. In another legend I learned as a child, Solomon, tested by the Queen of Sheba, is unable to tell the difference between imitation flowers and a real one until a bee lands on the living flower and saves Solomon's reputation. Solomon's ring is a token of his ability to see and interpret the natural world, down to its smallest messengers. Without this power, which the ring represents, will we lose the ability to tell the natural world from the artificial, and lose ourselves in the process?

It makes sense to me that the hoopoe that Solomon needs to find spends its time making barren rock bloom, spreading biodiversity, as it were. Solomon borrows this bird and harnesses its power for another purpose, just as he traps a demon to do his divine work, but he somehow loses control of these forces and they turn on him. Fitting that it is in a fish that he finds his divine ring at the end of the story—the natural world restores to him the order and balance that the ring itself is intended to represent—a ring that binds together the human and the wild, the natural and the unnatural. A ring whose meaning is easily distorted, as it was by Konrad Lorenz, but that is still a necessary symbol of harmony and natural order.

The hoopoe is a bird of paradox, just as we are creatures of paradox. When Edward O. Wilson says that civilization was purchased by the betrayal of nature, he is invoking this paradox. The trick for me, that birding embodies, is to value the paradox, not try to eliminate it. At the end of *The Conference of Birds*, the hoopoe and his small band of thirty survivors find what they are looking for and are annihilated in God's holy light. They make their pilgrimage, but they do not return from it. They are destroyed inside a higher, religious reality that destroys the paradox of human imperfection.

This is a beautiful mystical notion, but it is too much for me. The suicide bombers who kept blowing up buses during my trip to Israel also craved annihilation into a higher religious reality—though it was one leading them to murder, antithetical to Attar's Sufism. Persia, which nourished that beautiful ideal, is today a country that at the time of this writing is threatening to annihilate Israel and all the people who live inside it, a sense of divine mission utterly at odds with Attar's religious view. But then Attar himself suffered banishment for his heresies. Forcing God's hand by killing other people was alien to Attar, but not alien to religious dreams of purification. Extremism—of religion or materialism—of pure environmentalism or pure urbanism—is not the way. Edward O. Wilson frets, in his book *The Creation*, that the apocalyptic fantasies of American evangelicals will divert the attention of religious Christians from preserving the environment, which Wilson fears is harder to do when you dream of the earth melting away into a messianic future. The balance between heaven and earth is easily lost.

There's a humble, pragmatic response to *The Conference of Birds* offered by Robert Frost, that master of the diminished thing. In "Birches," he writes:

> *I'd like to get away from earth awhile*
> *And then come back to it and begin over.*
> *May no fate willfully misunderstand me*
> *And half grant what I wish and snatch me away*
> *Not to return. Earth's the right place for love:*
> *I don't know where it's likely to go better.*
> *I'd like to go by climbing a birch tree,*
> *And climb black branches up a snow-white trunk*
> Toward *heaven, till the tree could bear no more,*
> *But dipped its top and set me down again.*
> *That would be good both going and coming back.*

Frost, who seems to me so much the birdwatching poet of the twentieth century, is the poet of "toward" heaven, not "to" heaven. Looking up is the best we can do.

THEOLOGY AND NATURAL HISTORY—connected when Wallace began as a naturalist and severed by the time of his death on the eve of the First World War—still call back and forth to each other across the divide. Are birds the life of the skies because the skies have no other life—no angels, powers, thrones, dominions? No God? And is mere biology enough to account for morality and imagination and love and altruism and hope? And if it is enough, is it sufficient to sustain us? Can we live recognizing that we are the real life of the skies, projecting our hopes and needs upward into a void we cannot ever wholly accept? Or are birds the life of the skies because the very presence of life, the existence of biological processes, implies something that transcends biology, a sort of theology that, however unarticulated, or unacknowledged, is always lurking in us whenever we look up?

These are not resolvable questions, and they don't have to be. But they hover around birdwatching and explain an aspect of its appeal. Like the birds who go looking for a king and end up discovering themselves, birdwatching is always an unexpected as well as an expected quest, motivated by obvious needs as well as our deepest buried longings. Attar and Emerson and Dickinson and Tristram and Hume and Wallace and Thoreau and Frost were all searching for something when they looked at nature. It might have been a traditional idea of a creator who put us in charge of creation, or a mystical idea of a creator whose relationship to us is more opaque, or a creator who is utterly indifferent to us, or—and this is perhaps the most mystical of all possibilities, though it is most often championed by scientists like Edward O. Wilson—a creator who isn't there at all, but whose place has been taken by creation itself. None of these possibilities will go away in our post-Darwinian world, and we may need them all to save the natural world, and ourselves along with it.

19

AMERICAN HOOPOE

Still, he could *be found.*

—SAUL BELLOW,
"Looking for Mr. Green"

On April 29, 2005, *The New York Times* announced on its front page the astonishing fact that an ivory-billed woodpecker had been seen in the Big Woods of eastern Arkansas. "Back from the Dead," the headline declared, alongside a picture of the bird—not a photograph, which hadn't been secured, but a drawing that captured the grandeur of the creature. I cannot be the only person who was moved to tears by the news. After sixty years, the bird had been seen and therefore, potentially, saved. Here was an American hoopoe carrying a message from a scrap of wilderness to an urbanized, industrialized, suburbanized population. Here was a bird from beyond the grave, declaring what Solomon had written to Sheba: "Love is stronger than death."

Maybe. The future of the bird still hung in the balance. Only a male had been seen. Nobody knew if there was a breeding pair or sufficient quality habitat to let them breed if there was. But suddenly there was hope. I know I felt it.

Of course, I also felt a perverse disappointment. Was it because I wanted to find the bird myself, improbable as that could ever be? Or was it merely a writer's possessiveness? I'd written about the bird back in 2000, when it was a novelty, and I saw it as my property, my subject, my own private bird of paradise—even though many had written about the bird before me and I had no claim whatsoever. Birdwatching itself, vastly popular as it is, still feels like something I do alone, a kind of secret I share with the birds and a small group of the initiated, despite the many millions of others who do it, too. I feel like a hunter-gatherer when I bird, part of an ancient tribe, even though I'm a settled bourgeois city dweller who cannot read the stars, or even a compass, and have been known to jump when bugs land on me. Suddenly the ivory-bill was a media celebrity, and a buried, childish, primitive voice in me cried, "Mine!" Perhaps I didn't want the bird to be found at all, but to live forever in elusive mystery.

Perhaps, too, I did not want this bird of paradise to become a backyard bird again—accessible, available, earthbound. Though nothing could be more hopeful than to have the bird slip back to earth, to show up on a list of local birds alongside the Carolina wren or the chickadee. An ugly impulse, I know, to want to keep my private symbolism alive at the expense of the bird's actual salvation. I am reminded of Dostoevsky's Grand Inquisitor in *The Brothers Karamazov*, who decides it would be better, if Jesus returned to earth, to keep his return a secret and so keep alive the longing and illusion.

I'm not proud of the

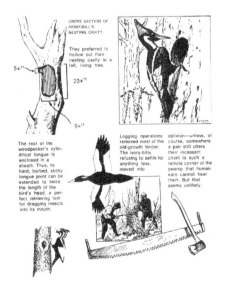

CROSS SECTION OF IVORY-BILL'S NESTING CAVITY.

They preferred to hollow out their nesting cavity in a tall, living tree.

5+"

20+"

8+"

The rear of the woodpecker's cylindrical tongue is enclosed in a sheath. Thus, its hard, barbed, sticky tongue point can be extended to twice the length of the bird's head, a perfect retrieving tool for dragging insects into its mouth.

Logging operations removed most of the old-growth timber. The ivory-bills, refusing to settle for anything less, moved into

oblivion—unless, of course, somewhere a pair still utters their incessant chant in such a remote corner of the swamp that human ears cannot hear them. But that seems unlikely.

undercurrent of unbecoming emotions, but I record them in the hope that they reveal more than a greedy and childish character but say something as well about our imperfect relationship to nature—our desire for conquest, as well as our capacity for wonder, and the way these two things often go together. The bird is the wild element we crave that erases the highway and the sadness of modern life. We look for it with a desperation born out of a desire to save it, and also to save ourselves from the civilization whose spread imperiled the birds in the first place. Of course that civilization also gave rise to our conservationist consciousness, our scientific curiosity, the very elements that urge us to rescue lost birds. And so we are forever torn between our desire to master and our desire to be mastered by nature. Edward O. Wilson puts a hopeful spin on this paradox in *Biophilia*, citing as an inborn human trait the desire to keep learning so that we can dispel old mysteries while giving birth to new mysteries that draw us forward: "A quiet passion burns, not for total control but for the sensation of constant advance."

This book is divided into two halves—backyard birds and birds of paradise. But it should be obvious by now that this separation is an illusion, or ought to be. Birds of paradise *are* backyard birds—the Aru Islanders were intimately acquainted with the feathered beauties that Wallace sailed thousands of miles, braving death and disease, to find. The hoopoe that filled my head with lofty dreams of Solomon and the Temple lived in a dirty hole in the wall near the Knesset in Jerusalem. These exotic birds may promise intimations of immortality, but they are subject to the same laws of nature that we ourselves are. That, actually, is what makes them so exciting.

By the same token, all backyard birds are really birds of paradise—embodiments of mysterious elements, the spark of life itself that, for all our science, we still cannot explain. Tennyson divined this when he wrote in 1869 a humble, almost childlike poem that was read aloud by a biology teacher when I was an undergraduate at Yale:

> *Flower in the crannied wall,*
> *I pluck you out of the crannies,*
> *I hold you here, root and all, in my hand,*
> *Little flower—but if I could understand*
> *What you are, root and all, and all in all,*
> *I should know what God and man is.*

At the time, I was vaguely embarrassed for the teacher trying to give his subject relevance with a poem that seemed archaic at best. I no longer feel that way. And I find it strange, in fact, that this poem is included in the *Oxford Book of English Mystical Verse*. It seems no more mystical than Darwin saying, "There is grandeur in this view of life, with its several powers, having been originally breathed into a few forms or into one." Certainly it is not more mystical than the recognition that every cell in the body holds the key to the entire body and all its genetic heritage.

In 1884, Tennyson, who followed scientific developments keenly and had a thorough grasp of evolutionary theory, invited Wallace to his home and had him explain what went on at séances. Wallace shared his experiences—the table rappings, the mystic writing. The Poet Laureate remained understandably baffled that there could be spirits everywhere who turned up only when a medium called, asking: "A great ocean pressing round us on every side, and only leaking in by a few chinks?" But his healthy skepticism did not keep him from believing that in the visible, material world there was mystery enough to make an ordinary wildflower a miniature Tree of Life.

The great trick of birdwatching, which gives it such large application, is holding things in balance. It is seeing infinity in the common, and pursuing a bird of paradise until it turns back into a backyard bird. It is, once again, all about binocular vision.

And so I made plans to go to Arkansas.

I enlisted two friends to go with me—Andy, from Florida, and Rob, from Pennsylvania. We'd all gone birding in southern Texas the year before, and it seemed the perfect follow-up trip. Andy is a professor of English literature and a passionate birder, but like me, he birds in the spaces his life allows—between children and marriage and teaching and writing and all the obligations of midlife. Rob, however—an old friend of Andy's from college—seems to do his work and his living in the spaces that birding allows. It was Rob who had organized our Texas trip, and he did it as if he were planning the Normandy invasion—everyone got a bound booklet including maps and bird lists with the birds ranked—yard bird, good bird, great bird, grail bird. There were birds on the list I did not know were birds, with names like green-breasted mango. He made the motel reservations, two to a room for maximum thrift.

Humbert Humbert, the pervert narrator of *Lolita*, while describing his mad flight with an underage girl across the United States, professes a preference for the "Functional Motel—clean, neat, safe nooks, ideal places for sleep, argument, reconciliation, insatiable illicit love." We also favored the functional motel. Our insatiable love was for the birds, but there was still a sense of driven pursuit and perhaps mild perversity. We started before sunrise and ended after dark, and driving five hours to see a duck (albeit a rare masked duck) was not considered extreme. Rob expected to see rare birds, almost as if he imagined that the birds would be looking for him as much as he was looking for them, as if they shared a common destiny.

Like many first-class birders, Rob combines type-A anality

with a totally Zen-like devotion to being out in the field. He would make a superb bird guide if he were willing to sully something as sacred as looking for birds with commerce. He has what Hemingway called *afición*—a knowledge and passion that retains a sort of spiritual purity. He wears his binoculars on an extra long strap so that they hang at his right hip, like a gunslinger's pistol, not thunking at his chest like the awkward necklace that gives birders their dorky reputation.

I may sing the praises of birdwatching, but Rob made me want to be a *birder*. Birding with Rob could actually be aerobic. There were hills to climb. Speed and stealth mattered if you were heading off a grazing flock of white-fronted geese. The ugliness of the landscape—some abandoned, urinous underpass that gave an unexpected glimpse of fulvous whistling ducks—was irrelevant to the larger purpose, which was to see birds. He set up his spotting scope with the swift efficiency of a soldier erecting an anti-tank gun. There were no aesthetic trappings—we always ate at Jack in the Box (a picture of the hideous fast-food clown was included in our booklet alongside various most-wanted birds) and everybody ordered the number 4 to save time and because we fell into ritualistic patterns. We became not ornithological outsiders but part of the great highway culture that had driven back nature in the first place—motels, fast-food restaurants, an undercurrent of nameless desire.

Kingbird Highway, Kenn Kaufman's memoir about his quest for a "big year," hitchhiking his way across eighty thousand miles, getting rides from truckers, doing anything he had to do in order to see every bird he could, is the anthem of that world. The very seediness was part of the romance—it wasn't a "natural" thing to do, but the surface squalor was connected to a deeper undercurrent of desire that in some sense transcended nature and got to the core of human behavior. Vladimir Nabokov discovered motels and highways while butterfly-hunting across America each summer, and when he wrote *Lolita*, it was the hunt for butterflies that informed Humbert's mad pursuit for an underage girl. And under the longing for butterflies something else, something older and nameless and primal: desire itself.

Birding, as opposed to birdwatching—despite my general insistence on the words' interchangeability—has a contemporary American acquisitiveness about it, fused to or perhaps fueled by ancient environmental cravings. Asked what he wants in *Key Largo*, Edward G. Robinson's gangster is unable to say until, prompted by Humphrey Bogart, he can only admit: "More. That's right. I want more." Birding is all about wanting more, though it has an ascetic element to it that gives it a paradoxical feeling of restlessness and self-denial, since you never get to keep your riches. It's all in the doing. And of course it has a natural element—the longing to see life, as Thoreau said, "pasturing freely where we never wander." The storm that sweeps through the Keys at the end of *Key Largo* and helps bring down Robinson's gangster would not undo a birder, who in some sense wants the storm in the first place. But it's the wild and the urban coming together in unexpected ways and places that makes modern birding what it is.

Wild America was the poetic name that Roger Tory Peterson gave the hugely influential book, published in 1955, that he wrote with British birder James Fisher about a year spent canvassing thirty thousand miles of U.S. territory (including an unsuccessful search for ivory-bills in the Big Cypress reserve in Florida). That book inspired a later generation of birders, but only two years later Jack Kerouac published *On the Road* and the cultural mood changed in ways captured perfectly by *Kingbird*

Highway, with its hybrid of the avian and the automobile. Put *Lolita*, *On the Road*, and *Wild America*—three gas-fueled classics of the 1950s—together and you will find a key to modern birding.

Rob gave birding its on-the-roadiness for me, but it was knowledge that set him apart—he knew every expected bird, so that he could home in on the bird that looked slightly different from the norm and thereby see the rarity, the vagrant, the unexpected. He looked for the exception, I looked for the rule. In this he had something in common with field biologists like Darwin and Wallace—it was noticing differences within a species that led to their breakthroughs. On my own, I would just have written "There are a lot of finches on these islands!" in my diary and felt pleased that I'd known they were finches.

In Texas, Rob and his friend Scott, another high-powered birder, had noticed a hawk on the far side of the Rio Grande that seemed just a little "off." At that distance I couldn't have told a hawk from a handsaw, but they stared across the river until they felt quite certain it was a roadside hawk, a Mexican bird that despite its pedestrian name is a rarity, at least when it crosses the border where American birders can count it. This bird obligingly did just that—luck is also a key part of birding. It flew across the river and landed on a telephone pole on the Texas side, where Rob and Scott studied it. I wrote down everything we saw: four black bars, four white bars on tail; white bars thicker than black on underside; yellow at base of bill; yellow eye, etc. Andy photographed it. The verdict: roadside hawk. They saw this bird right after Scott had said, "Why shouldn't we see something nobody else has?" They willed it out of the air.

Andy and I knew that Rob would see the ivory-billed woodpecker because he had kept himself pure—no articles, no profiteering. He was the chaste knight who would find the grail. Plus he had the chops—he would never be taken in by a pileated woodpecker and would not need to look only for the white trailing edge as the bird flew; he would know that there was more black on the face of an ivory-bill, he would gauge bill size and color. And he would use that most mystical of all birding tools—*jizz*.

The term is almost impossible to use out loud, because it is also slang for semen, and either makes birders seem geekily oblivious to street slang or contains the suggestion that birding is in itself vaguely pornographic; both possibilities of course are true. In any event, jizz (sometimes spelled "jiss," or even "giss," not that that helps) is often said to be an approximate acronym for "general impression size and shape," a British air force term originally applied to the identification of fighter planes too far away to see clearly but that could nevertheless be told apart by an aggregate of small indicators that together made a plane a Spitfire, say, rather than a Messerschmitt. Jizz is most clearly used in hawk watching, where you cannot tell the field marks of each hawk in a faraway kettle of birds but where enough of the bird's attributes—length of tail, stockiness of body, tilt of wing—are manifest, below the threshold of ordinary perception, so that jizz somehow whispers the name of the bird in your ear.

When you are birding well, it is as though the Force is with you and jizz offers the proof, telling your blood "wood thrush" or "cuckoo" before you've actually tallied, or even quite seen, any fieldmarks. As if there were a platonic spot inside you where the bird lives—as if, like the Simorgh in *The Conference of Birds*, the creature is somehow part of you, making the double meaning of "jizz" weirdly appropriate. Rob was a master of intuitive birding. The Force was with him, and he also had great eyesight, as well as a remarkable ability to refrain from eating or going to the bathroom, whereas Andy and I each traveled with a suitcase full of Zone bars and seemed to have to pee at every tree.

But life had caught up with Rob. His girlfriend had just had a baby, and at the last minute he decided he couldn't go. For some reason, hardcore birders often seem to be without children. They have dogs. This is either because they know the world is overpopulated or because doing the one thing that we most have in common with the birds is deemed an impediment to the freedom of movement required for a life of avian observation. (Wanting more can lead to having less.) Rob had been sucked into mammalian responsibility, and though Andy and I both felt that our children were the central fact of our lives, we were stunned by Rob's defection. We needed Yoda to guide us to victory.

But we went anyway. Though with an ironic frivolity that Rob would never have sanctioned—if only because it was a birdless waste of time—we flew into Memphis and began our trip with a visit to Graceland. The ivory-bill, after all, had been code-named Elvis by the search team from the Nature Conservancy and the Cornell Ornithology Laboratory that kept the secret for over a year. But after the mortuary gloom of Graceland, which looked like nothing so much as a funeral home run by prostitutes, and where the only birds we saw on the grounds were grackles, we were hungry for the Big Woods.

From Elvis's house it is an hour-and-a-half drive to Brinkley, Arkansas, a small town in the Mississippi Delta that declares itself, in a sign on I-40, "home of the ivory-billed woodpecker." In Brinkley, Andy and I stayed at the Mallard Pointe Lodge, which abuts the Dagmar Wildlife Management Area and caters mainly to hunters. The vast sitting room is filled with stuffed bobcat, cougar, multiple species of ducks, and, mounted above the extensive bar, the rear end of a deer. But the only other people staying there were birders looking for the ivory-bill, and the lodge was happy to have us.

At a store in Brinkley called The Ivory-bill Nest you can buy a T-shirt that says *Got Pecker?* on the front and, on the back, *We*

Do! Brinkley, Ark. But despite the store and the highway sign and the barbershop that offers an ivory-bill haircut—basically a Mohawk slicked to a point and dyed red—there were plenty of people in town who feared the discovery would lead to hordes of birders, closure of public lands, interruption of hunting.

You have to be a very small town indeed for a bird that may or may not exist to disturb your way of life, but if it is your way of life, chances are you want to keep it and are worried about intrusion. Hunting, and the feeling that the land is yours whether or not you own it, is still an aspect of Southern life. Arkansas has fewer than 3 million residents in the entire state—Brooklyn has almost as many people—and in the southeastern portion, part of the low-lying, fertile Mississippi Delta region, a Deep South culture thrived among rich cotton-growing soil, old-growth woods, and bottomland swamps. It was mired in slavery, Jim Crow, and the hardships of sharecropping, of course, but it provided, for blacks and whites, a distinct culture that even now persists, a sense of literal groundedness.

Going south to look for a bird meant going into the heart of an American paradox. Back in January 2002, when I found myself in Louisiana for a second time, stalking through various swamps on an organized ivory-bill search, I took a day off to visit Oakley, the plantation where Audubon painted some of his most famous watercolors, including the mockingbirds fighting a snake up in a tree. Above the dining room table where Audubon took his meals with the family, his head filled with visions of flight, hung a large wooden fan called a shoo-fly—something like an Indian punkah—that was operated by a slave child who pulled a tasseled cord during dinnertime. That same day, I drove up the "River Road," a stretch of about seventy miles between New Orleans and Baton Rouge on either side of the Mississippi, along which restored plantations can be found. "See the Old

South as you always imagined it," the brochure of one planta-tion house said, and if you imagined it without slaves or masters, I suppose that description would be accurate. But it was the New South, or rather, the Old-New South, that was compelling.

The landscape was a surreal mixture of elements—vast fields of cane (the same crop the slaves planted and harvested), cut to stubble at that time of year; huge, complex petrochemical re-fineries, all scaffolding and erector-set architecture, alongside wooden shacks and po'boy shops; a tiny graveyard set into a field against the backdrop of a factory that belched white smoke into a white sky; the levee on my right, with the river somewhere be-hind it (though when I scrambled up the bank, I found only driblets of water, boggy puddles, the mud crowded with egrets and killdeer). And then there were the restored plantations, smaller than I'd imagined, charming and chilling, like the gin-gerbread house in the fairy tale.

At Laura, an airy Creole plantation house designed by a Senegalese architect—"if you weren't lucky enough to own an architect, you could always rent one," the tour guide brightly in-formed me—the story of Br'er Rabbit was born, or at least recorded by an ethnographer who visited the slave cabins there and wrote down what he heard. But the story that kept haunting me as I drove up to Oakley was a different slave story, "The Peo-ple Could Fly," which begins, in Virginia Hamilton's retelling, with heartbreaking simplicity:

They say the people could fly. Say that long ago in Africa, some of the people knew magic. And they would walk up on the air like climbin up on a gate. And they flew like blackbirds over the fields. Black, shiny wings flappin against the blue up there.

Then, many of the people were captured for Slavery.

The ones that could fly shed their wings. They couldn't take their wings across the water on the slave ships. Too crowded, don't you know.

When a woman and her baby are cruelly whipped, the woman appeals to an old slave named Toby to summon the forgotten magic:

"Yes, Daughter, the time is come," Toby answered. "Go, as you know how to go!"

He raised his arms, holding them out to her. *"Kum . . . yali, kum buba tambe,"* and more magic words, said so quickly, they sounded like whispers and sighs.

The young woman lifted one foot on the air. Then the other. She flew clumsily at first, with the child now held tightly in her arms. Then she felt the magic, the African mystery. Say she rose just as free as a bird. As light as a feather.

The slave story has its terrible historical specificity that shames the listener with its naked longing for escape—its faith, not in human beings, whose evil must have seemed ineluctable, but in magic. But it has its secondary meaning, too, that speaks to us all now living outside that time, a dream of a world where nothing can tie us down, not gravity or history or fate. A dream of Eden, of angels, and of a time when we all had wings—or a time when we'll have them again. Perhaps as common as the wish to see birds is the wish to *be* them, though true birdwatching only works when you hold your human ground and face living between heaven and earth, with all its historical and political burdens.

In a memoir of growing up in the 1930s on a cotton farm in

the southeastern part of Arkansas not far south of Brinkley, Margaret Jones Bolsterli traces the "Delta of the mind" that grew out of the literal Delta. Though she herself felt she had to get out—to find, as she puts it, conversation rather than stories, not to mention a world that educated its women—she has her burial spot picked out on land her grandfather, who fought in the Civil War, purchased in the 1840s from an Indian. And although she subtitles her memoir "Reflections on the Making of a Southern White Sensibility" and gives a stark view of the Delta's nearly feudal ways when she was young—with its cult of the white woman and its rigid social hierarchies, punishing sharecropping system, abhorrence of being "common," outbreaks of sudden violence, imprisoning sense of history gone wrong, and gnawing unacknowledged guilt—she evokes rhapsodically the magical power of that world, its sense of cohesion and community and order, not merely social but, above all, natural, a society bound to soil so rich it was reported that a broomstick thrust into the ground would sprout. If the social world had an aspect of the medieval, the natural world was positively primeval:

> Barns and cribs to play in have been the salvation of many a lonely country child, but in addition to these, we had, within fifty yards of our back door, a living, seething swamp for our personal entertainment. It never seemed to occur to anyone that it might not be a good idea to let small children play in a swamp infested with thousands of poisonous snakes, partly because snakes were such a part of the scenery that nobody paid them any mind.

It makes sense to me that the ivory-bill could have survived in this world, and that the very things that made the South seem to the North, even after the Civil War, an area of darkness—pre-industrial, socially immobile, feudal—could make it, however unintentionally, environmentally ahead of its time, preserving the earth out of love and neglect.

Many years before I began birding, my wife and I, newly married, found ourselves in Georgia in summertime and decided on a whim to go to the Okefenokee swamp. I had not heard of ivory-bills at that point and did not know that the swamp had been home to ivory-bills, the last one seen there in 1942, when the refuge biologist and his wife observed one at close range. I liked the exotic sound of the word "swamp" and did not realize it wasn't just a morass of sinking earth but a whole ecosystem with trees and water and land and animals and birds. I did not know that 90 percent of the swamp's 400,000 acres had been logged by the time the Fish and Wildlife Service acquired it in 1936. But I wanted to go there, we both did, for mysterious reasons, to make contact with something old—older than the oldest building, older than the oldest painting, older than the oldest words.

Perhaps, having embraced the ordered idea of marriage and responsibility, we both wanted to go to a place whose name conjured disorder and primal chaos. Or maybe it was the primal, generative chaos that marriage also brings you closer to that made us want to glimpse an actual swamp. Our friends thought it was a hilarious place for newlyweds to go, but we did not.

The trip was a disaster. We arrived at noon and took a tourist boat through a few stagnant byways—it was so blazing hot that even the alligators refused to come out of hiding. I had no understanding of what a swamp was or what it did or why I was there or what to do once I was there. Baking in the still waters, I didn't care; we finished our little float and fled to our air-conditioned car. It was not until I started birding that I had a way of relating to swamps, of thinking about the life inside them, of realizing how central swamps are, how much I need them—and how much they need me.

Birding, in its own small way, had given me a place in the swamp, made me part of the fellowship of people drawn there for their own reasons, people with whom it turned out, however different our backgrounds, interests, and education, I had the most basic things in common.

20.

THE BIRD IS THE WORD

Haven't you heard about the bird?
Don't you know that the bird is the word?

—THE RIVINGTONS,
"The Bird's the Word"

There still are ancient pockets of the earth in the American South. One of these is Bayou de View, the euphoniously named corner of the Big Woods where the ivory-bill was seen on February 11, 2004, by Gene Sparling, a kayaker from the western part of the state, drawn to the swamp because he'd heard there were stands of thousand-year-old cypress trees. Floating alone down one of the bayou's mazelike channels, he saw a giant woodpecker foraging in an old cypress tree. He was low in the water in a camouflaged kayak and he watched the bird for close to a minute. Though he does not call himself a birder, he has more than a passing familiarity with birds and had dreamed in childhood of finding ivory-bills in the Big Thicket region of Texas. He knew the bird he was watching wasn't a pileated—he had those nesting on his property in Hot Springs, Arkansas, and this one was different.

Just as there is a logic to David Kullivan having seen the bird while out turkey hunting, so there is logic to Gene Sparling seeing the bird as he floated directionless through a swamp. Like the bird itself, he was drawn to old trees. He didn't have a particular goal and didn't mind if he got lost and had to camp on the damp bank of a bayou. Like the boy in the Faulkner story who removes his compass and puts down his gun and only then is rewarded with the appearance of the bear everyone else is hunting, Sparling had as much in common with the bird as with its pursuers.

Sparling included a cagey allusion to his sighting toward the end of an account of his trip that he posted on a canoe club website. He soon drew the attention of ivory-bill hunters who grilled him and decided that his sighting was credible enough to merit a visit to Bayou de View. These were Bobby Harrison and Tim Gallagher, two friends who had been searching for the bird for many years. Sparling led them through the bayou to the place where he had seen the bird. Not far from the spot, Harrison and Gallagher saw a black-and-white bird emerge from a side channel and fly across their path in bright sunlight. At the same moment they both cried out "ivory-bill." The rest is birdwatching history.

The secret was kept until April of the following year, which gave the Cornell Ornithology Laboratory and the Nature Conservancy and Fish and Wildlife time to coordinate and mount a proper search while securing as much of the surrounding land as possible. Access to the area surrounding Bayou de View was restricted, and was still restricted when Andy and I were there in March. We went in the company of Jay Harrod from the Nature Conservancy and Gene Sparling himself, who was working on retainer for the Nature Conservancy.

We put in at a spot called Woodfin and paddled in plastic canoes camouflaged green and brown. I sat in the front of Sparling's canoe, Andy sat in the front of Jay's. Sometimes we pulled in our oars and simply floated. We had binoculars at the ready, but it was hard to retain a sense of vigilant tension as you lapped along the dark water. Gene in particular, a trim middle-aged man with a close-cropped sandy gray beard and a baseball cap, had a way of imposing casual calm.

"I've got no place to go and all the time in the world to get there," he drawled lazily when I thanked him for taking the time.

We paddled through narrow, tree-lined channels. The water was beautiful and dark. The area had been logged, but incompletely, and from time to time one of those thousand-year-old cypresses rose out of the swamp, its head blown off by lightning or wind but putting out a new crown, which was pale red, the catkins hanging down. A bird broke the silence and rocketed toward a tree; Andy and I seized our binoculars, but it was a wood duck. There were a lot of them, colorful helmeted birds that nest, uncharacteristically for ducks, in tree cavities.

"If I had feathers like that I might be able to attract a mate, too," said Gene.

He and Jay sat paddling behind us like gondoliers, singing a slow familiar song, the banter of men on a Sunday outing.

"She went back to the boyfriend I didn't know she had. Someday she'll come back again and show up at my door—and she'll be welcome."

"I keep trying to remember the name of that girl you were seeing."

"I keep trying to forget it."

It was hard to avoid the realization that we were tourists. And yet you could not dismiss the feeling of *why not now, why not us?* After all, Tim Gallagher and Bobby Harrison had been tourists, too, led to the spot by Gene in order to see the bird, and they had done just that. But I envied the way Gene had seen it. He'd had no goal in that maze beyond simply being there. He was not trying to find anything, not even looking—or perhaps he was on a quest he had begun in childhood and forgotten the reason for.

Now, however, everything was routine. Sparling was doing the opposite of what had drawn him to the swamp in the first place. He told me he was amazed at the way names he invented on the spot to enter into his GPS as he searched the bayou in his new bird-hunting capacity—"crooked forest," "the power line"—took on a sort of permanence. I thought of the names in Central Park the birders use—mugger's woods, the vibrating tombstone, the rustic bridge—that no doubt began in the same offhand way. And now the bayou was getting parsed like Central Park.

Gene pointed out the "resurrection fern" that burst spontaneously into life after a rain, greening the bark of trees. He admired the way each cluster of cypress knees has its own character—some forked, some "octopus," some cloaked in moss. "Old people talking," he said.

We passed two volunteers in head-to-toe camouflage perched high in a blind.

"Nothing but turtles," they told us.

We floated into Paw Paw Lake, and Jay shared a story of Faulknerian density about a man who had built a still in the lake during Prohibition and designed it to sink. It had failed to sink far enough, and the man—a strapping fellow who was often seen heading off into the swamp with a hundred-pound bag of corn on each shoulder—was sent to prison in Atlanta. He was visited only by a single person, a neighbor visiting his son at a nearby college. In gratitude for the visit, he had on his deathbed given his neighbor right of refusal over the land, and that man, Woodfin, still lends his name to the place where we had started our excursion. The story didn't really have a point except that this primal habitat had a human history, too, as mythic in its way as the trees, and that eighty years ago a still was hiding in this swamp along with, perhaps, an ivory-bill.

We were shown a great protruding branch from which one of the searchers had seen the bird but failed to get a picture, because he was eating a ham sandwich. Our tour was in many ways a tour of missed moments. Gene Sparling's sighting was not definitive—it was only when Harrison and Gallagher saw it that it gained wider acceptance, in part because Gallagher was editor of *Living Bird*, the flagship magazine of the Cornell Lab of Ornithology, and persuaded his friend John Fitzpatrick—who is head of the lab—that he had really seen it. But their sighting was not really definitive either, since it wasn't photographed. Only when David Luneau, a professor of engineering, mounted a video camera on his boat and, without quite knowing it, caught a video of the bird was there material evidence. But even that evidence, though held up by Cornell as definitive when it made its 2005 announcement, had, by the time Andy and I went down to Arkansas, been declared inconclusive in an article in *The Auk* by Jerome Jackson, a noted ivory-bill expert. The debate continues, with some major birders, like Kenn Kaufman and David Sibley, backing Jackson, who suspected a pileated, and others siding with Cornell.

"Give me the ocular proof!" Othello roars in jealous rage to Iago. Birders need it, too, and the rarer the bird, the more they need it. My seeing the bird would add not a feather to the scale; only a picture would make a difference. But Andy had brought his fancy camera and held it on his lap.

From Paw Paw Lake we paddled into Stab Lake and up a channel called the power line that passed directly under Interstate 40. We heard the roar of trucks. Our ivory-bill had become an ovenbird.

On the way back, we had to paddle hard against the wind. "It's easier to push a fat woman down the stairs than up," said Gene, with such wry good nature that it didn't sound violent or misogynistic, just Southern.

All the way back we peered past tupelo and cypress trees, but we did not see the bird. Neither did I see it when I went out looking with David Luneau, who showed me the spot where he took his video—he'd tied a bandanna around a tree to mark it. The Luneau video has become the Zapruder film of ivory-bill studies, parsed and pored over and debated. I was careful to wear dark clothes for the outing—I'd met Luneau on an earlier search for the ivory-bill in 2003 and he had suggested I remove my electric blue fleece if I hoped to see the bird. Luneau has devoted a huge number of hours to the search and told me that in the mornings he spends twenty minutes on the elliptical trainer watching video footage from cameras he has mounted on various trees and the front ends of boats.

Andy and I tramped through woods and around lakes and into swamps, and we kept running into searchers who spent weeks and months doing what we were doing for a few days. We spent a night and day farther south at the White River Wildlife Refuge, another promising area whose second-growth trees have been growing since at least the thirties, when the refuge was created. We joined a team of paid searchers working six-month tours of duty. These were field biologists who moved around like migrant workers from conservation project to conservation project—"Everyone gets his start with the spotted owl," I was told.

One of the men coordinating the search was Tom Snetsinger, whose mother, Phoebe, is the *Guinness Book of World Records* record holder that Simon Baron-Cohen holds up as the female exception that proves the masculine rule of birding; before she died, in 1999, she had seen more species of birds than anyone else in the world. She is a double legend because, although a birdwatcher since the 1960s, she took up birding seriously after being diagnosed with terminal melanoma in 1981. Given less than a year to live, she decided to forgo treatment and take a planned birdwatching trip to Alaska. When she came back, she found her cancer was in remission. Year by year and bird by bird she defied all the predictions, keeping herself alive like a bird-watching Scheherazade. She did not die of cancer—the van she was riding in while pursuing birds in Madagascar overturned, killing her instantly. She had seen approximately 8,400 bird species—but of course she had never seen an ivory-bill. Her son Tom, who lives in Oregon, had gotten burned out on spotted-owl work and had come south for a change.

I envied the free-spirited searchers, living in communal grad-school grunge, unglamorously waking up before first light to spend entire days doing "transects" of the swamp. One of them had a tattoo on his leg that said "Less is more." They had room-mates, but there was a "shagging room" for conjugal visits. They cooked communally and posted communitarian articles on the re-frigerator and didn't just fret about the environment—they lived doing something about it, banding, counting, searching. I envied them, but I could not do it—my ratio of indoor to outdoor activity is reversed, for one thing. But I admired the businesslike seriousness with which they hunted through the woods—it wasn't a sport or a pastime, it was a job. Like policemen, soldiers, journalists, they daily came face-to-face with unglamorous reality, making their living in service of a world shrouded for most people in fantasy and delusion.

The Big Woods of Arkansas, where the ivory-bill was spotted, is, despite its name and 500,000 acres, an area that was quite thoroughly logged over a hundred years ago. It is intercut with highways and owes some of its preservation in the 1960s—in the area where the bird itself was seen—not to idealistic environmentalists but to a cantankerous, toothless dentist from Stuttgart (Arkansas, not Germany) named Rex Hancock, who swore like a sailor, loved to hunt waterfowl, and was afraid he'd lose his sport if the developers got their way.

This was explained to me by Dennis Widener, a man with bright blue eyes, close-cropped silver-white hair, and the sort of deep Southern accent whose molasses undertow starts tugging on your own vowels. Widener is the project manager of the Cache River National Wildlife Refuge, an area of the Big Woods that embraces thirty-three thousand acres of bottomland forest, including the euphonious Bayou de View. He grew up on a farm in west Arkansas, and his attachment to the land seems total. He spends most of the time reforesting the denuded areas of the floodplain.

If Gene Sparling, with his eye for giant cypress trees and his Huck Finn independence, is the ghost of the past, and the no-nonsense searchers represent the present, Widener is the ghost of the future. He led me and Andy to areas of the floodplain that had been mature forest until the 1960s, when soybean prices soared and farmers were so keen to clear and plant that they did not even log the old trees—they burned them. As prices fell and farming failed, groups like the Nature Conservancy began buying up the land, which, like the land reclaimed when the Huleh swamp was drained, is gradually being returned to what it used to be. Crop dusters wheeled like large birds of prey above us as we drove down dirt roads past stubble fields and toward the newly wooded areas that are slowly making the land, under human management, wild.

"It means something to see your handprint on the land," Widener told us as we tramped through young woods planted with hardwood trees, sweet gum and cypress and cedar. Though there was an abundance of woodpeckers, redheaded and red-bellied and hairies, it was unlikely there would be an ivory-bill. In a hundred years, however, if the bird survived, it might well live in these areas, since already there will be decaying trees for it to feed on and live in. The area still floods for four months a year—the natural hydrology of the floodplain is intact—and bears have begun to return to the region. They hibernate in trees and the young occasionally drown. But the bears can survive for months on floating acorns from the overcup oak—Widener held one up for us to examine. "God knew what he was doing when he made the overcup acorn," he drawled. He called our attention to a rock elm; it is believed that the seedpods make squirrels drunk. You can fill your hunting quota in one tree; you shoot one squirrel and the others simply keep eating.

Widener himself is a hunter. I know because I asked him. I asked every local person I met, actually—I knew the answer would always be yes, but I liked to see how people answered it. Margaret Jones Bolsterli recalls learning how to shoot when she was eight years old and that she and her brothers used to shoot snakes and turtles "by the thousands."

When I asked Widener if he hunted, we were sitting in Gene's Barbeque in Brinkley, where you can order an "ivory-bill burger," though nobody did. (I did, however, encounter the miracle of fried pickles for the first time.) He seemed wary, as if the question might be a trap. I don't blame him. There is a carpet-bagging aspect to the descent of people like me on the swamp and the culture around it.

"Yes, I am," he said at last, definitively but I thought a little defensively. I expanded on my gratitude to hunters for setting the conservation movement in motion in that area. It's only then that he told me about the dentist from Stuttgart whose hunting passion might have saved the ivory-bill, and then relaxed into the proper way to eat a squirrel: cut it up like a chicken, roll it in batter, fry it, make gravy out of the drippings and serve it with mashed potatoes. "Nothin' better," he said, with a beatific look on his face. Even Jay Harrod, the Nature Conservancy man who paddled Andy in Bayou de View and who had initially said, in response to my question, that he goes "deer camping"—it can't be called hunting, because he never hits anything—let down his guard and admitted that he likes to shoot squirrels with a .22 pistol.

At some point during this conversation a gray-haired man came up to us with a dead bird in a ziplock bag. He held it up over our food so we could all see what was inside—a tiny mossy bird with a yellow stripe on its head. He was eager to know what it was. We told him it was a golden crowned kinglet—you could even see the orange inside the yellow stripe, though the wing bars had been rearranged into zigzags and the feet were gone, just like those early specimens of bird of paradise called *apodia* by Linnaeus.

The man was a groundskeeper, and he had blown the bird a long way with his leaf blower before picking it up. He had never seen anything like it and felt it must be something very rare indeed. I showed him the bird in my Peterson guidebook and the range map that indicated the bird was a winter resident. The man was also a winter resident and seemed skeptical. "I'm seventy-two and I've never seen it," he kept saying, astonished.

When he left, Widener observed that a few years earlier that man wouldn't have bothered picking up the bird at all, but now, with ivory-bill awareness running high, everyone saw birds in a whole new way. The ivory-bill, whether or not it showed up again, had already given something to the town. It had created birdwatchers.

At Gene's they sell T-shirts with a picture of an ivory-bill and the phrase *The Bird Is the Word!* I asked Widener what that meant. He thought it was a religious statement, a kind of New Testament evocation—*in the beginning was the word*—and laughed. Certainly there is a strong current of Southern religious feeling in the region—that morning I'd noticed a billboard that said, "Jesus wants full custody, not weekend visitations." The owner of the Ivory-bill Nest gift shop, when I asked her, felt it was a reference to economic salvation, the promise of better business through the ivory-bill's recovery. Both can be true, of course.

The phrase is also part of a song written by the Rivingtons, a black rock 'n' roll/rhythm and blues group, in 1963. The song was stolen by the white Minneapolis group The Trashmen in 1964, which combined it with another Rivingtons song, "Papa-Oom-Mow-Mow," and produced a big hit called "Surfin' Bird" that's been covered by the Ramones and even by Pee-wee Herman.

There's a happy mixture of nonsense and sexual innuendo in those songs, but I think Widener is right to hear in the phrase a religious element, too. And why can't it be a pop song and an expression of theological longing and a dream of economic recovery all at the same time? It's like Graceland, where our trip started out. When you think of Graceland, you don't think of the Elvis who died fat on the toilet but of some vision of eternal youth and eternal desire, something American that comes from the fusion of African-American and pop culture, some deep-seated longing, half high and half low, half carnal, half religious. A fit confusion for something as old and new as birdwatching.

It was hard to leave the swamp, and not simply because we did not find the bird. It was hard because swamps are the sorts of places that lie on the periphery but are in fact central. They are a literal ecological necessity, doing the important work of wetlands, absorbing floods and breathing like a lung and giving a home to a staggering variety of animals and birds and plants. But they're psychological necessities, too. The shore of an ocean is where the water meets the land, but the swamp is where land and water have not quite separated yet; they are still in a primordial generative chaos, which has a thrilling, disconcerting quality that beckons in a deep way.

IN 1894, when Robert Frost was twenty years old, he published his first poem, "My Butterfly," and buoyed by this success (he received $15), he printed up two little booklets containing a handful of poems, one for himself and one for Elinor White, his high school sweetheart, whom he hoped to marry. He felt the booklet would persuade her that he had prospects, despite his having quit Dartmouth. Elinor was still in college, and Frost traveled to St. Lawrence University in Canton, New York, to persuade her to drop out and marry him. She did not receive him well—she was not allowed to entertain men in her room, she did not want to leave school, and she sent him on his way.

Frost suspected she was in love with another man. He destroyed the booklet he had made for himself and then, impelled by despair and rage, traveled, by steamer and train and then on foot, to the Great Dismal Swamp, which lies on the border between Virginia and North Carolina. His plan seems to have been to kill himself there, or simply to vanish somehow into the earth. He walked into the swamp until the road ended, but found a plank bridge that allowed him to cross a patch of water and keep going deeper into the swamp. Darkness came on. He lost his way.

But Frost did not die, nor, it seems, did he want to. Something happened to him in the swamp that changed his mind. He joined up with a party of duck hunters and found his way out, literally and emotionally. It was a slow trip back. He had no money, so he walked or hopped freight trains until, broke and exhausted, he fetched up in Baltimore three weeks later. His mother wired him money and he came home. The following year he married Elinor.

Frost never quite explained what happened in the swamp, though his poetry is an ongoing commentary on the event. When he wrote that he would like to get away from earth a while—but then return, tipped down from the top of a birch tree—or when he wrote about stopping by woods on a snowy evening, the forest beckoning with deathly allure—or when he found an abandoned woodpile and felt the "slow-burn odor of decay"—you can sense that, deep under the frozen New England earth, the Southern swamp is alive in him, a primal place where the poet lost and found himself again.

EPILOGUE (MAGIC HOUR)

What was the name of my best friend?

—EMERSON,

suffering from dementia, asking about Thoreau

Central Park, like the Old City of Jerusalem, is surrounded by walls punctuated by gates with poetic names. But unlike the gates of Jerusalem—or of European parks, for that matter—Central Park's gates are just breaks in the wall. Olmstead and Vaux wanted no ramparts or ornate entrances, they wanted the democracy of low sandstone walls with unobtrusive apertures that admitted everyone. The gates could have been named by Walt Whitman: Merchants' Gate, Miners' Gate, Artists' Gate. Though one or two have ostentatious flourishes, most of these twenty entrances are as unremarkable as their names are poetic: Mariners' Gate, Inventors' Gate, Warriors' Gate.

When I go birding in Central Park, I almost always enter through Hunters' Gate, on Central Park West and Eighty-first Street. This is partly because it is close to my apartment, but also because the first time I went on an organized bird walk, led by Starr Saphir, that is where we met, and it has since become my private birdwatching portal. There is no Birdwatchers' Gate, but there is a Naturalists' Gate, just a few blocks south, opposite the American Museum of Natural History. It is appropriate, though, to go birdwatching through a gate named for hunters.

When I used to visit my father in his nursing home, I would often go birding afterward, entering the park at 106th Street through Strangers' Gate, which leads up a flight of dark stone steps. This was an apt name, because my father was losing his memory. I was becoming a stranger to him, he was becoming a stranger to me, and most terrifying of all, he was becoming a stranger to himself.

It was soothing, in a chilly way, to fill my head with birds after one of those visits. There is a mechanical component to birding, ticking off the names of species, functioning not through conversation and explanation but through mute proximity to inarticulate life. The birds are like stars, pregnant with mystery but also remote, unfathomable. And so we give them names, like constellations, to make them familiar to us. We cling to that familiarity and need it desperately, but always alongside the familiar is the unfathomable. In the night sky we still see the light of dead stars, and in birds, too, there is the spark of something ignited eons ago, flashes of extinct forms that somehow put us nearer to our origins even as they baffle our desire for simple understanding.

Birding and memory go together. In a very basic way, I wanted to keep my mind alive to stave off my father's fate—forcing into my head black-throated blue and black-throated green, common yellow throat and yellow-breasted chat; the white tail band of a magnolia warbler seen from below, the chestnut undertail coverts of a catbird. I was greedy for birdsong—the buzzy rising scale of a parula warbler, the wooden whistle of an oriole, the harsh cry of a red-tailed hawk. D. H. Lawrence ends the prose poem that begins "Birds are the life of the skies" with the phrase "all birds have their voices, each means a different thing." To me each song meant the same thing, a sort of liquid memory poured into my mind.

The scientist Fernando Nottebohm, studying canaries at the Rockefeller University, determined in the 1980s that his birds were actually growing new brain cells in order to learn new songs. Dismissed at the time because they defied conventional scientific wisdom that adult brains do not change, his conclusions are now accepted and contain thrilling implications for human beings, since the Parkinson's disease and dementia that were erasing my father's brain progressed by killing neurons believed to be irreplaceable. If birds are capable of neurogenesis, the ability to grow new brain cells, perhaps humans are, too.

But memory and birding go together at a deeper level. When we bird, our bodies are remembering an older relationship to the natural world. Perhaps even our origins among the trees, a memory that draws us toward the very muteness that our conscious mind fears and avoids. It may be that Robert Frost, craving dissolution in the Great Dismal Swamp, was giving in to bodily memory to erase his conscious memory of loss and failure and heartbreak. There is no perfect resolution of these two types of consciousness—poetry was for Frost a way of mediating between them. Birdwatching is another.

Not long after I took up birding, my wife and I rented a house on a lake in New Hampshire. The woman renting us the house had recently been widowed and the house still bore the traces of her husband's illness—the cane leaning against the wall, the hospital bed in the spare room. There were also remnants of the couple's former life together. Her husband's parkas were still in the closet, his hunting caps were hanging on a hook, and on the bookshelf I found a copy of Roger Tory Peterson's *Eastern Birds* with her husband's name written on the first page.

In the front of the book was a checklist of American birds of the Eastern region; the man had checked off the birds he had seen. It was the list of someone who had not traveled much beyond New England. Of course he did not have to—one of the wonders of spring migration is that you do not need to fly South yourself to see neotropical birds in your own backyard.

There was something strangely affecting about the list—the fact, to begin with, that the watcher was no longer alive to add new names. But also the way in which the impersonal record of birds seen can become a sort of life monument. The unknown man's list for me took on a kind of personality. Here was a testament to his curiosity, to his urge to name the animals and participate in a community that is half scientific and half folkloric.

I never learned what he had done for a living, but I knew that in his spare time he had seen a red-bellied woodpecker and an evening grosbeak, and that he found it worthwhile to record his sightings. It gave him something in common with Adam in the Bible, namer of animals, and with Audubon and Wilson and all the American naturalists who had come up with names for birds as their contribution to the pioneer history of this country— memorializing themselves and their friends and wives and children in the process. And it gave him something in common with me. I had only just begun watching birds, and bird names still had the magical aura of something newly mastered. Writing them down on scraps of paper every time I went birding was as much a thrill as seeing the birds.

My first impulse that summer was to try to see birds that he had not managed to find and to complete his list for him. But my second impulse, more powerful (and easier), was to see the birds he'd already seen. And every time in the course of my two weeks in his house that I did see a bird whose name he had marked I felt weirdly linked to him. I was passing through the same place he had passed through in both a local sense and in a more metaphysical one; seeing those birds made me feel more alive at the same time that each bird whispered to me that my own list was finite and that what is not recorded is lost.

One generation comes and another generation passes away, but the earth abides forever. But what if the earth itself is passing away? And what if the animals, which we do not reckon as individuals but as ever-renewing species, should disappear along with it? How would I have felt if along with cedar waxwing and indigo bunting and great-crested flycatcher, this stranger had included Carolina parakeet and passenger pigeon and ivory-billed woodpecker? What if the birds he saw could never be seen again—by me or anyone else? What if the watcher and the watched disappeared together?

Toward the end of his life, Audubon developed dementia. The bird names he had mastered, several of which he had come up with himself, along with the birds he had seen in his long life, began to fly out of his head. Extinction is like that sadness amplified, as if the earth itself had the power to forget the animals that inhabit it, as if all awareness of a thing could be erased, not just in an individual mind but in God's mind.

There is a story from Audubon's early years that is a companion to the story of his memory loss. When he was nineteen years old, newly arrived in America and living on the Pennsylvania estate his father had bought for him, Audubon used to take long walks near the bank of the Perkiomen River. He discovered a cave where he would go with a book to read—often the animal fables of La Fontaine—and with paper and pencil for sketching.

Above the entrance to the cave one day in early spring Audubon noticed a small nest, attached with mud and lined with goose feathers. It was the nest of a pair of phoebes. Audubon was fascinated by these birds and watched them carefully.

He made many attempts to sketch these and other birds, but left them all unfinished. His failures, however, only strengthened his resolve to combine art and nature in some new way.

"Now in a moment I know what I am for," wrote Walt Whitman, inspired by a mockingbird's song toward the realization that he would become a poet. Audubon had a similar epiphany in his cave, studying his phoebes. "I looked so intently on their innocent attitudes that a thought struck my mind like a flash of light, that nothing after all could ever answer my enthusiastic desires to represent nature, than to attempt to copy her in her own way, alive and moving!"

He sometimes brought seventeen-year-old Lucy Bakewell, who shared his passion for nature, to the cave. Love of the natural world blurred with human love; it was in the cave, while the phoebes twittered nearby, that Lucy told him for the first time she loved him. Audubon later described the phoebes as if they were the ones in love: "Their mutual caresses, simple as they might have seemed to another, and the delicate manner used by the male to please his mate, riveted my eyes on these birds, and excited sensations which I can never forget."

In Audubon it is always hard to tell where the human ends and the natural world begins—this is a romantic carryover from his beloved fables of La Fontaine, but there is also something deeper, mythic in the confusion. In a rare love poem, "Never Again Would Birds' Song Be the Same," Robert Frost writes in the voice of Adam, describing the lasting effect that Eve had on the birds in the garden. Her soft eloquence, carried upward by "call or laughter," permanently adds to the sound of birds a human "oversound." The sonnet concludes:

> *Never again would birds' song be the same*
> *And to do that to birds was why she came.*

This is Frost's way of agreeing with Audubon that birds sing back to us an aspect of ourselves.

The phoebes in Audubon's cave are famous among birdwatchers because Audubon tied a silver thread around the legs of the nestlings as an experiment to see if the birds would return to the same spot. It is one of the first known instances of bird banding in America, and it was a success—in subsequent years the banded birds returned to the cave. The symbolism of the story remains deeply stirring. At the very moment when he was falling in love and pledging himself to another person, he was marrying the natural world, binding himself to these birds with a silver thread.

AUDUBON NEEDED this double marriage—we all do. I vividly remember in Central Park in 2003, not long after my father died, watching a phoebe. They are often the first birds to return to the park, and they are quite faithful to particular locations inside the park, just like Audubon's birds two hundred years ago. Audubon had watched these birds in a very different America, but here I was in a scrap of green inside a great city watching the same birds. It wasn't the continuity of the natural world only that consoled me; it was the continuity of human activity.

Audubon's cave haunts me. I see the young man sitting there with his long hair and wild hope, half eighteenth-century gentleman, half caveman, trying his best to knit the world together. Opening up before him, the world of birds and art and love and achievement. At his back, the shadow world that would engulf him in later years.

I've spent many years trying to find a children's book, or at least remember the name of it, that my father used to read to me and loved dearly. It was about a king who wanted to see something never before seen. His courtiers turn the palace and the country upside down trying to find a "new thing," but the king keeps responding, to whatever he is shown, "The thing that I want is not here!" Finally, one lowly member of the court brings him an egg, and as the king watches, the egg cracks and opens. A little chick emerges and the king is satisfied at last.

I don't know precisely why my father loved this story so much—he was not at all attuned to the natural world, and yet, as someone whose family had been murdered in the Holocaust, the creation of new life had a special, mystical resonance for him. Which is to say, he was of course connected to the natural world. Birding is all about the humble accumulation of new things. In a poem called "Proud Songsters," Thomas Hardy writes of a group of singing birds:

> *These are brand-new birds of twelve-months' growing,*
> *Which a year ago, or less than twain,*
> *No finches were, nor nightingales,*
> > *Nor thrushes,*
> *But only particles of grain,*
> > *And earth, and air, and rain.*

In Hardy's fanciful recipe for birds—grain, earth, air, and water—the missing particle, life itself, is what the poem, and the birds themselves, inspire you to feel and wonder at. Birds always have about them the sense of newness. In fall, when the leaves are dying and the birds are harder to see because their plumage is drab, there is an unexpected sense of abundance because migration includes the babies born in spring and summer making their first trip south. This is what the king and my father were looking for: more life.

But there is a beautiful and terrifying poem that my father was also very fond of, the shadow side of the children's book. It was written by the great Yiddish poet Avraham Sutzkever. It has no title and is included in a collection called simply *Poems from My Diary*:

> Who will remain, what will remain? A wind will stay behind.
> The blindness will remain, the blindness of the blind.
> A film of foam, perhaps, a vestige of the sea,
> A flimsy cloud, perhaps, entangled in a tree.
>
> Who will remain, what will remain? One syllable will stay,
> To sprout the grass of Genesis as on a new First Day.
> A fiddle-rose, perhaps, for its own sake will stand
> And seven blades of grass perhaps will understand.
>
> Of all the stars from way out north to here,
> That one star will remain that fell into a tear.
> A drop of wine remaining in a jar, a drop of dew.
> Who will remain, God will remain, is that enough for you?

Sutzkever was born in Vilna in 1913, spent his childhood in Siberia, and then returned as a young man to Vilna, where he became a poet. In 1941 the Nazis rounded up all the Jews and herded them into a ghetto—Sutzkever and a young rabbi were forced to dig their own graves by a sadistic Nazi who did not in the end shoot them. Sutzkever escaped the ghetto and became a partisan, writing as he fought—at one point scribbling a poem as he hid inside a coffin.

Sutzkever's entire body of work asks, again and again, "what to make of a diminished thing." Frost wrote "The Oven Bird" before Sutzkever was born; Sutzkever witnessed genocide, and the diminishment he wrote about was darker than even Frost's dark vision could imagine. But Sutzkever's Siberian childhood filled him with a love of the natural world, and he understood the natural world as part of the human world. In a poem about his murdered mother, written in the Vilna Ghetto in October 1942, he imagines her ghost saying to him:

If you remain
I will still be alive
as the pit of the plum
contains in itself the tree,
the nest and the bird
and all else besides.

Can a book about birdwatching sustain a reference to the horrors human beings inflict on each other? What sort of book would it be if it could not? After the ovens of Auschwitz, the ovenbird's question takes on darker overtones, but does not go away; it becomes only more urgent. More than ever we need to ask, for ourselves and for our children, what to make of a diminished thing. And we need to know that we are asking it about ourselves as well as about the world around us.

When Edward O. Wilson speaks of human beings in terms

of evolutionary history and notes that we have stone-age emotions, medieval institutions, and twenty-first-century technology, we may resist aspects of the characterization, but we know only too well what he means. There is genocide in Darfur as I write this, just as there was genocide looming when James T. Tanner published his study of the ivory-billed woodpecker in 1942. In the introduction to that book, Arthur Allen described the bird as a fit emblem of what America was fighting for—I would like to believe that is true, that our humanitarian struggles and our environmental struggles go hand in hand.

Are we a suicidal species? We must consider the possibility. Since 1945 we have had the technology to destroy ourselves, not metaphorically, but literally. We live inside a reality unimaginable by the men and women of the nineteenth century and of all the centuries before then. We have similarly reached a turning point, through industrialization, in our ability to destroy the natural world. It is worth quoting Wilson one more time, from his book *The Creation*, addressed to an unnamed evangelical minister as a plea to save the world:

> The Creation—living Nature—is in deep trouble. Scientists estimate that if habitat conversion and other destructive human activities continue at their present rates, half the species of plants and animals on Earth could be either gone or at least fated for early extinction by the end of the century. A full quarter will drop to this level during the next half century as a result of climate change alone. The ongoing extinction rate is calculated in the most conservative estimates to be about a hundred times above that prevailing before humans appeared on Earth, and it is expected to rise to at least a thousand times greater or more

in the next few decades. If this rise continues unabated, the cost to humanity, in wealth, environmental security, and quality of life, would be catastrophic.

Human beings have a double burden—we must worry about our impending extinction—as individuals, if not as a species—while worrying about the fate of the natural world around us. It is hard to balance these things—it may even be that anxiety about personal extinction leads us to indifference to the vulnerable world around us; people have conquered countries, cut down forests, extirpated animals, slaughtered human beings, all in the quest to shore up strength and power and keep the darkness of death at bay.

This of course is a failed strategy. Environmentally, our fate is intertwined with the natural world around us, and so the more we protect it, the more we protect ourselves. But the impulse to destroy and the impulse to preserve are alive in us simultaneously. We needed to subdue the natural world in order to thrive in its midst, but subduing it too fully will ultimately destroy us.

Robert Frost in the Great Dismal Swamp was not unique in contemplating suicide as a way of saving himself, marching toward the very darkness he feared being engulfed by. But in the end Frost settled down, as all of us must, in the mouth of Audubon's cave.

Birdwatching lends itself to private symbolism. I can't use Zeiss binoculars, although they are superb and the company even sponsored a search for the ivory-bill, because Zeiss made optics for the Nazis. (I use Leica, which also made optics for the Nazis, but less zealously, and even smuggled a few Jews out of Germany.)

Looking for the ivory-billed woodpecker, I inevitably found myself jotting in my notebook "I. B. Woodpecker," linking the bird to I. B. Singer, like Sutzkever a great Yiddish writer steeped in loss, obsessed with diminishment and survival. As if the bird I sought kept a culture alive in its song, though it doesn't even sing; it drums and makes a thin, tinny *ank*, a language that remains haunting and obscure.

But birdwatching is a world of small gestures that reflect larger worlds. My favorite place to watch birds in Central Park is Tanner's Spring, a humble little area not even located in the park's wooded interior but just off Central Park West, a hundred yards north of the Diana Ross playground. The spring, at the base of a slanting, mica-flecked rock, is perhaps ten feet long and three feet across. But it is a peaceful spot, hidden by trees and bushes. I find myself linking Tanner's Spring with James T. Tanner, the man who studied the ivory-bill in the 1930s. The name has nothing to do with him, of course, but still I find in my private association something more than the merely idiosyncratic.

There is a bench at Tanner's Spring, made from a slab of stone, and on a good day you can see an ovenbird, grackles, perhaps a Swainson's thrush, a magnolia warbler, a towhee taking a bath. I've seen a Blackburnian warbler, orange throat blazing, come down to drink. Flickers seem to like it. Some days, of course, there's nothing but starlings. Occasionally a sharp-shinned hawk perches nearby and shuts up all the birds.

Tanner's Spring has its human history as well as its natural history. This is where the residents of Seneca Village, the nineteenth-century community of African-Americans, drew their water before they were displaced to make room for Central Park in the 1850s. They were not a powerful community, they could not fight off eviction, and nobody knows where they went.

Some days it is harder than others to see the world in a grain of sand; Tanner's Spring looks like what it is, a puddle-sized splash of water, clogged with leaves, protected unaesthetically by a wire storm fence and haunted by human history. But most days, birdwatching continues to work its magic, my curiosity gets the better of me, and I can't stop looking. The birds that come to drink are real and wild. My daughters, whom I sometimes bring to the spot, are as real as the birds. And when I explain to my elder that once this was a spring that watered a village, and that a girl perhaps her own age came to the pump that must once have stood there to get water for her family, she understands, as only a seven-year-old can, that her imagination of an alternate world isn't a betrayal of reality but a way of doing it greater justice.

Birding is a world of small gestures, but small gestures can change the world. It sometimes occurs to me that the trees planted in Central Park—even the ones near Tanner's Spring—are in some cases more than 150 years old. They are old enough to support ivory-billed woodpeckers, in fact, if only the birds lived in this region. The unglamorous work that Dennis Widener is engaging in down in the floodplain of the Mississippi Delta might, in 150 years, provide the future habitat of the ivory-bill, and, if not an ivory-bill, then many other species that also deserve a home.

"If the East is to have wilderness it must restore it," Roger Tory Peterson observed in *Wild America*, in a chapter about Shenandoah National Park. "The second growth, now thirty, forty, or fifty years old, which clothes the Shenandoahs, will, while our sons are alive, become trees eighty, ninety, or one hundred years old. Our grandsons may see a forest approaching its climax." He wrote this in the mid-1950s, when trees in Florida, Arkansas, Louisiana that might now be supporting ivory-bills were still inching toward maturity. "Wild America" will always belong more to the past, and perhaps the future, than the present, but that doesn't mean it doesn't exist at all.

In Arkansas, Andy and I went to visit Lousiana Purchase

State Park, not far from Brinkley. Thomas Jefferson made the purchase in 1803, the year Audubon arrived in America. It doubled the size of the United States, adding land that extended from the Gulf of Mexico to Canada and including what is now Arkansas and twelve other states. There is a stone laid in 1926 marking the spot from which, in 1815, at President Madison's orders, the official survey of the entire Louisiana Purchase was begun. A spot was chosen by drawing a line from the confluence of the Arkansas and Mississippi Rivers and extending that line toward a line drawn between the confluence of the Mississippi and the St. Francis Rivers. The point at which these two lines met became the starting point for the survey.

This spot had been lost for many years until, in 1921, the original witness trees, two old sweet gums slashed by surveyors in 1815, were rediscovered in the course of a land dispute between two neighboring counties. Those trees are gone now, but the stone marker erected several years later still stands in the headwater swamp. You get to the marker by walking along a narrow boardwalk that carries you over black water, through stands of slender cypress and tupelo trees, several of which seemed no thicker than my legs. The area had obviously been cleared and recleared, though it is now growing slowly back.

It required a vast act of imagination, standing on the boardwalk, to conjure up the vision of 900,000 square miles of unexplored wilderness beginning at our feet. Of course it took imagination—if it were still wilderness, I would not have been standing there with bug repellant and binoculars. It was twilight, the soft end of day, and the smooth tupelo trunks were faintly purple. A red-shouldered hawk flew overhead. A barred owl called off in the distance. As we drove away, meadowlarks flew over our car.

At the opening of his book *The Song of the Dodo: Island Bio-*

geography in an Age of Extinctions, David Quammen proposes a very effective thought experiment: Take a beautiful Persian carpet and hack it into thirty-six pieces. You do not, he notes, wind up with thirty-six little Persian carpets but thirty-six unraveling scraps of useless material. Animals that need vast tracts of forest—a whole Persian carpet of land—cannot live in pieces of forest; those pieces can in fact no longer be called a forest.

I sometimes borrow this figure when I think about time fragmentation as well. Writers are always looking for unbroken tracts of time—Walt Whitman declared defiantly, "I loafe and invite my soul," and Thoreau, who ran off to find more time as well as more space, declared, "Time is but the stream I go a-fishing in" (whatever that means). We all need a certain quality of unbroken time, just as certain birds can live only in unbroken expanses of wilderness.

Standing on the boardwalk in Arkansas, I struggled to imagine the different shape time must have had in 1803—uninterrupted by telegraph or radio or telephone or television or instant messaging or air travel or electric lights. Certain thoughts can live—or at least thrive—only in unbroken tracts of time. One of the little gifts of birdwatching has been to anchor me, in a small new way, in natural time. Dawn and dusk matter differently to me now, and the seasons, tied to the arrival of birds and the departure of birds, bind me to the earth in subtle and important ways.

Charles Lyell, living in a quieter age, realized that wind and rain might over eons erode mountains, inspiring Darwin and Wallace to recognize that a single-cell organism might over time become a human being. I wonder if it is harder to imagine slow time in our own fast-paced world, a world that, with all its technological wizardry, seems more in line with a biblical account of creation—God spoke and it was so—than a creeping evolutionary model. Time, more than anything else, is the difference between *The Origin of Species* and Ovid's *Metamorphoses*. It was possible to understand this in Darwin's day and still believe that minute transformations taking place over vast amounts of time did not constitute a final answer erasing all mystery; evolution merely stretched the magic out over many millions of years.

Many days in New York City, if I haven't had time for proper birdwatching, I go to Tanner's Spring to sit on the stone bench for the last hour of light. This is a good time to see birds come for a final bath or a stealthy drink before vanishing into the branches. "Magic hour" is what the searchers I met in the White River Wildlife Refuge called the last hour of daylight, when each of them went out into the woods alone and sat down, as quietly as possible, near a possible roost hole, in the hope that, at dusk, an ivory-bill would appear. I know that what they did and what I do are very different. But they are also connected. Tanner's Spring is the merest echo of the Big Woods of Arkansas. But the Big Woods of Arkansas itself is the merest echo of what it used to be. And still they are all connected. Just as backyard birds are in fact birds of paradise. It just depends on your definition of backyard—and paradise.

Recently my friends Rob and Andy e-mailed me that a

group of scientists from Auburn University in Alabama have seen an ivory-bill in Florida, near the Choctawhatchee River, a remote area of the Florida panhandle. Perhaps we will go looking there. But even if we don't, other people will, awareness of the wild world will grow, and the Nature Conservancy will buy up land in the area—not the most picturesque land, but the land likeliest to sustain the bird. And if it can sustain that bird, it can sustain a lot of others.

We cannot change the world until we change our consciousness of it. What sort of species are we, and might we still become? The answer is still being written, even at this late date. This is the magic hour. There is still time, before the light fades and there is no longer anything left to see.

SOURCES

The outdoor world of birdwatching is bound to an indoor world of books, a paradox present in all great quests. "I have swum through libraries," says Melville in *Moby-Dick*, a story of high adventure that begins with the notes of a "sub-sub librarian." If I weren't such a slow reader, I would say that I have flown through libraries; in any event, there have been many books and articles. I am incredibly grateful to all the scholars and biographers and bird guide authors and artists who have made possible not only this book but my birding life. I will try to give a sense of the books and people I have consulted for this project, knowing that my list will inevitably be incomplete.

To watch birds you need only a pair of binoculars, and maybe not even those, but to be a birdwatcher you need a bird guide. I started with Roger Tory Peterson's *A Field Guide to the Birds of Eastern and Central North America*, which revolutionized birding when it first appeared in 1934 as *A Field Guide to the Birds*, though it has been revised many times since. For clarity and simplicity it is unsurpassed; it is a book I still use (along with *A Field Guide to Western Birds*), though I now also use the National Geographic field guide, which has eastern and western birds, as well as *All the Birds of North America*, the field guide of the American Bird Conservancy. I love the way *Eastern Birds: A Guide to Field Identification*, a Golden Field Guide from St. Martin's Press, fits in any pocket. I also love the illustrations by James Coe and the

OURCES

fact that Jim is a friend of my sister and brother-in-law, who once gave me a painting of a hairy woodpecker by Jim that hangs in my kitchen. When I wrote about birdwatching for *The New York Times Magazine* in 2000, David Allen Sibley's *The Sibley Guide to Birds* was about to come out and the book, with its delicate, nuanced illustrations, has lived up to all the fanfare. It is especially useful now that it has been broken into two pocket-sized editions, for East and West.

There are also guidebooks with photographs instead of drawings, and even though these seem to occupy a lower rung of utility in the birder hierarchy, since photographs of birds seldom capture the bird as drawings do (odd as that sounds), I often found myself consulting the National Audubon Society's *Field Guide to North American Birds: Eastern Region*, and the *Kaufman Field Guide to Birds of North America*, not so much in the field but on subways or at night in bed. *Hawks in Flight: The Flight Identification of North American Migrant Raptors*, by Pete Dunne, David Allen Sibley, and Clay Sutton, with illustrations by David Allen Sibley, was the first bird guide I read that suggested it was possible to identify birds too far away to see clearly with a new set of impressionistic yet oddly precise criteria (not that I've ever gotten good at it).

This is only a brief sampling of guidebooks. I have consulted many others, and also listened to *Birding by Ear* recordings, the excellent series of tapes and CDs put out by Peterson Field Guides. Fleshing out the field guides was a book I bought as soon as I got my first Peterson guidebook: *The Birder's Handbook: A Field Guide to the Natural History of North American Birds*, which combines detailed descriptions of all North American birds—including nesting habits, diet, and conservation status—with short, informative essays on natural history that include biographies of ornithologists and of individual species,

302

and that explains various ornithological concepts—mimicry, migration—helpful for birding. I've also found it useful to have on my shelf *Manual of Ornithology: Avian Structure and Function*, by Noble S. Proctor and Patrick J. Lynch, with an introduction by Roger Tory Peterson and illustrations by Patrick J. Lynch.

For the statistics about the number of birdwatchers on page 3 of this book, I am indebted to Richard Aiken at the U.S. Fish and Wildlife Service, who gave me the results of Fish and Wildlife's 2006 survey "hot off the computer" and explained to me how the figure of 47.8 million people watching birds translates to one in five Americans.

Edward O. Wilson's books—beginning with his autobiography, *Naturalist*—have had an enormous impact on me and this book. It was a chance assignment to review *Naturalist* in 1994, just as I began birdwatching, that suddenly gave me a context for what I had begun doing and led me to think about ideas like biophilia, which Wilson explored in his 1984 book of that title. Wilson's work gave me a way of thinking about human beings inside a natural context that is at heart Darwinian and yet seemed an opening up of human possibility, not a narrowing. I've quoted from several of his books, including *Consilience* and *The Creation*, but have read and been influenced by many more.

I read about the history of the compass in *The Riddle of the Compass: The Invention That Changed the World*, by Amir D. Aczel, though it was my brother-in-law Jon who taught me how to use one after my humiliation in the woods.

In writing about the ivory-billed woodpecker I consulted, as everyone must, James T. Tanner's classic study *The Ivory-billed Woodpecker*, published by the Audubon Society in 1942 (reprinted by Dover) and bought by me at great expense on eBay when I was first working on my ivory-bill story for *The New Yorker* in 2000, though the book is now back in print—perhaps like the bird itself. Roger Tory Peterson described his May 1942 sighting of an ivory-bill in the Singer Tract (which he called his most exciting bird experience) in his *Bird Watcher's Digest* column, under the title "Finding the Ivory-billed Woodpecker." The account appeared in the January–February 1988 issue. It has been included in *All Things Reconsidered: My Birding Adventures*, a collection of Peterson's essays edited by Bill Thompson III, the editor of *Bird Watcher's Digest*, whose *Identify Yourself* is an excellent birdwatching resource.

There has been a boom of ivory-bill books, or books that touch on the bird, in the last five or ten years, including Christopher Cokinos's *Hope Is the Thing with Feathers: A Personal Chronicle of Vanished Birds*, where I first read about the fate of the ivory-bill. There is also Scott Weidensaul's *The Ghost with Trembling Wings: Science, Wishful Thinking, and the Search for Lost Species*. Phillip Hoose's *The Race to Save the Lord God Bird*, though described as a book for young adults, is an excellent overview for grown-ups, too, and has wonderful pictures. *The Grail Bird: The Rediscovery of the Ivory-billed Woodpecker*, by Tim Gallagher, gives a lively account of the sighting of the bird in Arkansas, which I also learned about directly from conversations with Gene Sparling. That sighting was originally written about in *Science Express* on April 28, 2005, in an article by John W.

Fitzpatrick et al. titled "Ivory-billed Woodpecker (*Campephilis principalis*) Persists in Continental North America." There is a link to that and other ivory-bill articles, and frequent updates, on the website of the Cornell Lab of Ornithology: www.birds .cornell.edu/ivory. David Luneau, who took the contested video of the ivory-bill in Arkansas, maintains a very useful website at www.ibwo.org. He also was an invaluable, and generous, personal source of information for me. Jerome A. Jackson's *In Search of the Ivory-billed Woodpecker* offers a comprehensive natural history of the bird. Jackson also wrote a skeptical assessment of the bird's Arkansas rediscovery in the January 2006 issue of *The Auk*. Jackson is joined in his skepticism in a comment by David Sibley et al. in the March 17, 2006, issue of *Science*, which in turn is rebutted by Fitzpatrick and company in the same issue. The debate continues.

For first telling me that Faulkner's "The Bear" contains a reference to the ivory-billed woodpecker, I am indebted to Robert Bendick, Regional Managing Director, Southern U.S. Conservation Region, of The Nature Conservancy; he had come to Arkansas with his daughter to look for the bird. (He also shared with me his insights about Southern writers and the conservation movement.) There are also older accounts of the ivory-bill, including Alexander Wilson's amazing description, which appears in his *American Ornithology* and is quoted at length in *Hope Is the Thing with Feathers*. There is also Audubon's famous account from his *Ornithological Biography*. For this and other Audubon citations, I used the beautiful Library of America edition of Audubon's writing, edited by Christoph Irmscher, as well as *Audubon: Selected Journals and Other Writings*, edited by Ben Forkner.

––––––––

Audubon himself has been well served by biographers in recent years. I am indebted to Richard Rhodes's *John James Audubon: The Making of an American*, along with William Souder's *Under a Wild Sky: John James Audubon and the Making of "The Birds of America"* and Duff Hart-Davis's *Audubon's Elephant: America's Greatest Naturalist and the Making of "The Birds of America."* I am grateful to *The New York Times Sunday Book Review* for having given me a chance to write about all three of these books together in 2004. My thinking about Audubon as an artist of resurrection was no doubt influenced by Harold Bloom's 1992 *The American Religion: The Emergence of the Post-Christian Nation*, in which he speaks of the resurrected Jesus as a sort of cornerstone of American religion.

Mark V. Barrow, Jr.'s *A Passion for Birds: American Ornithology After Audubon* was enormously helpful in explaining how the bird-killing of Audubon gave way to the bird preservation of his successors, such as Frank M. Chapman and even Theodore Roosevelt, both of whom are written about well in Barrow's book. For background on the post-Audubon world of birders, I am indebted to Joseph Kastner's 1986 *A World of Watchers*. Kastner's lively, informal popular history of American birdwatching introduced me to the Bronx County Bird Club, which made me feel a sense of urban fellowship when I was just beginning to watch birds in Central Park and was feeling mildly freakish. Predating Kastner's book by thirty years—and actually dedicated to Ludlow Griscom, one of the founders of modern birdwatching—is the excellent *Birds and Men: American Birds in Science, Art, Literature and Conservation, 1800–1900*, by Robert Henry Welker.

Stuck into my copy of *Elizabeth Bishop: The Complete Poems, 1927–1979* is a piece of xeroxed paper with an excerpt of the letter from Elizabeth Bishop, quoted in this book, in which she writes about Darwin and the nature of poetry. It has been stuck in there since 1984, when I took a poetry class at Yale with Charles Berger. It was in that class that I first read Bishop's "Brazil, January 1, 1502," quoted twice in this book. (I would have loved to be able to quote Bishop's wonderful poem "Sandpiper" about that little bird running along the beach "in a state of controlled panic," but there wasn't quite a place.) I am grateful to Professor Berger for both the poem and that excerpt about Darwin, which has meant more and more to me over the years as I have read more and more Darwin, and has become a sort of extra poem in the book, combining as it does an awareness of how the scientific mind and the poetic mind overlap. (In her letters, Bishop writes a fair amount about birds, and describes to Marianne Moore her excitement in 1941 upon receiving a copy of Peterson's bird guide as a Christmas present from Robert Penn Warren; she offers to get a copy for Moore.) Charles Berger's class also included a section on Robert Frost, and it was then I first read "The Oven Bird," a poem that has haunted me ever since and that is a touchstone for this book.

My good friend Sam Magavern called to my attention the Coleridge biography that traces the origin of a line in the poem "Frost at Midnight"—that book is *Coleridge: Early Visions*, by Richard Holmes.

Walt Whitman was wonderfully taught in college, too; I was extraordinarily lucky to have Richard Brodhead and Harold Bloom, among others, as my teachers. I found David S. Reynolds's *Walt Whitman's America: A Cultural Biography* particularly helpful for broadening my sense of Whitman's world. I have used the Library of America's edition of Whitman's poetry and prose, edited by Justin Kaplan, whose *Walt Whitman: A Life* was also valuable to me. John Burroughs's writings about Whitman, published in Whitman's lifetime, are remarkably astute. Though Burroughs certainly figures in the biographies of Whitman I have read—and gets his own chapter in Kastner's *A World of Watchers*, where he is described taking bird walks with Walt Whitman, who scribbled down Burroughs's observations—I "discovered" Burroughs years ago in the American Museum of Natural History, which by rights should be considered a source for this book as well. There is a little display devoted to Burroughs just off the hall of Northwest Coast Indians that includes some of the books I have quoted here—*Wake Robin* and *Birds and Poets*—as well as a stuffed passenger pigeon. Burroughs is also written about well in Welker's *Birds and Men*, in a chapter called "'John O' Birds': John Burroughs." In my discussion of Burroughs and Whitman, I have plucked a quotation from Abigail Adams about American birds from Alfred Kazin's *On Native Grounds*. Welker's *Birds and Men* has an illuminating chapter about Thoreau, quoting Emerson's account of Thoreau's using his spyglass to look at two rose-breasted grosbeaks. I have also, in writing about Thoreau, consulted numerous biographies, including Henry Seidel Canby's *Thoreau*, Richard Lebeaux's *Thoreau's Seasons* and *Young Man Thoreau*, and most especially Robert D. Richardson, Jr.'s *Henry Thoreau: A Life of the Mind*. It is there I discovered Thoreau's deathbed comment—"One world at a time"—which serves as the epigraph for Chapter 6, and the haunting quotation from Emerson, suffering from Alzheimer's, asking about Thoreau. Richardson's splendid *Emerson: The Mind on Fire* was also useful. I used several editions of Thoreau's writing, most consistently the Modern Library's edition of *Walden and Other Writings* and the Princeton University Press editions of Thoreau's journals. There are multiple sources

for the story about the Baal Shem Tov and the woods that I relate to Thoreau, but I have relied on, and quoted from, *Major
Trends in Jewish Mysticism*, by Gershom Scholem.

Charles Darwin's *The Voyage of the Beagle* and *The Origin of Species*
are central to this book, and I have used the old Penguin Classics
versions of those volumes that I've had for years. Mary DeJong,
at the American Museum of Natural History, kindly located for
me John Gould's image of Darwin's rhea, which was drawn from
the remains of Darwin's feast and appears as plate 47 in Volume
Three of a work whose title is almost as long as Darwin's voyage:
*The Zoology of the voyage of H.M.S. Beagle, under the command of
Captain Fitzroy, R.N., during the years 1832 to 1836*, "published
with the approval of the Lords Commissioners of Her Majesty's
Treasury; edited and superintended by Charles Darwin, Esq.,
M.A. F.G.S., corresponding member of the Zoological Society,
and naturalist to the expedition."

Janet Browne's wonderful two volumes of biography of Dar-
win, *Charles Darwin: Voyaging* and *Charles Darwin: The Power of
Place*, were enormously helpful, as were *Charles Darwin's Letters:
A Selection*, edited by Frederick Burkhardt, with a foreword by
Stephen Jay Gould. Many books about Darwin, including *Darwin's Dangerous Idea: Evolution and the Meanings of Life*, by Daniel
C. Dennett, and, from another direction, *Finding Darwin's God:
A Scientist's Search for Common Ground Between God and Evolution*, by Kenneth R. Miller, lurk in the background of my thought
and writing. Miller's book is notable for being both a refutation of
intelligent design theories by a respected cell biologist and an argument for the compatibility of Darwinian ideas about evolution
with religious faith. *Darwin, His Daughter, and Human Evolution*,
by Randal Keynes, Darwin's great-great-grandson, brought home

how central the death of Darwin's beloved ten-year-old daughter, Annie, was to his darkening religious views. This notion was reinforced by an interview with Ralph Colp Jr., a surgeon, psychiatrist, and Darwin historian, in the November 2005 issue of *Natural History*, devoted to Darwin, where Colp states simply, about Darwin, that "Annie's death seemed to him so unjust that it precipitated his loss of belief in God."

Bill McKibben's *The End of Nature* is alluded to only in the chapter "Audubon's Monkey," but its formulation of a transformed relationship between humans and "the wild" had a profound effect on my thinking about the natural world. The essay I wrote about birdwatching for *The New York Times* in 2000 was called "Birding at the End of Nature," and I have retained that echo for this book as well. Leo Marx's *The Machine in the Garden: Technology and the Pastoral Idea in America* addressed similar themes when it was published in 1964; its focus on the nineteenth century gives it a different orientation, though one well suited to my argument.

For the information about Abraham Cahan's birdwatching, I am grateful to my good friend Professor Nancy Sinkoff, who discovered that Cahan watched birds in Gerald Sorin's *The Prophetic Minority: American Jewish Immigrant Radicals, 1880–1920.*

I first learned that Theodore Roosevelt was a birdwatcher by walking, time and again, through the entrance of the American Museum of Natural History that contains the glass display containing a snowy owl, shot and stuffed by Roosevelt, standing beside a pair of Roosevelt's old binoculars. In that display case is a placard with an anecdote related by Roosevelt's younger sister, Corinne, about his bursting into a cabinet meeting with news of a chestnut-sided warbler, which I have quoted in this book. I have also been informed (and delighted) by Edmund Morris's *The Rise of Theodore Roosevelt* and its sequel, *Theodore Rex*, as well as David McCullough's *Mornings on Horseback: The Story of an Extraordinary Family, a Vanished Way of Life, and the Unique Child Who Became Theodore Roosevelt*. The statistics about the amount of land set aside by Roosevelt comes from the website of Theodore Roosevelt National Park, www.nps.gov/archive/thro/tr-cons.htm.

Opposite the display with Roosevelt's snowy owl is one devoted to Roosevelt's travels, and it was there I first saw the map tracing his 1913 Amazonian expedition and vowed I'd one day use the title *The River of Doubt*—now taken, alas, by Candice Millard's *The River of Doubt: Theodore Roosevelt's Darkest Journey*, a gripping account of Roosevelt's near-fatal Amazonian travels. Roosevelt's own writing was useful to me, too, especially his essay "My Life as a Naturalist," published in the *American Museum Journal* in May 1918. In his autobiography, Roosevelt writes about how his mother, Martha—who was raised on a slave-owning plantation in Georgia, and who, in Roosevelt's words, remained "completely unreconstructed"—told him slave stories like those about Br'er Rabbit when he was a boy, linking Roosevelt more than I imagined to the paradoxes of Audubon's Southern experience. (It was in fact Roosevelt's uncle, Robert Roosevelt, who also learned slave stories from Roosevelt's mother and who first published those stories in *Harper's Weekly* before they were made famous by Joel Chandler Harris.) Roosevelt's review of Alfred Rus-

sel Wallace's *The World of Life* I found quoted in Ross A. Slotten's
The Heretic in Darwin's Court: The Life of Alfred Russel Wallace.

Roger Tory Peterson—whose *Wild America*, written with James
Fisher, I discuss toward the end of this book—wrote beautifully
on several occasions about his life-changing encounter with a
flicker, including the March–April issue of *International Wildlife*
in an essay called "My Top 10 Birds—Favorite Avian Subjects of
Artist Roger Tory Peterson."

Simon Baron-Cohen's *The Essential Difference: Male and Female
Brains and the Truth About Autism*—which I discovered in a
bookstore one day because I mistook the author for Sasha
Baron-Cohen—was one of several books that, like Edward O.
Wilson's work, placed human nature in the context of biological
nature in ways I've found connected to birdwatching. (I would
add Melvin Konner's *The Tangled Wing: Biological Constraints on
the Human Spirit*.) Kenn Kaufman's classic birding memoir
Kingbird Highway seemed to set in motion some of the biological principles laid out by Baron-Cohen and was in any case a
book I read early in my birding life that inspired me to travel beyond Central Park to see birds.

Though falconry appears only fleetingly in this book, I think it's
important for birders to encounter this sport, which makes overt
certain things implicit in birding—though birders never cross
the line and borrow a bird from the wild. It was falconers, comfortable with tricking wild things back into wildness, who saved
the peregrine falcon from extinction. I would recommend Frank

Lyman Beebe and Harold Melvin Webster's encyclopedic *North American Falconry and Hunting Hawks*, Emma Ford's falconry memoir *Fledgling Days*, and Stephen Bodio's electrifying *A Rage for Falcons*.

In writing about Robert Frost—who dreamed of being carried away by an eagle when he was a boy—I profited from several fine biographies, including Jay Parini's *Robert Frost: A Life*, a nice balance to Lawrance Roger Thompson's dark though informative view of the poet. John Elder's *Reading the Mountains of Home* is not only a beautiful reading of "Directive," one of Frost's great late poems, but also a wonderful model of how a poem can work like a compass.

I used *The Poetry of Robert Frost*, edited by Edward Connery Lathem, because I've had it since childhood.

Thornton W. Burgess's *The Burgess Bird Book for Children*, published in 1919, refers to "Teacher the Oven Bird," written about in my chapter on Frost. The book was graciously lent to me by my daughter Ariella, who received it on her fifth birthday from my friend Susan Miron. Two of the book's illustrations are reproduced here—a bobolink, for Emily Dickinson on page 195, and the ovenbird on page 299. The artist, Louis Agassiz Fuertes, was one of the great bird artists of the twentieth century; according to Roger Tory Peterson, it was a Fuertes painting of a blue jay, given to him in seventh grade, that turned him into a bird artist. There are several other Fuertes illustrations in this book, all generously sent to me by Mark Madison, Ph.D., historian at the U.S. Fish and Wildlife Service's National Conservation Training Center, who also located for me the Fish and Wildlife pamphlet from the 1970s about the ivory-billed woodpecker, a page from which appears on page 254.

———

The story of Leonardo da Vinci and the kite is quoted from Volume 2 of *The Notebooks of Leonardo da Vinci, Arranged, Rendered into English, and Introduced by Edward MacCurdy*.

I first learned about Alfred Russel Wallace while reading David Quammen's exhilarating jeremiad, *The Song of the Dodo: Island Biogeography in an Age of Extinctions*. Wallace, like birdlife, is powerfully present in the culture and yet simultaneously eclipsed, and I am grateful to *The New Yorker* for giving me a chance to explore the life and work of this great naturalist, whose time has come again. There have been at least five biographies published since 2000, along with two first-rate anthologies of Wallace's work that function as partial biographies and give a sample of a writing style so fine that Joseph Conrad kept his copy of *The Malay Archipelago* on his night table, borrowing liberally from it for several of his own books, most notably *Lord Jim*. The titles of Wallace biographies tend to enact, as well as relate, their subject's predicament: *The Forgotten Naturalist*, by John G. Wilson; *In Darwin's Shadow*, by Michael Shermer; *The Heretic in Darwin's Court*, by Ross A. Slotten; *An Elusive Victorian*, by Martin Fichman. Only Peter Raby's 2001 biography blurts out its subject without waiting for a subtitle: *Alfred Russel Wallace: A Life*. It was reading Raby's excellent book about nineteenth-century naturalist-explorers, *Bright Paradise*, that I learned about Wallace's friend Richard Spruce hiding his face in his hands as he pulled away from the tropics for the last time. And it was Raby's Wallace biography that contained an account of Wallace's conversation with Tennyson about spirits of the dead.

In addition to Wallace's own writing—his two-volume autobiography, *My Life: A Record of Events and Opinions; The Malay Archipelago; Island Life*—I was helped by two excellent anthologies, *Infinite Tropics: An Alfred Russel Wallace Anthology*, edited by Andrew Berry, with a preface by Stephen Jay Gould, and *The Alfred Russel Wallace Reader, A Selection of Writings from the Field*, edited by Jane R. Camerini, with a foreword by David Quammen. The University of Chicago's edition of Robert Chambers's *Vestiges of the Natural History of Creation and Other Evolutionary Writings*, with a fine introduction by editor James A. Secord, helped me understand not only the way this eccentric book shaped the thinking of both Darwin and Wallace but also the way exuberant amateurs, proceeding by hunches, can have as big an impact on science as anybody else. An older, somewhat conspiratorial study, Arnold C. Brackman's *A Delicate Arrangement: The Strange Case of Charles Darwin and Alfred Russel Wallace*, was also useful. Charles H . Smith, professor and librarian at Western Kentucky University in Bowling Green, operates an excellent website, *The Alfred Russel Wallace Page* (www.wku.edu/~smithch/), which offers Wallace news, biographical information, maps and photographs from Wallace's work, and links to electronic versions of Wallace's work, including the "Ternate essay" that Wallace sent to Darwin. I am grateful to Professor Smith for helping me locate the image of Wallace, taken in Singapore, that appears in this book.

I am incredibly grateful to my friend the artist Tobi Kahn for access to his treasured volumes of *Cassell's Book of Birds: From the Text of Dr. Brehm*, by Thomas Rymer Jones. Based on the work of the German zoologist Alfred Edmund Brehm, this four-volume work (bound in two) was published in England in 1869, just five years after Wallace returned from the Malay Archipelago,and the extraordinary engravings and hand-colored plates—

several of which appear in this book, though only, alas, in black and white—gave me a glimpse of the reverence with which these exotic species were reproduced in Victorian England. Tobi also allowed me to use his lavishly illustrated copy of *The Museum of Natural History: Being a Popular Account of the Structure, Habits, and Classification of the Various Departments of the Animal Kingdom*, by Sir John Richardson, William S. Dallas, and T. Spencer Cobbold, published in 1860—it is there that I found the image of the hoopoe that appears in Chapter 18.

In writing about Emily Dickinson I used *The Complete Poems of Emily Dickinson*, edited by Thomas H. Johnson, and a number of excellent biographies, including Alfred Habegger's *My Wars Are Laid Away in Books: The Life of Emily Dickinson*, and Richard B. Sewall's *The Life of Emily Dickinson*. Most useful of all for my purposes was Roger Lundin's *Emily Dickinson and the Art of Belief*.

In writing about birdwatching in Israel, I found the encyclopedic knowledge of Yossi Leshem, director of the International Center for the Study of Bird Migration in Latrun, invaluable, whether he was explaining that Shimon Peres took his name from a lammergeier vulture or sharing information about the diversity of Israel's migration or simply including me in his many e-mails, one of which contained the astonishing photograph of a speared stork that appears in this book. Leshem's book *Flying with the Birds*, written with Ofer Bahat, was also helpful in giving me a fuller picture of bird life in Israel. I also drew on *Birds in the Land of the Bible*, by Uzi Paz, with photographs by Yossi Eshbol. Hadoram Shirihai's monumental *The Birds of Israel* was also enormously helpful. I also made use of the article "Lake Hula—Lake Agmon," by Tamar Zohary and K. David Hambright, published in *Ariel: The Israel Review of Arts and Letters.* My source for Melville's Levant journal was Volume Fifteen of *The Writings of Herman Melville,* the Northwestern-Newberry edition, edited by Howard C. Horsford with Lynn Horth.

I wish someone would write a biography of Henry Baker Tristram. I learned what I could from fleeting references in Darwin and Wallace biographies, and from Judith E. T. Tarrant's monograph, written for the Durham Country Local History Society, "The Reverend Canon Henry Baker Tristram: Naturalist, Freemason and Churchman," which draws on an unpublished memoir of Tristram by his granddaughter. I am grateful to John Banham, secretary of the Durham County Local History Society, for sending me the monograph. I was also greatly helped by "Natural Selection Before the Origin: Public Reactions of Some Naturalists to the Darwin-Wallace Papers," by Richard England, published in the *Journal of the History of Biology* (June 1997). It is from this paper that I learned that Tristram, in 1893, acknowledged Darwin as "our great master." I was also helped by I. Bernard Cohen's "Three Notes on the Reception of Darwin's Ideas on Natural Selection" in *The Darwinian Heritage,* published by Princeton University Press. It was in Errol Fuller's encyclopedic and beautifully illustrated *Great Auk* that I saw the photograph of young Tristram—who owned a great auk egg—dressed like Lawrence of Arabia. Gorgias Press has reissued a number of Tristram's books, including *Bible Places; or The Topography of the Holy Land, Travels and Discoveries in Palestine and Jordan, The Land of Israel: A Journey of Travels in Palestine,* and *The Natural History of the Bible.*

The bestiary I refer to for medieval views on hoopoes and owls is T. H. White's 1954 *The Book of Beasts: Being a Translation from a Latin Bestiary of the Twelfth Century*. White's 1951 *The Goshawk* is also a superb book about falconry, and in a deeper way a meditation on wild animals and human beings.

I learned about Elliott Coues and the sparrow war from Joseph Kastner's *A World of Watchers*, which gives the sparrow war its own chapter; from Barrow's *A Passion for Birds: American Ornithology After Audubon*; and from Paul Russell Cutright and Michael J. Brodhead's full-length biography, *Elliott Coues: Naturalist and Frontier Historian*. Coues has a walk-on part in Michael Shermer's *The Heretic in Darwin's Court*, where Wallace and Coues, two spiritualist-naturalists, meet in Washington, D.C.

Yehuda Amichai's poem about the Huleh swamp appears as section 2 of the long poem called "Once I Wrote Now and In Other Days: Thus Glory Passes, Thus Pass the Psalms," in the collection *Open Closed Open*, translated by Chana Bloch and Chana Kronfeld. James P. Smith took me to find Hume's tawny owl in Eilat and added to my education about the birds of Israel. His excellent illustrations appear in two books that have also helped me: *A Guide to the Birding Hot-Spots of Northern Israel* and *A Guide to the Birding Hot-Spots of Southern Israel* published by the Society for the Protection of Nature in Israel and the Israel Ornithological Center.

For the critique of Konrad Lorenz and information about his Nazi connections, and the meaning of those connections for his work, I am indebted to Boria Sax's paper, "What Is a 'Jewish Dog'?: Konrad Lorenz and the Cult of Wildness," published in 1997 in *Society & Animals: Journal of Human-Animal Studies*. Sax's book *Animals in the Third Reich: Pets, Scapegoats, and the Holocaust* elaborates on those ideas in fascinating detail.

With the exception of Emerson's own translation, the translations from Farid ud-Din Attar's *The Conference of Birds* are by Afkham Darbandi and Dick Davis. Margaret Jones Bolsterli's *Born in the Delta: Reflections on the Making of a Southern White Sensibility* gave me a wonderful cultural context for the world that may have preserved the ivory-bill.

The story "The People Could Fly" appears in Virginia Hamilton's superb collection *The People Could Fly: American Black Folktales*, published by Knopf.

I am grateful to Michael Specter's "Rethinking the Brain: How the Songs of Canaries Upset a Fundamental Principle of Science" in the July 23, 2001, *New Yorker*, for an overview of the work of Fernando Nottebohm. And to Nottebohm's own "A Brain for All Seasons: Cyclical Anatomical Changes in Song Control Nuclei of the Canary Brain," from the December 18, 1981, issue of *Science*. Nottebohm, and canaries, are also written about in David Rothenberg's lively and informative *Why Birds*

Sing: A Journey Through the Mystery of Bird Song. I also learned about birdsong from *The Singing Life of Birds: The Art and Science of Listening to Birdsong*, by Donald E. Kroodsma.

The poem by Avraham Sutzkever that begins "Who will remain, what will remain?" appears without a title in *A. Sutzkever: Selected Poetry and Prose*, translated from the Yiddish by Barbara and Benjamin Harshav, in the section called "Poems from My Diary (1974–1985)." The lines from Sutzkever's poem "Mother" appear in *Burnt Pearls: Ghetto Poems of Abraham Sutzkever*, translated from the Yiddish by Seymour Mayne and introduced by Ruth R. Wisse, who helped me track down this poem.

The New-York Historical Society's Seneca Village website, www.nyhistory.org/seneca, was useful for learning about Central Park before the park was there. So was the website of the Central Park Conservancy: www.centralparknyc.org/virtualpark/the greatlawn/senecavillage. I gained a better understanding of the modern park, where I do so much birding, from Marie Winn's *Red-Tails in Love: A Wildlife Drama in Central Park*, and I still consult Tom Fiore's excellent contribution, "Birds Through the Year in Central Park," in the section called "A Wildlife Almanac" in the back of Winn's book whenever I forget what week in April to expect a Northern waterthrush, or when in May there might be a mourning warbler. (I call the blackpoll one of the last of the warblers to arrive in the park, though Fiore identifies the mourning warbler, and I've no doubt he is correct, but since I almost never see those, I've stuck with the blackpoll.)

ACKNOWLEDGMENTS

Once again, I am deeply grateful to my editor, Jonathan Galassi, for his patience, intelligence, and encouragement, and his ability to see the forest *and* the trees (and, of course, the birds). His former assistant Jim Guida went beyond the call of duty in his helpfulness, particularly when it came to choosing and organizing the art for this book. Zachary Woolfe stepped in when Jim left and has been enormously helpful. Sarah Chalfant, my agent and friend, has, as always, helped bring this book into being.

I am grateful to editors at *The New York Times Magazine*—beginning with Adam Moss, now at *New York Magazine*, and Gerry Marzorati and Katherine Bouton—for allowing me to write about birds back in the 1990s, and to David Remnick and Henry Finder at *The New Yorker* for sending me to Louisiana to write about the ivory-billed woodpecker. *The New Yorker* also let me try out my ideas about Alfred Russel Wallace, and I am particularly grateful to Leo Carey for his insights there. Anne Fadiman helped me shape a piece for *The American Scholar* on birding in Israel that I drew on for this book. And Chip McGrath and Caroline Herron allowed me to write the first piece about birdwatching I ever wrote—a tribute to guidebooks for *The New York Times Book Review*. The excellent bird walks of Starr Saphir and Steve Quinn in Central Park started me off as a birder.

On various trips to Louisiana and Arkansas to look for the ivory-billed woodpecker, I was treated with unfailing generosity and kindness by David Kullivan, James Van Remsen, Vernon Wright, Bill Vermillion, David Luneau, Gene Sparling, Jay Harrod, Robert Bendick, Nancy DeLamar, Scott Simon, and Dennis Widener, among many others. The list of birders and ornithologists I have interviewed at various times is long; I am grateful to them all, and am still inspired by conversations with George Fenwick, Kenn Kaufman, Paul Kerlinger, and Pete Dunne. George Butler, whose masterful film on the ivory-bill had not been released at the time of this writing, screened his film for me (and caught an error in the proofs for this book).

Yossi Leshem not only drove me all over Israel, pointing out birds, he has remained enormously generous with his time and expertise. My knowledge of Israel's birdlife was also expanded by Amotz Zahavi, James P. Smith, and my cousin Gil Nachshoni, who first took me to see griffon vultures in the Golan Heights.

Jerry and Roberta Silbert invited me to the Menunkatuck Audubon Society's "Biodiversity Day," and even put me up in Guilford.

Keith Winsten, my old college friend and now the executive director of the Brevard Zoo in Melbourne, Florida, showed me Micronesian kingfishers years ago. My friend Andy Furman, who shares my love of birds, shared with me his birding friends Scott Lewis and Rob Stone, too—they allowed me to join them on a Texas birding trip and freely shared their knowledge and camaraderie. Other dear friends have been helpful, too—Sam Magavern is responsible for my discovering the Harry Smith anthology, the biography of Coleridge quoted in this book, Madeira Canyon in Arizona, and an astonishing number of other things. Josh Weiner began sending me bird poems back when I thought I was creating an anthology, and never stopped. Cindy Spiegel, as always, offered all sorts of sage and calming counsel. So did Jonathan Mahler, Jonathan Wilson, Jeff Goldberg, Blake Eskin, David Taylor, and Robin Cembalest, who lent me her visual expertise. Julie Cohen shared her enthusiasm, and her piping plovers. David Rosenberg first told me about the Hula swamp project and shared many of his deep insights about the natural world. John Dorfman pointed me to *The Conference of Birds* years ago.

I am very grateful to my good friend Stephen Dubner for his early reading of this book. My Nextbook colleagues have been wonderfully supportive; and I am particularly grateful to Arthur Friend and Mem Bernstein for giving me my home at Nextbook, and to Julie Sandorf for her friendship and support.

Assembling the art for this book introduced me to a whole new dimension of bookmaking. I am especially grateful to Mark Madison at the U.S. Fish and Wildlife Service, Mary de Jong at the American Museum of Natural History, Bill Thompson III at *Bird Watcher's Digest*, Leslie Wilson at the Concord Free Public Library, and the photographers Hanne and Jens Eriksen, Don Riepe, and Yoav Perlman. India Amos, art director of Nextbook, generously helped me scan several of the images in this book.

Tobi Kahn's generosity, with his books and everything else, is boundless. George Blumenthal made the photographing of images from Tobi's delicate books possible by providing digital photography services. It was at Tobi and Nessa's table that I heard Steve Shaw talk about the warblers in Central Park. Steve's enthusiasm and encouragement started me on my birding life.

The New York Society Library has, as always, been a refuge, and also a splendid source of material for this book.

My family by marriage has long been a source of love and encouragement, and the Michigan clan was my bridge to Point Pelee. My wife's parents, Tova and Jimmy Springer, and my brother-in-law Jonathan Springer immeasurably enrich life in New York.

I am incredibly lucky to have in my life the dedicatees of this book—my sister Anna; her husband, Jon; and their three children, Isaac, Celia, and Ella: they offer constant love and support, as does my mother, Norma, who taught me more about literature, and nature, than I own up to. My daughters, Ariella Rose and Avital Leah, inspire me in every conceivable way, and this book is as much a letter to them as it is anything else. And finally, nothing would be possible without my wife, Mychal Springer. In the immortal words of Johnny Cash, "Mother Nature's quite a lady, but you're the one I need."

ILLUSTRATION CREDITS

p. 8: World Trade Center as seen from Jamaica Bay. Photo by Don Riepe/American Littoral Society.

p. 22: Ivory-billed woodpecker, painted by Alexander Wilson, in his *American Ornithology*. From the archives of the Ernst Mayr Library of the Museum of Comparative Zoology, Harvard University.

p. 29: Yellow-rumped warbler, painted by Louis Agassiz Fuertes. Courtesy of U.S. Fish and Wildlife Service, USFWS/National Conservation Training Center.

p. 40: Painting of Carolina parakeets by John James Audubon. Collection of the New-York Historical Society.

p. 63: Mockingbird, painted by Louis Agassiz Fuertes. Courtesy of U.S. Fish and Wildlife Service, USFWS/National Conservation Training Center.

p. 75: Photograph of ivory-billed and pileated woodpeckers by Jonathan Rosen.

p. 88: Thoreau's telescope, leaning with his flute against a volume of Alexander Wilson's *American Ornithology*. Courtesy of Concord Free Public Library, photo by Alfred Hosmer.

p. 102: Gaucho chasing rheas. Courtesy of American Museum of Natural History Library.

p. 103: Drawing of Darwin's rhea by John Gould. Courtesy of American Museum of Natural History Library.

p. 110: Self-portrait of John James Audubon in buckskin, sketched in 1826 when the artist was in Liverpool.

p. 128: Theodore Roosevelt in buckskin, 1884. State Historical Society of North Dakota 0410-127.

p. 131: Theodore Roosevelt in 1915, on the beach at Breton National Wildlife Refuge in Louisiana, the second oldest refuge in the country. Courtesy of U.S. Fish and Wildlife Service, USFWS/National Conservation Training Center.

p. 142: Engraving of falconer from *Cassell's Book of Birds*. Courtesy of Tobi Kahn.